CROSS-CULTURAL TOPICS IN PSYCHOLOGY

Edited by LEONORE LOEB ADLER
and UWE P. GIELEN

Foreword by Ronald Taft

PRAEGER

Westport, Connecticut
London

Library of Congress Cataloging-in-Publication Data

Cross-cultural topics in psychology / edited by Leonore Loeb Adler and
Uwe P. Gielen.
     p. cm.
   Includes bibliographical references (p.   ) and index.
   ISBN 0–275–94524–3 (alk. paper).—ISBN 0–275–95062–X (pbk.)
   1. Ethnopsychology.   2. Psychology.   I. Adler, Leonore Loeb.
II. Gielen, Uwe.
   GN502.C77   1994
   155.8—dc20   93–40574

British Library Cataloguing in Publication Data is available.

Library of Congress Catalog Card Number: 93–40574
ISBN: 0–275–94524–3
       0–275–95062–X (pbk.)

First published in 1994

Praeger Publishers, 88 Post Road West, Westport, CT 06881
An imprint of Greenwood Publishing Group, Inc.

Printed in the United States of America

The paper used in this book complies with the Permanent
Paper Standard issued by the National Information Standards
Organization (Z39.48–1984).

10 9 8 7 6 5 4 3 2 1

This book is dedicated to all those individuals who are working for a better understanding of cultural differences and similarities.

Contents

Foreword

Ronald Taft

Scholars of human behavior have for a long time been curious to learn to what degree members of outgroups (i.e., other cultures) have the same characteristics as their own people. In the past, with typical ethnocentric arrogance scholars made the underlying assumption that the outgroups would be different in most respects and, by implication, peculiar if not inferior. The traditional emphasis in cross-cultural study used to be on the differences between the scholar's own culture ("civilization") and that of other people ("barbarians"); but today, as a result of repugnance to the myths of racial superiority, scholars have learned to be less judgmental than in the past. Perhaps we now lean too far on the relativistic side in that we avoid making judgments about the psychologically relevant and important question: Do some cultures and cultural institutions provide better than others for the welfare and mental health needs of individuals? This is an aspect of cross-cultural psychology that would warrant more attention, but this would require treading much delicate ground.

Modern cross-cultural psychologists often place as much emphasis on the similarities in the behavior of people in different cultures as they do on differences. The search for similarities arises to a large extent from a belief in the underlying unity of the human race in the midst of the diversities that manifest themselves on the surface. Implicit in the study of similarities is the assumption that universals in human behavior are waiting to be discovered once we have developed psychological concepts appropriate for making generalizations across different cultures. Studies of the same phenomena across cultures can serve to establish which psychological principles are broad in their application and which are rather specific to a particular culture. Cross-cultural replications of studies initially based on only one culture provide information on the possible value for an understanding of human behavior of the theory on which the study is based. Psychologists are more and more being confronted with the specter that practically all of our knowledge is culture bound, excepting for those findings that are as much physiological as psychological. The growing tendency among developmental, cognitive, personality, and social psychologists to test their findings cross-culturally arises partly from the need to establish limits in the populations to which the characteristics of a particular sample can be generalized. Considering that the typical samples used in studies by cognitive, personality, and social psychologists tend to be quite narrow culturally (e.g., American, urban, educated), it should not be surprising that there is a growing realization of the value of cross-cultural studies for a science of psychology.

Many of the studies referred to in the present volume fall into the category of "similarity" research concerned with the study of the cultural generalities of findings and the limits of generalization. In contrast to the concentration on similarities and their limits, the emphasis in much cross-cultural research is the traditional one of studying how members of different cultures vary in their behavior. This type of research tends to be interested in the interaction between a culture and the particular psychological characteristics being studied, and it could just as well be called cultural psychology as cross-cultural psychology. Studies that concentrate on differences in the behavior of members of different cultures have two main aims. One is to study the nature of the particular cultures themselves; the other is to throw light on the way in which culture impinges on individuals. Cultural psychology deals with the process by which a child becomes enculturated and also how the behavior and performance of individuals reflect the influence of their culture. This approach to cross-cultural psychology frequently finds itself at the intersection of psychology and anthropology where a knowledge of both fields is useful for understanding the results of the investigation.

A special case of cultural psychology is the study of how individuals respond to situations where they are in transition between their original culture and another that differs from it in some important respects. This occurs in several types of situation, for example, where a traditional culture is eroded through contact with another dominating society, as in colonization; where a traditional culture is transformed into a modern one; or where an immigrant is acculturated to the host society. All these transitional situations are examined in this book.

Leonore Loeb Adler and Uwe P. Gielen are to be congratulated on having planned and organized this collection of chapters. Their content reflects the diversity of cross-cultural psychology.

Preface

Leonard W. Doob

Why should you read this book? Look at the Contents and you will immediately discover topics with which you may already be acquainted: They range from emotion and moral reasoning to human beliefs and personality, from language and child development to gender and mental health. Ah, yes, but the approach here is cross-cultural. Consequently, these topics are given more than a twist that will be useful as you contemplate your self and your society.

This Preface is not argumentative—of course not, a scholarly preface never ever argues—rather, it is unabashedly personal. Let me begin with some scattered autobiographical notes. As I sat uncomfortably in a large German auditorium on a few occasions and listened to Hitler during his campaigns to attain political power in 1930–32, my thoughts often competed with what he was shouting. I wondered whether we Americans could ever tolerate such a skillful demagogue. In the lectures by the founder of a new psychology at the university I was attending there, I tried and failed to find an explanation for the support being given Hitler. Later during those rallies it seemed that what I was being taught by another savant concerning utopias and ideologies provided some insight into the Nazis and their beloved leader. More than a decade later as British and U.S. planes began heavy and continual bombardments of Germany and other occupied European countries, colleagues and I in a Washington war agency decided, that Fortress Europe, which the Nazis were claiming could never be breached, was in fact turning out to be a "Fortress without a Roof" (*eine Festung ohne Dach* sounded pungent). Had we who devised this propaganda line been inspired by psychology and the social sciences? In the mid-1950s I was doing what I considered research on acculturation in East Africa and learned that the colonial power at that time was affecting the Baganda and the Luo only superficially: Intensive interviewing revealed to me, I thought, that the cultural values of most, but not all, these good people remained unscathed. For the past quarter of a century as the editor of a psychological journal, I have been trying vainly to assess the scholarly contribution of "experiments" that obtain data in contrived laboratory situations from U.S. undergraduates who usually receive course credit or a token fee for participating under ethically approved procedures.

Each of the learned studies or expositions in this book in front of you introduces theories and issues more profound than my own. All of us, however, when confronted with a Hitler or a learned treatise, inquire whether the research will guide us helpfully in the future. We solve or resolve a communication or a practical problem and then question the source and validity of our increased wisdom; insights are rare and treasured. Those strangers from our own or another country whom we love or hate may or may not be different from us, and we are puzzled. Experiments inside or outside laboratories are intriguing, yet then again we may wonder whether all the details of any contrived or real experience are ever repeated. And so as we seek assistance from many sources in the past, we are perplexed.

Cross-cultural social science can be one of the sources. Privately you believe that you yourself are quite unique and that others, though they differ from you, are also similar in some respects. After you become acquainted with cultural areas at a distance, you may well be skeptical concerning findings based upon the behavior or verbal responses of North Americans and Europeans. Indeed, we admire culture-bound studies even without abandoning a skeptical reservation concerning their applicability to other peoples: A well-designed and controlled experiment accomplishes its own objective. Really, does it?

After experiencing cross-cultural studies you and I as well as our peers may raise puzzling and baffling but intriguing and useful questions concerning what social scientists, reporters, and other informants generally tell us. If their data come from our shores or from lands like ours, we wonder whether their findings or arguments are valid elsewhere. We know these communicators often avidly seek and uncover universal truths, yet we realize they are overgeneralizing when they express their findings in the present tense and thus imply that all people at the moment and not merely college sophomores think, feel, or act as they recklessly suggest. Some of us blush or writhe when authors express appreciation for low correlations that account for little of the variances but are "statistically significant" possibly only because a large number of informants have been tapped.

Cross-cultural research suggests how individuals react to conditions different from those prevailing in Western-oriented societies. Maybe someday we shall be like them in some respects, or they will be like us. Times and people change. Recalling that platitude shocks me and should shock you when an investigator or a conventionalized, respectable abstract fails to reveal even the year when a study was conducted. The date of publication does provide a clue to the context, although often there may be a noteworthy time lag before the paper, the book, or the mass-medium piece has been composed, approved, and transmitted publicly.

The advantages of studying people not yet completely affected by the so-called West are or should be self-evident. Such people may not have been plagued by pollsters on a street or over a telephone, and hence as respondents they may or may not be more forthright or they may simply not provide what they deem to be respectable or anticipated replies to questions posed during interviews. In contrast is a frequently used technique in modern experimentation that resorts to a make-believe approach. What would you do if blinkblank? A fictitious account—called a scenario or script these days, as the method is later described to readers—is read by the hapless subjects, who are asked to pass judgment on what allegedly happened in the story. Studies in this tradition almost always conclude with a lame plea for future research and then immediately and seriously suggest the nature of the research to be conducted in a similar or dissimilar methodological rut.

And the challenge of language in cross-cultural research? We realize that the same words have different connotations for persons in the same society, a situation that often is many times greater when different languages must be employed. A conscientious backtranslation is supposed to solve that problem: One person translates from language A to language B, and another person independently backtranslates from B to A. The original and the back-translated version are compared, and discrepancies are thus discovered. But obviously both translators have been trained in the same tradition, so that when *equator* is translated into a language that does not possess that single word but resorts to "belt around the middle of the land," then the latter is backtranslated into the former, thereby losing some of the expression's subtle connotations.

Have I been exaggerating the limited value of considerable but not all research on peoples residing in the West? Yes, the reply must be, if our interest is limited to those peoples and the limitation is explicitly admitted. But problems arise, even in Ohio, Florida, and Texas, concerning the universality or applicability of diligent findings. Glance at the eleven studies devoted to *Generalizing from Laboratory to Field Settings*—edited by Edwin A. Locke (Lexington, MA: Heath, 1986). If there is a slip 'twix a U.S. laboratory and a U.S. field, surely the slippage must be greater between data from the United States and data from the land of the Zulus.

Cross-cultural research has its own imperfections too. While the value of replicating a finding from one society to another may be highly desirable or necessary, theoretical challenges remain. Why replicate in a particular society and not elsewhere? Perhaps the investigator happens to be spending a sabbatical there, or likes the scenery or the friendly people. In addition, some aspiring principles must be tested not merely in two or three societies but in a representative sample of the world's societies selected systematically from a commendable and convenient source such as the Human Relations Area Files. Even then, however, the traits, values, or behavior being surveyed, as critics have sometimes suggested, are perforce ripped out of their cultural context.

In my view, biased and now expressed, in short, puzzling problems will, must, and should forever challenge us. This book's authors demonstrate the importance of investigations and ponderings that transcend Western boundaries. Have they brought Nirvana a bit closer? You decide, please, after reading what follows.

Part I

History of and Methods for Cross-Cultural Studies

1

Introduction to Cross-Cultural Psychology

David Yau-Fai Ho

Cross-cultural psychology has a long past but only a short history. Psychologists have had a longstanding interest in the impact of cultures on individuals. For instance, how do child-rearing practices influence personality formation in various cultures? Do speakers of different languages have different patterns of thought, as claimed by the Whorfian hypothesis? Is the Oedipal complex universal? As an organized intellectual discipline, however, cross-cultural psychology is no more than two or three decades old. A developmental milestone was the establishment of the International Association for Cross-Cultural Psychology in 1972, when its inaugural meeting was held in Hong Kong.

Today cross-cultural psychology is firmly established as a psychological science. Yet most students of psychology probably complete their studies, even at the graduate level, without coming into formal contact with cross-cultural psychology. More seriously, many psychologists still regard it as peripheral to the concerns of mainstream psychology. The reason is that psychology has always aspired to be a universal science. Traditionally, it aims to produce an abstract body of knowledge transcending temporal and spatial dimensions. Presumably there is nothing "cross-cultural" about the facts of, say, conditioning, and maturation, and individual differences. The same assumptions of regularity or lawfulness governing behavior would apply regardless of historical and cultural context. True enough, people behave differently in different cultures. But that is of central concern to cultural anthropology, not psychology.

Our contention is that no serious psychologist can remain indifferent to and ignorant of cross-cultural psychology. Psychology is distinct from the physical sciences in that the agent of investigation is also the object being investigated:

It is the study of human beings by human beings. It studies not only human behavior but also conceptions about human behavior, including our own—that is, the question of how psychological knowledge, including that about the self, is generated. Culture enters into the generation of psychological knowledge because of its pervasive influence on both behavior and conceptions of behavior. As we shall see, cross-cultural psychology is much more than the intellectual luxury of studying people's oddities in exotic cultures. It challenges mainstream psychology to a self-examination and to make good its claim of being a universal science.

CROSS-CULTURAL PSYCHOLOGY DEFINED

Cross-cultural psychology is the scientific study of human behavior and mental processes, including both their variability and invariance, under diverse cultural conditions; its primary aims are to investigate (a) systematic relations between behavioral variables and ethnic-cultural variables and (b) generalizations of psychological principles.

This definition embodies a number of important notions. First, cross-cultural psychology is a science, by virtue of the scientific principles and methods it employs. We may go as far as to say that cross-cultural psychology owes its gain in stature largely to its methodological contributions to psychological science.

Second, unlike cultural anthropology, cross-cultural psychology is not primarily concerned with the comparative study of cultures per se, that is, the enduring characteristics that mark a culture apart from other cultures. It is still focused on the individual and thus retains its identity as a psychological science. The units of comparison are not modal or normative patterns at the collective or population level but the psychological functioning of individuals across cultures. However, it insists on adopting a perspective of crucial significance: The individual is not regarded as an abstract entity to be studied without reference to culture; accordingly, the unit of analysis is now the individual-in-a-cultural-context.

Third, as in general psychology, included in the scope of investigation are both observable behavior and mental processes that cannot be directly observed but must be inferred from behavioral or physiological observations. Animal behavior is excluded, presumably because culture is unique to humans. More importantly, the scope of investigation is explicitly enlarged to include, ideally, the total range of human behavior and mental process under all known cultural conditions. Virtually nothing about life's secrets in diverse cultures is left untouched—not even unusual behavior under extreme cultural conditions. The enlarged range of observations forms the foundation for attaining the two stated aims.

Fourth, by definition a comparative framework is always operative. Both differences and similarities in psychological and social functioning across ethnic-cultural boundaries are studied. Strictly speaking, however, cross-ethnic and cross-national comparisons do not qualify as cross-cultural research unless relevant cultural variables have been included.

Comparison is thus the hallmark of cross-cultural psychology. It should be noted, though, that all scientific investigation entails comparison. The significance of a phenomenon can be gauged only against a background of patterns, regularities, or uniformities established after prolonged observation. Cross-cultural psychology goes to an extreme in delineating conditions under which legitimate, systematic comparisons across cultures can be made. It pays special attention to questions of comparability of samples and equivalence of measures used in different cultural contexts. Probably it is in answering these questions that its methodological contributions will be most strongly felt.

THE STRENGTHS AND PROMISES OF CROSS-CULTURAL PSYCHOLOGY

Cross-cultural research is far more ambitious than merely to catalog behavioral differences across ethnic-cultural groups. The scope of investigation is enlarged, giving substance to the claim that psychology is a universal science of human behavior. We are compelled to recognize the inadequacy of basing our knowledge on research conducted within only one culture or under a limited range of cultural conditions. We are thus challenged to examine the completeness of psychology as a body of knowledge about human beings. Ideally, the scope of investigation should be panhuman—that is, inclusive of the entire range of human behavior under all known cultural conditions.

Obvious advantages follow from conducting research in diverse cultural conditions. The range of cultural variables is increased, especially if extreme or unusual cultural environments are included. The likely result would be a corresponding increase in the range of observed behaviors. Consequently, we lay a more solid empirical foundation upon which theories may be constructed.

Let us consider, for instance, the advantage of increasing the range of cultural variables in estimating the heritability of the intelligence quotient (IQ)—a research problem that continues to be hotly debated. Heritability is a statistical concept derived from genetics. A coefficient of heritability, which ranges from 0.00 to 1.00, tells us the percentage of variance accounted for by genetic factors. Many investigators have put the value of the heritability coefficient for human ability or achievement around .80, which is rather high. But is this a fair estimate? Research on the heritability of the IQ has been plagued by a host of methodological problems. Here, we shall consider only one: the sampling of populations. Most of the research has been conducted in Euro-American societies. Suppose we extend the sampling to the entire universe of populations, including those living under Stone Age conditions. (This requires the construction of IQ tests that have panhuman applicability—in actuality, far from being achieved.) The range of environmental variables would be immensely increased. Consequently, in all likelihood a much lower value of heritability coefficient would be obtained. The point is that a finding about heritability is applicable only to the population where the study was made. Furthermore, if the environmental characteristics of the population change over time, the finding is applicable only to the generation studied. In sum, the finding is subject to both spatial and temporal limitations.

We can also test the generality of psychological laws or principles. For example, are Piaget's stages of intellectual development invariant across cultures? And Kohlberg's stages of moral development? The degree of generality may be assessed by their range of applicability, that is, by delineating the cultural conditions under which they remain valid or become invalid. Suppose we have a principle stating that there is a specific pattern of relations among several variables. We find that the pattern of relations is highly similar across the cultures studied. It would be reasonable to conclude that the principle tested has a high degree of generality.

In testing the generality of a principle, one recommended approach is to maximize the variance of variables through sampling from heterogeneous populations. This makes it more likely to include subjects with widely different attributes. Thus the variance of their attributes, including those not directly related to the principle being tested, has been maximized. A principle validated under the condition of maximized variance is said to be robust. In contrast, the approach of Berry and Annis (1974) is to minimize the variance. This is analogous to an experiment in which experimental manipulation is reduced to a point where effects may no longer be observed.

Panhuman variability and invariance in psychological functioning can be established with confidence only when observations have been made under a sufficiently wide range of cultural conditions. Principles presumed to have panhuman validity, that is, invariance across all known cultural conditions, are universal generalizations. They are especially significant because the quest for universal principles has been a longstanding aim of psychological science. In practice, however, panhuman validity is difficult to demonstrate. What is required is that no major exception is found in a sizable number of diverse cultures investigated.

Another promise of cross-cultural research stems from its inclusion of and emphasis given to ethnic-cultural variables, in addition to the usual variables of psychological functioning. Investigating systematic relations between these two classes of variables is now brought into the research agenda. These relations may be causal or merely correlational. If causal relations are entailed, usually psychological variables are regarded as the effects, or dependent variables, and cultural variables as the causes, or independent variables.

The reason is that traditionally behavioral scientists are interested in how culture shapes psychological functioning. However, there is no intrinsic reason why this has to be so. A fertile area of investigation awaits our attention: How does the psychological and social functioning of individuals collectively affect cultural processes and translate into cultural change?

If our research agenda were successfully followed, cross-cultural psychology would attain the status of a mature science. The promise is no less than a coherent body of knowledge about behavior-culture interactions involving both individual and collective phenomena. These interactions are of unsurpassed significance in behavioral science because they tell the story of how human character and culture create each other. If culture is defined as that part of the environment created by human beings, then we create environments that, in turn, make us human. In short, human beings are both the creators and the products of culture.

ANALYTIC CONCEPTS USED IN CROSS-CULTURAL PSYCHOLOGY

Cross-cultural psychologists have introduced three important terms that serve as analytic concepts: *emics, etics,* and *theorics.* Emics are culture-specific concepts; they apply in a particular culture, and no a priori claim is made that they apply in another. The emic approach aims to describe and interpret behavior in terms that are meaningful to members of a particular culture. Etics are culture-invariant concepts or universals; or, if not entirely universal, they apply to more than one culture—many more. They may be used to analyze emic phenomena. The etic approach aims to make valid cross-cultural comparisons and is characterized by the discovery of true universals in different cultures. Etics that are assumed, but have not been demonstrated, to be true universals have been called imposed etics (Berry, 1969, p. 124) or pseudoetics (Triandis, Malpass, & Davidson, 1972, p. 6). Such etics are said to be usually only Euro-American emics indiscriminately, even ethnocentrically, imposed on the interpretation of behavior in other cultures. A true etic, in contrast, is empirically and theoretically derived from the common features of a phenomenon under investigation in different cultures. Berry (1969, p. 124) called this a derived etic. At an even higher level of analysis, general principles are formulated to explain or account for systematic variation as well as invariance in human behavior across cultures. Naroll (1971a) proposed that the term *theorics* be applied to this level of analysis. Berry (1980, p. 13) defined theorics as "theoretical concepts employed by social scientists to interpret and account for emic variation and etic constancies."

An example may be used to illustrate the meanings of emics and etics. The term *face,* which is Chinese in origin, may be cited as an example of emics. An emic approach would investigate face behavior in Chinese society, as perceived by Chinese people. Ho (1976) has argued, however, that the concept of face has universal applicability. In terms of two interacting parties, face is defined as "the reciprocated compliance, respect, and/or deference that each party expects from, and extends to, the other party" (p. 883). In terms of the emic-etic distinction, we would say that the emic conceptualization of what constitutes face and the rules governing face behavior may vary considerably across cultures; however, inasmuch as the concern for face is culturally invariant, the concept of face is an etic. The reader may also find it a challenging intellectual exercise to think of some examples of theorics. It may be observed that the term *theorics* is itself a theoric. More interesting is to note that the term *emics* is not an emic, and the term *etics* is not an etic; both are indeed theorics, abstract constructs used to interpret and explain culture-specific and universal phenomena respectively.

The emic and the etic approaches may be combined in cross-cultural research. An example of this research is Osgood's (1967) study of cross-cultural comparability in attitude measurement via multilingual semantic differentials. Methodologically, it has been proposed that the combined emic-etic approach consists of three stages of inquiry: "Initially, the researcher identifies an etic construct that appears to have universal status. Secondly, emic ways of measuring this construct are developed and validated. Finally, the *emically defined* construct can be used in making cross-cultural comparisons" (Davidson, Jaccard, Triandis, Morales, & Diaz-Guerrero, 1976, p. 2, italics added). An objection may be raised, however. In itself, to begin by identifying an etic construct calls for an ethnocentric or, more precisely, a culturocentric judgment. It would be better to begin with no presuppositions about universals; instead, universals are to be discovered. Emics pertaining to a domain of behavior from different cultures are first gathered and examined; among these, emics that appear to be similar across cultures suggest the existence of a universal.

An approach without presuppositions has been described by Ho (1988, pp. 56–62). It is advocated by some Filipino psychologists and appears to be well suited to the emic level of investigation, particularly during the initial stages. One begins with no preconceptions, no hypotheses, and no claim to any foreknowledge. One does not even entertain notions of the procedures to be followed, what one is searching for, or even the goals to be reached. There is only a global, undifferentiated notion of the subject matter to be investigated—which is subject to change as one proceeds. In fact, one does not even presume to know what questions should be asked, let alone the answers; that is, one admits not only that one does not know but also that one does not know what one needs to know. One proceeds as if one were in a state of total ignorance. With such an intellectual attitude, the researcher attends to the phenomena as they appear, without interpretation, as a starting point. The raw data consist of what people say and do, as well as the labels and conceptual schemes they use to interpret behavior. The researcher is then guided by the data obtained to discover what concepts need to be clarified, what the relevant variables are, and what measures can be suitably used. Further investigations, leading to reformulations, may be necessary before arriving at a formal research plan.

A cross-cultural psychology that relies solely or primarily on Euro-American concepts cannot be expected to achieve its stated aims. Unfortunately, however, a perusal of the literature reveals a paucity of theorizing with the use of concepts that are non-Western in origin. We would argue that cultures should be treated not only as targets of investigation but also as sources of intellectual nourishment. Concepts from each culture may be regarded as potentially useful, both as emics for interpreting behavior native to that culture and as alien concepts for interpreting behavior in another. We need to hold no prejudice against alien concepts as necessarily ethnocentric. On the contrary, borrowing alien concepts is in the spirit of cultural cross-fertilization and may result in a creative synthesis of native and alien ideas. In the same spirit, Ho (1988, pp. 62–64) argues that the richness of Asian concepts (e.g., face), pregnant with psychological and sociological meanings, may be more fully exploited to provide fresh ammunition for innovation in the behavioral sciences.

CONCEPTUAL AND METHODOLOGICAL ISSUES

Using the concept of culture as an explanatory construct is full of intellectual traps. We shall attempt to answer three broad questions. First, how can the concept of culture be used to explain psychological phenomena in a meaningful way? Second, how can the units of culture be defined, and what are the difficulties involved? Third, how can cultural variables be measured?

Culture as an Explanatory Construct

How do we interpret empirically established differences in behavior between cultural groups? The temptation is to explain, all too readily, the group differences on the basis of cultural differences. It would be wise to resist this temptation and to reflect on the intellectual traps of invoking the concept of culture as an explanatory construct. To begin with, very often cross-cultural or cross-ethnic differences decrease or even disappear when socioeconomic class is controlled. For example, Cashmore and Goodnow (1986) found that differences in parental values between Anglo-Australian and Italian parents in Australia decreased when indicators of socioeconomic status were taken into account. Lambert (1987) reported a similar finding in a study of child-rearing values in ten countries. Now suppose we systematically control for other potentially relevant factors, such as age, sex, and intelligence, as well. Differences that survive elimination may then be attributed to cultural differences. In effect, culture is treated as a residual variable. It explains the yet unexplained portion of the between-group variance. But has it now become a wastepaper-basket construct—a victim of having been invoked to explain too much?

In its crudest form, a simplistic yet overinclusive cultural explanation reduces to a facile notion: People in Culture A behave differently from people in Culture B, because Culture A is different from Culture B. For example, if Chinese are found to be more authoritarian than Americans, it is because Chinese culture is presumed to be more authoritarian than American culture. But what has been explained? An attempt at a full explanation would trace the difference in authoritarianism, a personality variable, to differences in socialization; in turn, differences in socialization could be traced to specific differences in cultural values, which must then be identified. Available evidence suggests that in Chinese culture, attitudes toward filial piety may indeed be linked to attitudes to child training (Ho & Kang, 1984), as well as to authoritarianism (Ho & Lee, 1974). The Confucian ethic of filial piety is, of course, markedly different from the corresponding American ethic governing intergenerational relationships.

Thus, to revitalize explanatory potency of the culture concept, we need to go beyond global explanations. A more satisfactory account of cultural effects requires conceptual linkages between culture and psychological functioning. The concept of internalization is useful here. It deals with the crucial question: How do cultural influences originally external to the individual transform into psychological forces operating within the individual? We need to gain a knowledge of how cultural differences translate into differences in the individual's psychological experience. In turn, the causal links between individual experience and personality formation—a classic psychological problem—will have to be investigated.

The Boundary Problem in Unit Definition

The literature of cross-cultural research is replete with studies that classify individuals arbitrarily according to the national or ethnic groups to which they belong. Common practice is, however, a poor guide to sound research. National or ethnic group membership does not necessarily correspond to cultural group membership. Multicultural or multiethnic groups may live in the same country, and some ethnic groups living in different countries share the same culture; also, cultural or subcultural diversity may be found within ethnic groups, and different ethic groups may share elements of the same culture. Cross-cultural studies are, therefore, not to be confused with cross-national or cross-ethnic studies.

The enterprise of cross-cultural research implies the existence of distinct cultural units with identifiable boundaries. In attempting to define these units, we confront the boundary problem. A cultural group is supposed to refer to a group of individuals who share a common culture. But what is "common," and what marks a culture apart from other cultures? It is, for instance, misleading to speak of the Indian culture as if it were a single monolithic entity, when in fact India is so rich in ethnic, linguistic, and religious diversity. This brings us to the question of how cultural boundaries may be delineated. Time, place, and language are obviously three differentiating factors of basic importance. Naroll's (1970) approach to unit definition, which has gained widespread recognition, employs the *cultunit* concept. A cultunit encompasses "people who are domestic speakers of a common district dialect language and who belong either to the same state or the same contact group" (p. 248). The double-language boundary method is proposed to establish language boundaries (Naroll, 1971b). Instead of trying to establish one boundary between two language communities, we proceed in two directions: from language A to language B, and from language B to language A. If a boundary is established in both directions, that is, if mutual unintelligibility is indeed found, we may treat the two language communities as two cultunits.

For cross-cultural research, classification based on well-defined cultural units is an improvement over that based on national or ethnic group membership. But cultural boundaries are not static, especially in the modern age of accelerated cultural changes and exchanges. Unit definition runs into serious difficulties when a culture is undergoing rapid changes or when cultures come into contact with each other. Cultural contacts, often in conflict, result in acculturation, the process—which may be bidirectional—whereby members of a cultural group learn and assume the behavior patterns of another cultural group to which they have been exposed. They may also lead to biculturalism or even multiculturalism, in which individuals are exposed and enculturated to more than one culture. These phenomena have not received the attention they deserve, but they do pose intellectual challenges to cross-cultural psychology. For instance, does it make sense at all to speak of cultural boundaries within the bicultural or multicultural mind?

Toward the Multidimensional Measurement of Cultural Variables

Classification is only one of the many steps of scientific inquiry; and the definition of cultural units, even if satisfactorily achieved, is only a step toward mature cross-cultural research. Unfortunately, in too many research studies, culture is still treated as a nominal variable: That is, individuals are assigned into groups on the basis of their cultural group membership. Observed group differences in behavior are then explained by reference to cultural differences between the assigned groups. Note that the behavioral differences are obtained from empirical results, but the cultural differences are presumed on the basis of a prior knowledge of the cultures compared.

An approach that reduces culture to the status of a nominal variable is inherently limited. First, categorical assignment presumes that each subject belongs to one, and only one, cultural unit. This presumption is untenable in the case of bicultural or multicultural individuals. Second, subcultural variations arising from potent factors such as age, sex, and socioeconomic class are ignored. More fundamentally, within-group individual differences in enculturation, and hence in the extent to which culture is internalized, cannot be dealt with. Cultural differences are thus reduced to differences in kind, not in degree. Third, culture is treated as a unidimensional variable; the multidimensional nature of cultural processes (e.g., language acquisition, socialization, and cultural cognition) is not addressed.

As social psychologists know, the group to which an individual belongs is not necessarily the same as the reference group with which the individual identifies. Cultural group membership per se, it should be pointed out, is not a psychological variable, but internalized culture, cultural identification, and cultural orientation are—just as age, sex, and socioeconomic class are not in themselves psychological variables, but psychological maturity, gender, and class identification are. Internalized culture may be defined as the cultural influences operating within the individual that shape personality formation and various aspects of psychological functioning. Individual cognition, for instance, is shaped by internalized cultural beliefs. A research example may be found in Ho (1977). Using Chinese popular sayings, each stating a stereotyped belief, a scale was constructed for measuring culture-specific belief stereotypy, a psychological construct referring to the persistent tendency to hold beliefs in a rigid, undifferentiated, and oversimplified manner. The concept of cultural identification acknowledges that individuals may differ in the extent to which they identify with the cultural traditions of their group. And the concept of cultural orientation reaffirms a measure of autonomy in one's preference for various cultural patterns, perhaps even in articulating one's own transcultural value system. These concepts liberate us from the rigidity of looking at people solely in terms of their cultural group membership.

A great deal more work will have to be done to develop multidimensional, quantitative measures of cultural variables. Three main classes of cultural variables are of special interest to cross-cultural psychology: (1) *exposure,* the quality and quantity of how an individual is actually exposed to the external culture (e.g., child-rearing practices); (2) *enculturation,* the process of how an individual learns from, adapts to, and is influenced by the culture to which he or she is exposed, and (3) *internalized culture,* a consequence of enculturation. Note that exposure refers to cultural processes external to the individual, in itself without reference to psychological functioning. In contrast, enculturation and internalized culture pertain at once to both external culture and internal psychological functioning, thus serving as conceptual links between these two domains.

The psychological approach to the study of cultural processes, it is now clear, differs from the anthropological. Psychologists certainly need to be better informed of the work of cultural anthropologists. They are also equipped to make a distinctive contribution in their own right. The psychological conception of culture is not the culture external to the individual, but the cultural internalized as a result of enculturation within the individual. Introducing the concept of internalized culture opens the door to a new territory of thought. Interest is now focused on how culture is experienced and internalized by the individual. Thus the psychological conception gives full recognition to individual differences in cultural processes. Given their penchant to measurement, psychologists are in a position to show how such processes can be measured, a necessary step for gaining fuller psychological knowledge.

NOTE

The author gratefully acknowledges the financial support he received from the Committee on Research and Conference Grants, University of Hong Kong, in the preparation of this chapter.

2

A Brief History of Cross-Cultural Psychology

John D. Hogan and Aldo Tartaglini

Cross-cultural psychology is a relatively new discipline, but its creation was inevitable. The potential for enhancing the science of psychology through the interdisciplinary collaboration of anthropology and sociology is so immense, the only reasonable question can be: Why did it take so long?

Without this collaboration, the explanatory value of large segments of psychology is restricted in important ways. Some of the most basic issues in scientific psychology have a limited empirical backbone without a knowledge of behavior across cultures (e.g., the nature-nurture controversy). Even widely accepted theories of development, most of which purport to have universal explanatory power (e.g., Jean Piaget and Lawrence Kohlberg), remain unfinished until their validity is confirmed through cross-cultural observations. "The scientist, no less than the most unsophisticated layperson who knows only his or her own society, becomes prey to ethnocentric judgments" (Segall, 1979, pp. 22–23).

In addition, cross-cultural research provides the opportunity to explore psychological issues that are otherwise difficult to explore: How do important variables manifest themselves when their contexts are different? How general are "general" laws of psychology? What can be learned from "natural" experiments which cannot be reproduced in the laboratory? (Triandis, Malpass, & Davidson, 1973).

These are not easy questions for the traditional experimental psychologist. In fact, they are almost impossible to solve by the old methods. The conventionally trained psychologist is raised in a tradition that places the laboratory at the core of the science and touts the most exquisite controls as a goal. The new experimental psychologist must be willing to go beyond these historical emphases and adapt to broader, often less-controlled, techniques.

To psychology's credit, it has shown a willingness to respond to the challenge, although its response has been tardy and far from unanimous. Now it is possible to ask less naive questions of the data, and the importance of these questions has not gone unnoticed. The amount of cross-cultural research published in recent years has become massive (Adler, 1977; Brislin, 1983). Klineberg (quoted in Segall, 1979, p. v) says that now "the significant material would fill a fair-sized library, with contributions by psychologists from many different countries." The question is: What forces led to this point?

THE BEGINNINGS

Jahoda (1977) and Klineberg (1980), in two surveys of cross-cultural psychology, describe the development of the discipline, with sources selected from ancient times through the mid-1970s. Klineberg, in particular, notes that many of the earliest writings display an interest in cross-cultural issues. This is true for a variety of fields, from history to art and philosophy, despite the formal label under which the writings were produced.

At its most basic level, cross-cultural research had its inception when one group, with certain folkways and language, began to observe another group with somewhat different characteristics. When the observations became part of a record, usually with a view to promoting the superiority of one of the groups, the history of cross-cultural psychology began. For example, Aristotle is cited for his judgments on the superior contributions of populations living around the border of the Mediterranean Sea. The Arab scholar Ibn Khaldun is mentioned for his conclusion, based on a survey, regarding the superiority of his own people. Many such notions would find later expression in the belief that certain groups were less developed than others but would be able to advance in the direction of modern civilization.

Nevertheless, a history of remarks aimed at group differences does not constitute a field of study. The remarks remain largely random comments until organized in some systematic way. This systematization occurred only in recent times. It should be remembered that psychology itself did not emerge as a separate area of scientific study until the latter part of the nineteenth century, when it found its first clear expression in Germany. Some have argued that it was during that same period, also in Germany, that the first formal glimmerings of cross-cultural psychology (as a subdiscipline of social psychology) were seen.

THE EMERGING DISCIPLINE

Segall (1979) states unequivocally that the roots of social psychology lie in the nineteenth century, nourished mostly in Germany by such works as

J. F. Herbart's *Lehrbuch zur Psychologie* (1816). Herbart argued that the individual could be understood only in a social context and that psychology must embrace the methods of science to pursue the systematic description of ethnic groups.

In 1860 began the publication of a journal that embodied many of Herbart's ideas: *Zeitschrift für Völkerpsychologie und Sprachwissenschaft* (Journal of Folk Psychology and Language Science). A scholarly work, the journal was founded and edited by Lazurus and Steinthal and was published for thirty years. It had a broad range of articles that included group behavior, the psychology of culture, comparative studies, and a special emphasis on language.

Another German, Wilhelm Wundt, best remembered as the founder of experimental psychology, devoted many years to writing on customs, myths, and the relationship between a language and its people. Wundt published his *Völkerpsychologie* (Folk Psychology) in a series of ten volumes over a period of 20 years (1900–1920). As Adler (1989) has pointed out, these volumes do not constitute a cross-cultural treatise as is sometimes believed, nor is their title properly translated into English as "Folk Psychology." Nonetheless, she describes the work as Wundt's "mega-contribution to the discipline." Herbart's and Wundt's contributions to social psychology are now rarely mentioned, except in a historical context.

Whereas anthropologists and sociologists seemed willing to look to the findings of psychology, many psychologists remained oblivious to data outside their limited subfields. Consequently, the earliest experiments in cross-cultural psychology were for the most part conducted not by psychologists but by anthropologists using psychological techniques. Because of the difference in their background, the data-gathering techniques and interpretation of these workers would often differ from that of the traditional psychologist. For example, many of the early anthropological/psychological researchers questioned the emphasis on objective methods and the quantification of data, considering such procedures of doubtful utility.

Although it is clear that many events anticipated the development of cross-cultural psychology, as a part of social psychology, and that several choices could be made in identifying its formal introduction, "most psychologists now date the beginning of social psychology from 1908. That year saw the almost simultaneous publication of two textbooks with 'social psychology' in their titles, one by the psychologist William McDougall (1908), and the other by the sociologist E. A. Ross (1908)" (Segall, 1979, p. 29). The first textbook in social psychology to be written from a comparative, cross-cultural approach was *Social Psychology* by Otto Klineberg, and it would not appear until several decades later (Klineberg, 1940).

FRENCH AND BRITISH INFLUENCES

The inspiration of scholars from many countries affected the direction cross-cultural psychology was to take—sometimes by omission. For example, French sociologists of the nineteenth century paid little attention to the power of culture, concentrating instead on the effects of suggestion. Several important works gave the discipline a focus that would last until the mid-twentieth century. Emile Durkheim's (1897) *Le Suicide* emphasized the harmful effects of society. Durkheim believed that individual behavior was under the control of society. His was a sociologically oriented perspective that did not clearly distinguish between culture and social structure. Gustave LeBon's (1895) *The Crowd* emphasized the notion of a group mind, whereas Tarde's (1903) *The Laws of Imitation* highlighted abnormal aspects of social psychology. Because the influence of the French was greater than that of the British and Germans, the result was to retard development of a more normative, culturally-oriented social psychology (Segall, 1979, p. 31).

Among the British contributors, the work of W. H. R. Rivers (1864–1922) is particularly noteworthy. While teaching at Cambridge, Rivers was persuaded to participate in an expedition to the Torres Straits in 1899, an area located between New Guinea and Australia. Organized by A. C. Haddon, an anthropologist, the expedition also included C. S. Myers, William McDougall, and C. G. Seligman, each of whom would attain a level of celebrity in his own right, although not all connected to anthropology. McDougall, in particular, would later promote ideas directly at odds with a cultural interpretation of behavior. But it was Rivers's work on intelligence and sensory acuity among "primitive people" (Rivers, 1901) that has been called "the first modern empirical cross-cultural psychological study" (Jahoda, 1982, p. 19). Much of Rivers's subsequent writing reinforced the view that training in psychology was essential to success as a field anthropologist. One of his most visible students, A. R. Radcliffe-Brown (1881–1955), supported this position early on but later came to repudiate it. Instead, he adopted Durkheim's view and focused on the search for general laws of society.

Another great British contributor to early cross-cultural psychology was Bronisław Malinowski (1884–1942). Born in Poland and educated in Cracow, he received a Ph.D. in physics and mathematics, became enthralled with J. G. Frazer's *Golden Bough* (1890), and subsequently found himself studying experimental psychology under Wundt at Leipzig. Later he traveled to London, where through the efforts of Seligman, of Torres Straits fame, Malinowski was able to obtain support for fieldwork in New Guinea. A second trip to the Trobriand Islands near New Guinea followed. When World War I broke out, Malinowski stayed put, resulting in a longer stay and a greater immersion in the culture than he had originally intended. Much of Malinowski's later work was to find its origin in this second trip, including his attack on the universality of Sigmund Freud's Oedipus complex. He would continue to stress psychological processes throughout his career, although his focus often had a group emphasis to it.

The early work on methodology in cross-cultural research also owes a debt to Great Britain. J.W.M. Whiting (quoted by Price-Williams, 1979) identifies the first cross-cultural methodological paper as that by Edward Tylor in 1889, given at the Royal Anthropological Institute of Great Britain. The first application of the cross-cultural method in testing a hypothesis, according to Whiting (also quoted by Price-Williams, 1979) was a paper on alcohol and anxiety by Horton (1943).

FRANZ BOAS AND THE U.S. INFLUENCE

German-born Franz Boas (1858–1942) moved to the United States early in his career and came to dominate American anthropology. Throughout his career he retained an active interest in the psychological aspects of anthropology, challenging many of the positions psychologists took as a matter of course. Klineberg (1980, p. 36) called this a breakthrough in the relations between psychology and anthropology, one that would be continued by the students of Boas, who included Edward Sapir, Ruth Benedict, and Margaret Mead. Boas is "regarded as the founder of what became known as 'psychological anthropology' which flourished in America at a time when Radcliffe-Brown's influence in Britain had led to coolness and skepticism regarding the contribution of psychology" (Jahoda, 1982, p. 27). Boas asked that cultures be understood in their own right, not as a rung in a hierarchical ladder of evolution, nor as a genetically inferior cluster, but simply as a qualitatively varied entity.

The students of Boas began to apply his principles to a great many areas. Sapir became well known for his work in language, particularly the way in which language affected perceptions within a culture. This work would be carried on by his illustrious student, Benjamin Whorf. Sapir also studied the relationship between anthropology and psychiatry. Benedict focused on culturally derived notions of abnormality and, later, on studies of national character. Mead had the most directly visible impact on psychology. She began by attacking the theoretical concepts of G. Stanley Hall as they related to adolescent development, showing them to be of questionable validity when applied to other cultures. Later she would perform a similar function for several other cherished psychological concepts.

OTHER NATIONAL INFLUENCES

Although the influence of Western Europe and the United States on the history and evolution of cross-cultural psychology has been great, the contributions of other nations should be noted. A survey of articles published in the *Journal of Cross-Cultural Psychology* from 1970 to 1979 revealed that

52 countries were represented, 28 of which were neither European nor the United States (Lonner, 1980a). Some countries have been contributing for many years; others, no less important, have found a voice more recently. As another example of the geographically diverse contributions to the field, at a conference organized in New York in 1975, Leonore Loeb Adler brought together 76 social scientists from 12 countries on six continents.

In New Zealand at the end of World War II, Ivan Sutherland and Ernest Beaglehole began to develop a distinct "New Zealand psychology," combining anthropological and psychological approaches. James Ritchie, a student of Beaglehole, investigated the Rakau Maoris, the study of which "must surely be one of the first empirical studies of an indigenous tribal group made from a psychological viewpoint" (Shouksmith, quoted in Sexton & Hogan, 1992). Lise Bird has studied gender roles in New Zealand and Aotearoa (Bird, 1993), and Corey Muse has written about culture in Western Samoa (1991).

Other countries view themselves as natural laboratories for cross-cultural research and have produced books and articles to demonstrate that viewpoint. Among these countries are Hong Kong, a place where Eastern and Western cultures intersect, surrounded by political uncertainty; Israel, with its mixture of immigrants from different regions and cultures; Canada, a country of two distinct languages and customs; Australia, with its contrast of white Australians and Aborigines; and the United States which has long been a so-called melting pot of ethnic and cultural diversity. Other countries such as Iran, Egypt, New Guinea, and Taiwan have also made similar claims for uniqueness.

All of this should serve as a reminder. Although it is true that the literature in cross-cultural research is dominated "by individuals from relatively affluent, Western, predominantly English-speaking countries" (Lonner, 1980a), the significant contribution of other countries cannot be denied.

THREE POPULAR AREAS OF RESEARCH: DEVIANCE, PERCEPTION, AND PERSONALITY

Cross-cultural researchers have shown a tendency to focus on a limited number of areas. Three of the more popular areas are discussed next.

Deviance

Cross-cultural psychology has been concerned with conceptions of deviant behavior virtually from its beginnings, a tradition that Marsella (1979) has traced to the writings of the eighteenth-century philosopher Jean-Jacques Rousseau. Rousseau's conception of humankind as naturally good (along with the corollary that institutions are responsible for making humanity "bad") is cited as evidence that Rousseau was among the first to consider "the role of cultural factors in the etiology of mental disorders" (Marsella, 1979, p. 234).

During the nineteenth century, physicians interested in social reform commented on "the price we pay for civilization," suggesting that modern patterns of social organization were associated with an increase in mental disorders (Marsella, 1979). More refined attempts to explore the role of cultural factors in mental disorders began to appear in the early twentieth century. For example, Kraepelin noted cultural differences in the expression and frequency of mental disorders among various populations in Indonesia in 1904. Reports on "culture-specific disorders" such as *latah* (Van Brero, 1895), *mali mali* (Musgrave & Sison, 1910), and *arctic hysteria* (Brill, 1913) were published, as was research on the existence of "Western" disorders in non-Western cultures (e.g., Cleland, 1928).

Marsella (1979) notes that the first epidemiological studies of mental disorders in various cultural groups began to appear in the 1930s and 1940s, with estimates of the rates of mental disorders in countries such as Germany (e.g., Brugger, 1931) and Japan (e.g., Akimoto, Sunazaki, Okada, & Hanashiro, 1942).

The concept of normalcy itself became another major issue, that what was abnormal in one culture could be viewed as normal in another (e.g., Benedict, 1934). The next 40 years witnessed the emergence of research focused on the role of cultural variables in the etiology and the expression and treatment of mental disorders (e.g., Carothers, 1948; Yap, 1951; Leighton, Lambo, Hughes, Leighton, Murphy, & Macklin, 1963; Kleinman, 1977). Several journals concerned with the cross-cultural study of mental illness have also appeared, including the *International Journal of Social Psychiatry* and the *International Mental Health Research Newsletter*.

Perception

Studies of perception in relation to cultural factors have been of particular importance in the history of cross-cultural psychology also. The literature in this area is vast; hence only a few of the more pertinent studies are mentioned here. A more comprehensive review can be found in Deregowski (1980).

Cross-cultural studies of perception first began to appear at the turn of the century. Early efforts ranged from anecdotal reports of differences in perception of orientation among Malawi housemaids (Laws, 1886) to the more sophisticated reports on visual and auditory acuity (Rivers, 1901) and on the perception of geometric illusions, color, and form among the subjects of the Torres Straits expedition (Deregowski, 1980). The same expedition included a study of time perception (Myers, 1903) and an investigation of cutaneous sensation (McDougall, 1903).

Other notable pieces of research in this area have included investigations of perceptual constancy (e.g., Thouless, 1933), closure (e.g., Michael, 1953), binocular disparity (e.g., Bagby, 1957), pictorial perception (Hudson, 1960), and retinal pigmentation (e.g., Silver & Pollack, 1967). More recent efforts include cross-cultural responses to the Ponzo Illusion (Kilbride & Leibowitz, 1975, 1977, 1982; Brislin & Keating, 1976), perception of spatial relationships (Nicholson & Seddon, 1977), and factors influencing orientation errors (Jahoda, 1977).

Personality

The origins of cross-cultural personality research have been traced to descriptions of "primitive peoples" found in the writing of pre-Enlightenment European explorers, traders, and missionaries. Speculation about the psychological attributes of the "savage" were used to justify European dominance over native peoples (Bock, 1980). During the nineteenth century Social Darwinism fostered the notion that differences between European and non-European cultures reflected evolutionary processes. White Europeans were considered superior; nonwhites were "ranked according to their resemblance to white Europeans and their physical differences were related to levels of cultural development" (Bock, 1980, p. 9).

The birth of anthropology during this period saw a departure from racist interpretations of intercultural differences, although many early anthropologists continued to think of culture in terms of progressive levels of development, and people at a given level were thought to share similar psychological features. Lewis H. Morgan, one of the pioneers of this movement, associated specific psychological development with each level in a series of progressive cultural evolutionary stages. Another scholar, Sir Edward Tylor, argued that human thinking became progressively more rational as cultures evolved from simple to more complex forms (Bock, 1980).

Franz Boas asserted that primitives and civilized people did not have fundamentally different ways of thinking; he rejected the idea that racial and cultural differences reflected different evolutionary stages. Edward Sapir, influenced by Gestalt psychology, emphasized cultural and behavioral patterns of organization and suggested that a given personality organization or "configuration of experience" is a microcosm of its "official" culture. Benedict and Mead also became known as "configurationists," that is, they attempted to associate "cultural elements with aspects of personality" (Bock, 1980, p. 80).

The 1930s and 1940s witnessed further developments, including a new approach based on the concepts of basic personality structure and modal personality, which can be seen in the works of Abram Kardiner, Ralph Linton, and C. DuBois. Cross-cultural researchers began using projective tests such as the Rorschach during this period, a tactic that remained popular through the 1950s. For example, DuBois used the Rorschach as a means of studying the modal personality of the Alorese in the Dutch East Indies. Other researchers employed the Thematic Apperception Test in combination with the Rorschach (e.g., Gladwin & Sarason, 1953). This period also saw the emergence of "national character" studies (e.g., Benedict, 1946), which used the methods of basic and modal personality studies (Diaz-Guerrero, 1977; Bock, 1980).

Other areas of extensive cross-cultural investigation have included psychological testing, memory, cognitive style (Ahmed, 1989); field independence (Witkin, 1975); emotion, authoritarianism, attitudes (Graubert & Adler, 1982; Adler, Denmark, & Ahmed, 1991); developmental issues (Adler, 1977, 1982, 1989); and competence.

MODERN DEVELOPMENTS

Although many social psychologists continue to look exclusively within their own cultures for their source of inspiration and study, some prominent exceptions have arisen. One outstanding case was the emergence of an extraordinary group of interdisciplinary researchers at the Institute of Human Relations at Yale University during the 1930s and 1940s. Strongly empirical, and using Hullian learning theory as their major theoretical emphasis, they produced a number of classic contributions. Among these was the establishment of the Human Relations Areas Files, which permitted the exploration of a host of cross-cultural hypotheses. For instance, from these files was to emerge the classic Whiting and Child book (1953) describing child-rearing practices across cultures and the effect of these practices on adult personality.

Although there were few textbooks in social psychology that stressed the effects of culture, even into the 1950s, there is one exception worth noting—that by Kluckhohn and Murray (1953). "It was built around a simple premise: 'Every man is in certain respects like all other men, like some other men, like no other man' (p. 53). With these words Kluckhohn and Murray expressed the need for a social psychology that encompassed anthropology, sociology, and psychology" (Segall, 1979, p. 33).

Interest in cross-cultural psychology has continued to grow in the closing years of the twentieth century, nurtured in part by a world made smaller by mass communication and rapid transportation. It seems fair to conclude that the "missionary goals of cross-cultural psychology have been attained, even though all Western psychologists may not have been converted" (Doob, 1980, p. 70). With these goals attained, the field of cross-cultural psychology has finally entered the mainstream of the discipline of psychology.

3

Research Methods for Studies in the Field

Nihar R. Mrinal, Uma Singhal Mrinal,
and Harold Takooshian

"Tell me the environment in which you live, and I will tell you who you are." Cross-cultural researchers might well agree with this maxim from philosopher José Ortega y Gasset. This chapter offers a concise overview of the array of field methods available to those who study behavior cross-culturally, along with sources for more detailed information on each. These methods include various forms of experimentation, observation, sampling, assessment of personality and ability, surveys, and techniques of attitude measurement.

To what extent must researchers adapt their methods when working cross-culturally? This simple question has two aspects. In theory, the basic philosophy of science underlying social research has a certain universal quality, which transcends specific cultures (Kerlinger, 1986, pp. 3–41, 279–343). In practice, however, methods often need to be adapted to fit different cultural contexts where, for example, the same survey or experimental situation in one culture has a different meaning within another (Bond, 1989; Segall, Dasen, Berry, & Poortinga, 1990). This duality of theory and practice was expressed quite forcefully by Donald Campbell in his 1975 presidential address to the American Psychological Association (APA), in which he went so far as to chastize the scientific study of individual behavior as misdirected unless psychologists pay greater attention to progress within parallel behavioral sciences—anthropology (culture), sociology (social structure), and biology (genetics and evolution). He felt that to ignore the truths revealed by these other disciplines is to produce a distorted picture of the individual's behavior and mentality—this, even while psychologists continue to use proven, standardized techniques from their century-old arsenal of research methods.

EXPERIMENTATION

Experimentation is the backbone of research in psychology, its most commonly used method (Aronson, Ellsworth, Carlsmith, & Gonzales, 1990). It has a few defining features. The experimenter creates or manipulates an independent variable (IV) to observe its effect on the dependent variable (DV) in order to establish a causal relation between the two. Moreover, the experimenter strives for total control of the situation—including random selection and assignment of subjects to test groups and elimination or monitoring of any unwanted, extraneous variables (EV). In double-blind experiments, neither researcher nor subject is aware of the specific hypothesis, nor the group being tested. Aronson et al. (1990) offer a detailed volume-length guide to general principles of experimentation. Experiments come in at least three forms: laboratory, field, and quasi-experiments.

Laboratory experiments are done in a controlled setting—if not a laboratory, at least some classroom or other space over which the research has control of the environment—access, sound, lighting, temperature, and so on.

Field experiments occur outside of a controlled space—perhaps on the streets, in factories, or in offices—manipulating the IV in a more "natural," if uncontrolled, setting. Whereas laboratory experiments are deliberately artificial, field experiments gain in realism what they sacrifice in control. Moreover, field subjects typically do not know they are being studied, so their behavior is more free of the "demand characteristics" commonly found in a laboratory. Bickman and Henchy's (1973) *Beyond the Laboratory* offers models of field experimentation, including cross-cultural work.

Quasi-experiments are a particular type of field experiment. *Quasi* means "almost"—a design halfway between true experiment and correlational study. In a school, for instance, the researcher often cannot randomly select or assign pupils to treatment groups, so self-selection reduces the potency of any findings; one is not sure whether the obtained difference is due to treatment variation or to selection differences. Cook and Campbell's (1979) book *Quasi-Experimentation* is the classic that offers creative techniques to enhance our inferential powers in quasi-experimental designs.

Overall, experimentation is a pivotal technique in cross-cultural comparison because of its precision. Note, for example, that our behavior can be viewed in three very different ways: as a product of our internal dispositions (genes, biochemicals, personality traits), as a result of our situational context (physical and social environment), or as an outgrowth of the interaction of these two (dispositions within situations). These three factors can be experimentally separated for testing. For example, to see the effect of some specific reward on people in culture A and culture B, subjects in both cultures can be assigned to two different praise or reward conditions, making a 2 × 2 between-subjects factorial design (two cultures times two rewards). The main effects of A and of B can be studied separately, while the A × B result is the interaction effect. Thus, experimental method can replicate identical situations across cultures to compare directly not only the what but the why of cultural differences. As George Cuvier noted, "The observer listens to nature, but the experimenter can question her, and force her to reveal her secrets."

OBSERVATION

In observational studies, the researcher passively observes ongoing behavior in a natural setting. Unlike the experimenter, the observer does not create the situation; the subjects are self-selected and normally do not know they are being studied. Thus, observation offers total realism in place of the total artificiality of the experiment (Kerlinger, 1986, pp. 347–363). This is necessary when systematic manipulation of an IV is simply beyond the control of the researcher or when ethics prohibit its manipulation (as in morbidity studies). Here, a relationship between two or more variables is tested by monitoring both the IV and the DV; if change in one (the predictor) is found to be associated with another (the criterion), a link between them is posited.

Observation is typically an "unobtrusive method" because it studies subjects' behavior without their knowledge, thereby reducing the "reactive" biases inherent in experiments, surveys, and obtrusive observation. In experiments, for instance, people "react" when they know they are being studied, thus distorting their natural behaviors (Bochner, 1980). In surveys, too, people often act differently than they may in private; when asked their opinion publicly, they often give "socially desirable" answers, if not other distorted replies based on their own particular "response style"—ingratiating, acquiescent, suspicious, hostile (Sechrest, 1975). Such sources of error haunt obtrusive methods.

There are at least a few different types of observational research. In *structured observation,* the researcher is objective and detached from his or her subjects of study, for example, counting the frequency of a certain behavior in such a way that any other observer would count the same result. In *clinical observation,* the researcher is also detached from his or her subject of study but highly subjective, for example using "gut" impressions to better understand the why as well as the what of subjects' behavior. A pioneer of this clinical approach is the Tavistock Institute in London, where clinical observers apply the psychoanalytic concepts of individual pathology to better understand problems within industrial and other "neurotic" organizations.

A third method is *participant observation,* in which the researcher is immersed within the subject of study (Berry, 1969), for example, by becoming a member of a street crowd in order to study crowd behavior. Although unusual in psychology, participant observation is certainly a favored method within cultural anthropology. It has been used in three types of research: process research, theory-generating research, and case studies. Here the process means what happens over a period of time; in contrast, outcome research describes the end point or result. When we have little knowledge of the process, process research is useful. Participant observation is useful to verify theory. Case study has been used to study language development in babies, personality disorder, and community reactions to disaster. A key method in psychoanalysis, case study may involve a single person or a group of persons, animals, organizations, or events.

Participant observation has been criticized on various grounds. The emotions of the participant observer may color the data. When the participant observer is from some other race, for instance, he or she easily attracts the attention of the target group, and may thus face such questions as "Who are you?" and "What are you doing here?" In such research it is therefore wise to have distribution copies explaining one's role and the research plan and ensuring participants of the measures used to safeguard confidentiality. The researcher should decide whether the emphasis will be qualitative or quantitative (counting variables). Finally the researcher should design units of observation in terms of time, space, people, and events.

Time Sampling. In traditional time sampling the observation times are preselected. Munroe and Munroe (1971) found faults with traditional ways of time sampling because of display tendency. They preferred to be unobtrusive by approaching the settings quietly, unannounced. Known as spot observation, this method catches the subject unaware. Of course, prior permission should be obtained in such studies.

Event Sampling. Event sampling includes a sequence of behavior. Not only the actual behavior but the whole sequence is studied—before, during, and after the event. The Munroes used this method in their observation of infant behavior, recording the incidence, frequency, and duration of infant crying. They used a predetermined record form in which they noted the onset of each crying bout; the duration of each bout, the identity of the caretaker, and the character of the response.

Ethology. Ethology emerged from zoology as the systematic observation of the behavior of organisms and of how such behavior contributes to the preservation of the species. For example, the ethologist may film and then analyze the actions of newborns—their grasping reflex, search for the nipple, facial expressions, and other fixed action patterns and releasers. Another example common in cross-cultural work is analysis of gestures and greetings—some culture-specific, others more universal. Eibl-Eibesfeldt (1989) offers a magisterial survey of cross-cultural research in the tradition of ethology, much of it conducted in non-Western cultures.

Ecological Psychology

In the ecological approach, behavior is viewed as the result of interaction between the individual and his or her environment. The ecological approach is a particular brand of observational research pioneered by Roger Barker and his associates (1963, 1968; Barker & Wright, 1951, 1955), and it is based on the view that the total setting in which behavior occurs should be understood. For example, Edward Hall's (1959, 1966) pioneering research on proxemics studied how personal space varies across cultures, with four "distances" common between two speakers: intimate, personal, social, and public (see also Little, 1965). Whiting and Whiting (1978) studied socialization of children simultaneously in six different societies. Although Hall and the Whitings do not use the term *ecological psychology* for their research, their anthropological techniques exemplify the same approach to ecological psychology and behavioral mapping enunciated in the copious writings of Roger Barker and his associates.

SAMPLING

Cross-cultural comparison requires representative and equivalent samples across cultures, lest the results be misleading or ambiguous. This requires a sampling frame—some definition or enumeration of each full population (Henry, 1990).

Probability Sampling

Probability sampling is essential if the results of the sample are to be generalized to a larger population. The assumption of many statistical tests is that the data have been collected according to the rules of probability. Probability sampling types include simple, stratified, and stage sampling.

In a *simple random sample,* each unit or individual has an equal chance of being selected from the entire population. To get a sample of 100 from a population of 5,000, the researcher selects every "n-th," or fiftieth, individual. It is routine here to use a random-numbers table, Statistical Package for Social Sciences (SPSS), or a computer-generated source of random numbers to aid in selecting the 100.

In a *stratified random sample,* the population is divided into strata, or subparts, such as men or women, or juniors or seniors. For this, a list of each stratum is required and every n-th case is sampled, moving from one stratum to another. Thus the population of the sample remains proportionate to the strata in the general population.

Stage sampling, or area sampling, is used when the investigator is working with a large population. First, the areas are selected on the basis of nation, state, or region. Second, blocks are selected within the areas. Finally, housing units may be selected. For example, in a survey of schoolchildren, first districts, then schools, then classrooms, and finally individual children are selected. At each stage selection is random.

Nonprobability Sampling

When it is not possible to produce a sampling frame of the population, nonprobability (nonrepresentative) samples may be necessary (Sechrest, 1970). These techniques sacrifice generalizability of the results for convenience in recruiting available subjects. In cross-cultural research, particularly in anthropology, such nonrandom samples are common because of factors such as limited budget and time pressure; such sampling is also used in pilot studies or as pretesting prior to larger studies.

In *convenience sampling*, the researcher recruits the most convenient "warm bodies" prepared to cooperate—people in a school, bus or train station, park, office, or factory.

In *purposive sampling*, or *judgmental sampling*, also known as selective or deliberate sampling, subjects are selected to meet the preset criteria of the investigation.

In *quota sampling*, the researcher wants to be sure that included are some minimum number of persons from preset subgroups, such as specific age or sex; but unlike stratified probability sampling, a sample frame is not used for quota samples. Subgroups are identified, an arbitrary size per subgroup is set, and the first individuals to fill the quota are selected.

In *cluster sampling*, particularly for large-scale surveys, adjacent units or clusters may be selected—such as three adjoining housing units in a large housing complex.

In *snowball sampling*, the researcher selects a few subjects who possess the desired qualities, then uses these to ask the names of other people who have the same qualities. For example, left-handed people may suggest left-handed friends to enlarge the sample.

Expert choice sampling is similar to *judgmental sampling*, except that an expert selects the sample based on personal expertise with the group.

Selection of Units

Selection of Cultures. To compare some behavior across two or more cultures, how should the specific cultures be selected? This requires prior knowledge of the cultures. Detailed information about world cultures can be obtained from the Human Relation Area Files (HRAF) in two manuals. The *Outline of Cultural Materials* (Murdock, 1971) consists of 700 subjects categories under 79 major sections. The *Outline of World Cultures* (Murdock, 1975) classifies them into eight major geographical regions—Asia, Europe, Africa, Middle East, North America, Oceania, Russia, and South

America. The anthropological survey of India is a prime source on India's tribes and its people. Frazier and Glascock's chapter on aging in cross-cultural perspective extensively discusses how the difference in selection strategies by psychologists, anthropologists, and sociologists has influenced their conclusions about the nature of aging in different types of societies.

Community Selection. The selection of a Primary Sampling Unit (PSU) should be based on judgment. It is culture in miniature. Various key criteria—like size, type, characteristics, representativeness, replicability, age, and sex—should be considered. At least three problems complicate the selection of PSUs (Lonner & Berry, 1986). First is the continuous variation in culture and language over broad geographical areas. The Tharus, for example, spread from Nainital in India to Janakpur in Nepal and are divided into three subgroups: Rana, Dangora, and Katharia (Singhal & Mrinal, 1991). Ranas think themselves superior to most. The Gonds are also spread throughout India and nothing is common among them except the generic name. The second difficulty in sampling is nomadism—members of the same group may not remain in one place. Third, there may be ethnic variation within the basic cultural groups. It is suggested that single community should be assumed as representative of the culture as a whole and whenever there are differences due to ethnicity, acculturation, religion, or language the different groups may be selected.

Selection of Individuals. A sample should be representative as well as equivalent. In cross-cultural research, getting this kind by sample is difficult. Osgood, May, and Miron (1975) note the relationship between these two is opposite—if efforts are made to increase representativeness, equivalence drops, and vice versa. In India a representative sample requires proportionate numbers of many castes, religions, and languages. It will also have many illiterates. This sample would hardly have an equivalence with the representative sample of any other country. Although Indian college students may have high equivalence with the students of other countries, they are certainly less representative.

In fact the sampling strategy should depend entirely upon the purpose of research. Osgood favored maximization of equivalence and preferred subjects who can read, who are homogeneous, and who are accessible—hence average high school adolescents. The representative sample in cross-cultural research is inappropriate except in particular circumstances, such as opinion polls or some sort of national or community survey. Judgment should be emphasized.

ASSESSMENT OF PERSONALITY AND ABILITY

The study of the relationship between culture and personality has been a major subject of investigation in psychology and anthropology. Here, the researcher has to encounter at least four basic realities (Guthrie & Lonner,

1986). First, not a single theory of personality can be generalized across cultures. There are the analytic theories of Freud, Jung, Erikson, and Sullivan; the learning theories of Dollard and Miller, and Skinner; and the humanistic theories of Rogers and Maslow—each differing widely from the others. All the theories have a Western orientation that may be inappropriate for non-Western cultures. Second, broad and sweeping terms like *modal personality* or *national character* have proven unsatisfactory. In fact, all cultures have a wide range of personalities. Third, there is no substitute for a detailed knowledge of the cultures under investigation. Library or brief "airport" visits do not serve a meaningful purpose (Campbell, 1964). The fourth reality is that samples in cross-cultural studies may not be ideal; take, for example, college students, urbanites, or other volunteers who have become quite familiar with various tests and scales; they may understand the five-, seven- or nine-point scales, whereas their compatriots may not understand much beyond the extremes of good and bad. Some researchers nonetheless favor college student samples as a safe choice because of their ease of comparison cross-nationally (Sechrest, Fay, Zaidi, & Florez, 1973).

Selection of a Measurement Procedure

A novice researcher may pick up some familiar test, administer it, and then try to connect the result with some theory. In reality the selection of a test should be the last step in planning research. Measurement is a means to an end, not an end in itself. A measurement procedure is selected to answer a question, test a theory, or reveal the relationship among specific variables modified by culture.

There are many difficulties in cross-cultural research design. Equating measures of both antecedent and consequent variables in two or more societies is difficult. Even if one decides to study his or her own culture, the conditions within cultures do not always remain the same. This problem could be reduced by doing various parallel studies in different societies.

Plenty of measurement techniques assess personality. Behavior is not only a function of dispositions; situations also play a major role in determining behavior (Mischel, 1968). Filipino subjects, for instance, could not rate their friends in the absence of a particular situation (Guthrie, Jackson, Astilla, & Elwood, 1983). Americans, on the other hand, tend to be situationist in explaining their own behavior and dispositional in judging others' behavior (Jones, 1976).

The researcher may choose a personality test on the basis of some theoretical formulation. For example, a psychoanalyst will favor the Rorschach Ink Blot Technique, or the Thematic Apperception Test (TAT), whereas a trait theorist will favor the Eysenck Personality Questionnaire (EPQ), Minnesota Multiphasic Personality Inventory (MMPI), or 16 Personality Factors (16 PF). Some common cross-cultural tests are the Adjective Check List

(ACL), California Psychological Inventory (CPI), EPQ, Rotter Internal-External (I-E) Scale, Strong-Campbell Interest Inventory, Personality Research Form (PRF), and State-Trait Anxiety Inventory (STAI). Most tests are Euro-American in origin, so the researcher is advised to administer them only after proper translation and adaptation if used in a different culture. Rich sourcebooks for finding valid, reliable tests are *Tests* (Sweetland & Keyser, 1983), Anne Anastasi's classic textbook *Psychological Testing* (available in many languages), and the journal *Educational and Psychological Measurement*.

Ability tests can be used cross-culturally too. Indeed, various so-called culture-fair, or nonverbal, tests of intelligence and aptitude have been available since the 1920s (Sweetland & Keyser, 1983)—the Beta II, Science Research Associates (SRA) Nonverbal Form, SRA Pictorial Reasoning Test, Raven's Standard Progressive Matrices and Advanced Progressive Matrices, Cattell's Culture-Fair Intelligence Tests, the D–48 or D–70 Dominoes Tests. Two cautions belong here. As Anastasi (1988) notes, being nonverbal does not make a test culture-fair; indeed, bias may enter at many stages of the research process—test design (pp. 297–309), administration (pp. 355–362), interpretation (pp. 66–67), and use. In addition, culture-fair tests seem to have only "moderate" reliabilities and validities compared with more traditional, culture-specific tests (e.g., Takooshian, 1985).

ASSESSMENT OF PSYCHOPATHOLOGY

Ralph Linton (1956) notes, "The test of relative normalcy is the extent to which the individual's experience has given him a personality conforming to the basic personality of his society." This cultural relativism among anthropologists is based on two types of evidence: (1) Normal behavior in one society may be considered abnormal in another. Zuni Indians consider as disordered behavior the initiative and drive normally expected by white Americans. (2) Some forms of psychological disturbance found in other cultures, such as *amok, koro,* or *latah* among the Malaysians and *Dhat* syndrome in India, are not widely known. (Khubalkur, Gupta, & Jain, 1986).

Researchers have been interested in various facets of cross-cultural difference in psychopathology—incidence, prevalence, course, treatment, and symptom cluster. Some cultures view mental disease as punishment or possession by particular gods and accordingly treat such illness through religious ritual, including chanting or punishment, carried out by local shamans. To know the accurate incidence, prevalence rate, and course of mental illness is a difficult task (Gurland & Zubin, 1982). Many patients are treated at home by private doctors because of the social stigma attached to mental illness. Patients from lower socioeconomic status are more likely to visit hospitals.

Culture and Pathology

Cultural factors are especially notable when studying psychopathology cross-culturally, since even common disorders often have culture-specific symptomology. With depression, for example, a North American patient may experience hopelessness, helplessness, guilt, suicidal ideation, feeling of worthlessness, loss of interest in various activities, and loss of ability to experience pleasure. Yet a depressed Nigerian has heaviness or heat in the head, a burning sensation in the body, a crawling sensation in the head or the legs, and the feeling that the belly is bloated with water (Ebigno, 1982). Thus a depression scale developed in one culture may be invalid in another. Researchers should develop their own test—a time-consuming process—or else use methods like observation to assess psychopathology (Sartorius, Shapiro, & Jablensky, 1974). This issue is discussed further in Juris Draguns' Chapter 14.

TRANSLATION

Cross-cultural research often requires translation of an existing instrument so that a concept can be compared. This is safe as well as economical, but the research may miss many aspects of the phenomena of other cultures. The researcher's originality is also reduced. In translating a Euro-American instrument, some modifications are required. Some items may be excluded, others added. Two sets of guidelines must be followed in this regard, one for the original test developers and a second for the translators.

Constructing an Original Test

For researchers who know in advance that their new test will be used for cross-cultural comparison, Brislin, Lonner, and Thorndike (1973) and Brislin (1980) provide guidelines for preparing easy-to-translate materials. They recommend using brief items with one dominant idea per sentence, and active rather than passive voice (which is clearer to understand). Not to confuse the translator and the respondent, repetition only of nouns, not pronouns, is suggested. The researchers recommend avoiding metaphors and colloquialism because they may not have equivalents in the target language. Subjunctive forms like *should, would,* and so on, are also to be avoided. The key idea should be followed by an additive sentence because some respondents in the target culture may require more information. Prepositions and adverbs indicating where and when, such as *upper, lower, beyond,* and *frequently,* should be avoided, since the target language may not have adequate equivalents. Possessive forms should be avoided because the target language may not have a clear understanding of the concept of ownership. Words indicating vagueness should be avoided like *probably, perhaps,* and *maybe*. Two different verbs in a single sentence should also be avoided. Finally, words most familiar to the translators should be used.

Item Modification

Many personality tests like MMPI and CPI are diagnostic in nature, which is not apparent from the content. In translating these types of test the emphasis should be on intent and not on content. The results obtained with the translated instrument should be subjected to multivariate analysis.

Translation

Back-translation and centering is essential in translating an instrument. A team of bilinguals is required. Bilingual A translates items from the source language (say, English) to the target language (say, Hindi); bilingual B then translates it back in the original language English blindly. This process of decentering—so-called, since no language is the center of attention—is repeated for several rounds.

English	Hindi	English	Hindi	English
Bilingual	Bilingual	Bilingual	Bilingual	
A	B	C	D	

After some rounds the original English version and last back-translated English version are compared. Any discrepancy is an indication of the fact that the concept is not fit for translation. After discussion this discrepancy may be removed. Finally, the results obtained with the translated material should be subjected to multivariate analysis to see the appropriateness of translated material.

SURVEYS: QUESTIONNAIRE AND INTERVIEW

Whereas experiments and observations test overt behavior, surveys are well suited to assessing intangibles—one's attitudes, beliefs, expectations, and values (Fowler, 1993; Kerlinger, 1986, pp. 377–388). Surveys, which measure what people say about themselves, may be in the form of written questionnaires or oral interviews.

Questionnaire

Construction. Questions directly related to the topic are included. The questionnaire should be made appealing. It should be as short as possible to save the time of both researcher and respondent. Questions related to all the aspects should be included. Instructions should be brief. There may be many issues raised by respondents, and the investigator should be ready to deal with them.

Format. The questionnaire normally includes a cover letter stating the purpose of the research, its importance, and the vital need for the respondent's help regardless of his or her opinions. Questionnaires should be as brief as possible (one page is ideal) and contain three essential elements in this order: introduction, body, demographics. The introduction offers the title of the survey, its general purpose (but not specific hypotheses), its sponsor, directions for completion, the anonymity of responses, warm thanks, and possibly an address or phone that an interested respondent might contact for further information. A succinct example follows.

WOMEN'S OPINION SURVEY. Women around the world seem to have divided opinions about the feminist movement. We are researchers from the United Nations who would appreciate your frank opinions on the 20 statements below. For each item, circle whether you Agree (**A**), Disagree (**D**), or have No opinion (**N**). This survey is anonymous. Thank you.

The body of the questionnaire is its scale items. The third section, demographics, follows the scales so as not to influence the answers and to record the possibly relevant profile of the respondent—age, education, gender, occupation, race or cultural group, income, religion, and so on.

Questions. The body of the questionnaire may contain various types of questions, such as open-end, closed-end, contingency, and matrix questions. In open-end questions, appropriate space is left for respondents to pen their answer. This space should be neither too long nor too short. For handwritten answers, clear lines may be printed. Open-end questions run greater risk of unanswered questions, which are more difficult to code. In some cases open-end questions provide no alternative. In closed-end questions, the respondent is forced to select from a list of preset responses. For this reason closed-end questions are also known as forced-choice questions. An exhaustive list of possible answers should follow the question. For example, to a question about religion, possible answers may be Hindu, Muslim, Sikh, Parsee, Buddhist, Catholic, Protestant, Jewish, other, none. For an attitudinal item such as "How good a job do you think the new Prime Minister is doing?" the possible range of answers is Excellent, Very Good, Good, Fair, and Poor (Do Not Know can be included). Contingency questions depend upon responses to earlier questions. A question such as "What methods do you adopt for birth control?" may be contingent on the question, "Have you ever done anything to delay pregnancy?" The researcher may present a set of questions with similar answers, such as Strongly Agree, Agree, Disagree, Strongly Disagree, or Cannot Say. This format saves time and space and makes the questionnaire easier to answer. But the respondent may follow a pattern, like marking every Agree or Strongly Agree.

To minimize the response pattern some questions may be reversed so that the respondent may give consistent answers by agreeing with some and disagreeing with others.

Order of Questions. To increase cooperation, care should be taken in the order of the questions. Start the survey with interesting, nonthreatening items. Challenging items belong at the end of the questionnaire. Similar questions belong together. Finally, make the questionnaire visually attractive.

Interview Schedules

In some situations questions are spoken to the respondents, with answers recorded by the investigator (Kerlinger, 1986, pp. 438–448). The structured interview schedule is best seen as an oral questionnaire. The interview schedule requires instructions for the interviewer, especially if the interviewer is some hired assistant rather than the investigator. Wording of question should be easy to understand by both the interviewer and the respondent. Response categories should be clear, not vague. The order of question should interest and motivate respondents. Various techniques such as ranking, rating, paired comparison, or semantic differentials may be used in the answer choices.

The Interviewer. An ideal interviewer is one who can adapt the standardized questionnaire to the unstandardized respondent. Such interviewers are assertive and persistent in getting the answer from respondents. They are not amused, shocked, or surprised after hearing respondents' answers. They restrain prejudice and suppress their own opinion (Converse & Schuman, 1974). They have a solid understanding of the purpose of the research and are committed to completing the interview whatever the situation. Rehearsals are essential before the real interview, by pilot interviewing a few friends first, then asking which items are unclear and in need of revision or asking whether there are any questions that were expected but not asked. This is essential not only to improve the wording of the interview questions but also to become more familiar with the interview situation. The interviewer's personal features—like age, sex, race, dress, color, background, or accent, for example—may affect the interview situation and should therefore be minimized. Whenever the situation is difficult or dangerous, the ideal interviewer uses good judgment in deciding whether to continue or stop the interview. He or she maintains neutrality. Finally, when the interview is over, the interviewer thanks respondents for participating.

ATTITUDE MEASUREMENT

An attitude may be defined as a predisposition to behave in a certain way toward a specific object. Attitude has three components: belief, evaluative (or feeling), and behavior (Myers, 1993). The object of the attitude may be any social stimulus—another person, group, organization, program, policy, or social issue. One rich source of attitude scales of potential use in cross-cultural work is Robinson, Shaver, and Wrightsman's (1991) collection of over 100 original public-domain instruments, most of them tested for reliability and validity, on an array of topics: subjective well-being, self-esteem, shyness, depression, loneliness, alienation, trust, locus of control, authoritarianism, sex roles, and values. The most common attitude-scaling techniques are reviewed below (Judd, Smith, & Kidder, 1991; Kerlinger, 1986, pp. 449–467).

Thurstone Scale. In the Thurston scale, a large number of items are rated on favorability by "judges." Statements are then piled into 9 or 11 piles from the strongest measure, say 11, to the weakest, say 1. The researcher then determines an average score for each item from the average responses of judges. If there is disagreement between the judges regarding some items, the items are rejected. The final items are selected from different piles to give good coverage of the attitude. This method of scaling is one of the oldest, yet most time-consuming, and it is not often used today.

Likert Scale. The Likert scale (1932) is the most widely used scaling method. It is very simple: Each item or statement is followed by five or seven ordinal answer categories, such as (1) Strongly Agree, (2) Agree, (3) Do Not Know or Undecided, (4) Disagree, (5) Strongly Disagree. When the statement is followed by four or six ordinal answer categories—omitting the neutral category—the method resembles a forced choice. Scores are summed and averaged. A Likert scale may also be scored as "+2, +1, 0, −1, −2." Through factor analysis, the set of items can be clustered into factors. Bem's Sex Role Inventory (1974) is an example of this, as are the authoritarian personality scales (Adorno, Frenkel-Brunswik, Levinson, & Sanford, 1950).

Bogardus Social Distance Scale. The Bogardus method (Bogardus, 1925) has been widely used to measure and compare prejudices toward ethnic, occupational, and religious groups. The Bogardus social distance scale is made up of the items indicating degrees of acceptance of a "target" group. As an ordered or ranked scale, it has been criticized on the ground that it does not measure the actual distance between the various points on the scale.

Figure-Placement Task. Once used by Kleck, Buck, Goller, London, Pfeiffer, and Vukcevic (1968), and Adler and Iverson (1975), this tool was later modified by Adler and Graubert (1976), and Graubert and Adler (1982) for cross-national research. This instrument is used to measure projected social distance in millimeters. A colored round sticker of ¾ inch is placed at the center of an 8½ × 11 inch page of white paper. Atop each page a brief sentence identifies the sticker: "The sticker below represents a mental hospital." In place of "mental hospital," various stimulus items may be printed. Along with the booklet the subject is also provided a card with the same number of stickers as the stimulus items, of the same color, size, and shape, which in the instructions read as "your self." Subjects are instructed to place the "self" sticker "any place on the page." Later the distance between the two stickers, the "stimulus item" and the "self," is measured. Physical and interpersonal spacing, as well as projected social distances, are recognized as reflections of attitudes toward individuals or objects; close or near spacing represents positive and warm feelings, whereas far or large distances indicate negative or cold attitudes.

Guttman Scale. Like the Bogardus Scale, the Guttman scale is also a proximity technique. Statements are presented in ascending order, each representing a higher degree of the attitude in the preceding statement. A person who responds to item 4 should agree with all lower items—3, 2, and 1—whereas rejection of item 4 means that all statements higher on the scale (from 5 to n) are rejected. Then a scalogram is prepared and a reproducibility value is calculated, Reproducibility = 1 − (Number of errors/Number of responses). A reproducibility of 90 or more is deemed satisfactory.

Visual Attitude Scale. Various pictorial or graphic formats (in place of words) may be used to measure agreement in a Visual Attitude Scale. The respondent has to mark a check on a line with numbers or words. For example, Bem's Androgyny Scale (1974) uses this. So does the "Ladder of Life," assessing optimism and pessimism (Watts & Free, 1974, in Lindsey, 1975), in which the bottom step, 1, is the "worst possible life," whereas step 10, at the top, is the "best possible life."

Smiling Faces. Butzin and Anderson (1973) developed a "Smiling Faces" rating scale, with seven faces. In the center is the neutral face; on one extreme is a strong smiling face, on the other a strong frowning face. The authors also developed four scales having 15 faces each, to be used on a young male child, a young female child, an adult male, and an adult female, keeping in mind the tribal, rural, and illiterate population.

Forced-Choice Scales. A pair of statements is presented to the respondent, who must check the more acceptable one. The choice is forced, since the respondent must select one statement. The following is an example: (a) One should always be willing to admit mistakes. (b) It is usually best to cover up one's mistakes. Rotter's internal-external control scale (1966) is a forced-choice scale.

Semantic Differential Scale. The semantic differential scale arranges a list of adjectives in pairs of opposites, such as active-passive, prohibitive-permissive, or narrow-wide. The scale was developed by Osgood and his associates (Osgood, Suci & Tannenbaum, 1957). The following is an example:

Obstructive (1)—(2)—(3)—(4)—(5)—(6)—(7) Helpful

Here (1) is very closely related to obstructive, (2) is quite closely related to obstructive, (3) is only slightly related to obstructive, (4) is equally related to obstructive and helpful or completely irrelevant, (5) is slightly relevant to helpful, (6) is quite closely related to helpful, and (7) is very closely related to helpful.

"Own Categories" Technique. Muzafer and Carolyn Sherif (1969) developed a technique that asked respondents to pile up statements that belong together. They found that highly involved subjects used fewer categories in sorting statements into piles. They also found that highly involved respondents found a greater number of statements objectionable. This method is more valid and less subject to bias.

Sociometric Technique. In the Sociometric Technique, each member of the group writes down or tells the investigator whom he or she would like to work with or wants as a leader or partner in some task.

Sociogram. In a Sociogram a matrix is prepared having the names of the group members in rows and columns. The columns contain the names of the persons choosing, and the rows repeat the same names. When a person named in the column chooses a person named in the row, a check is marked in the corresponding box. This way the choices of each subject are summed up. A sociogram may be prepared from this matrix. A variation of this matrix is to place all the names in a circle and then connect by a line all the names that have interpersonal interacting with each other; in this way the most "liked" persons can be identified.

CONCLUSION

Like APA President Donald Campbell, psychologists increasingly seem to recognize that psychology must take cultural diversity into account in order to have a veridical understanding of individual behavior. The advertisement for a new introductory textbook noted that it "shows how sociocultural contexts influence the way people think, feel, and behave. Culture, ethnicity, race, and gender issues are woven throughout the authors' presentation of classic and contemporary research" (Allen & Santrock, 1993). To the extent that cross-cultural research will become more common in psychology's future, it is important for both the natural and social scientists among us to adapt our methods for the work ahead.

4

Language and Communication

John Beatty

Communication generally means the sending of a message in such a way that a receiver understands the message transmitted by a sender. Those acts in which information is communicated are rather complex. When a communicative act is broken down into its constituent parts, each part can be seen as a variable, which if altered in some way changes the nature of the message being sent. The following parts or variables can be isolated: a sender, a message, a code in which the message is sent, the medium through which the code is sent, the context in which it is sent, and a receiver. Each of these constitutes a variable in the communicative act. By changing the variable, the nature of the message is altered in some way.

Consider the following statement made by a police officer to a driver of a stopped car: "Let me see your license and registration." In this example, the variables are filled in the following way:

sender	the police officer
receiver	the driver
message	the request for specific materials
code	language (in this case specifically English)
medium	speech
context	official, at a car stop

Changes in any of the variables may alter the nature of the message. If the sender is not in fact a police officer but a civilian, the request may be handled quite differently than if the sender is actually the police. If the driver of the car is the chauffeur for the limousine being driven in a cavalcade with the president of the United States riding in the back seat, such a request is likely to meet minimally with the police officer's suspension.

One suspects that the police officer would be sent to psychological services for help if instead of speaking English the officer spoke in Croatian, or if instead of speaking the officer approached the car and attempted to transmit the message in a different code, say through gesture in pantomime. Even simply shifting the medium and writing the request would likely be seen as strange. In a different context, a police officer's making such a request of the president while touring the Capitol would definitely be considered bizarre.

This is not to say that any or all of these scenarios might not happen, but one would need to construct a highly specific context that would allow the other variables to be considered rational. If a police officer suspected that the driver of the presidential limousine were an imposter and an agent of a foreign government, then the question coming in a language other than English is reasonable.

Such situations, where contexts are generally seen as out of the norm are often called marked contexts. They require the construction of some situation before they are seen as acceptable.

PARTICIPANTS IN COMMUNICATION

Various cultures define different possibilities for the variables. Senders occur in all communicative acts and may vary as to age, sex, position, occupation, and so on. The implications of having or being a specific sender clearly can alter the message.

In English-speaking societies, when Mr. John Smith and Ms. Jane Doe meet, they can address each other in a number of possible ways. Even the decision as to which one speaks first can be significant. Consider the implications of each of the following sets of greetings, for instance.

> Good morning, Mr. Smith.
> Good morning, Ms. Doe.
>
> Good morning, John.
> Good morning, Ms. Doe.
>
> Good morning, John.
> Good morning, Jane.

In the first, one might conclude that the speakers are formal or distant but relatively equal in status. In the second, Ms. Doe has status over John, and in the third, the speakers appear more equal and informal or close because they are on a first-name basis.

The Japanese book *Kojiki* contains an episode in which the sex of the person speaking first is crucial! Thus in Japanese, as in English, who speaks first can communicate a great deal. However, in Japanese, formality and distance are not linked. One can be formal and close, formal and distant, informal and close, or even informal and distant. Immediately it is apparent that the categories used in analyzing the English situation are not quite comparable to the ones required in Japanese, where in fact far more possibilities exist.

Many titles are possible in Japanese: *-san, -sama, -kun, -chan,* and so on. Each of these can be suffixed to one's name regardless of one's sex—Japanese does not distinguish Mr. from Miss, Mrs., or Ms. In addition, Japanese can affix these titles to either the family name or the given name, and to occupational titles as well. Hence one can address someone, male or female, with the family name of Watanabe "Watanabe-san," "Watanabe-sama," "Watanabe-kun," or "Watanabe-chan." If the person's given name is Hajime, one can also use "Hajime-san" or "Hajime-sama." In addition, all these titles can be affixed to occupations. The Japanese word for fish store is *sakanaya (sakana* is "fish"; ya, "store"). The person operating such a store can be referred to or addressed as *sakanaya-san,* meaning "Mr. Fishmonger," "Mrs. Fishmonger," "Miss Fishmonger," or "Ms. Fishmonger." These various titles do not reflect formal versus informal or equal or skewed status distinctions the same way English does.

Similarly, various cultures will define various statuses and contexts differently. Any attempt to assume that a category that exists in one society will exist in another is dangerous.

CODES

Codes occur in many forms. The most common (and most studied) is language, but others, such as gesture, touch, smell, distance, and actions, are exploited regularly by people in all cultures. The following are indications of the kinds of codes and the variables contained within them (after Beatty & Takahashi, 1993).

Body Language, Gesture, and Posture

Body language deals largely with the human body as it is used for communication. Different parts of the body can be used to carry different symbolic meanings. Hair is one of the more common parts used: Hair length and style can send messages about age, gender, political position, and so on.

The use of body position and movement for communicative purposes is also part of this variable. The way the body is held and moves can convey a good deal of meaning. One has only to look at Greta Garbo in *Camille,* when she is told that she must give up her lover. At first she fights the idea, but then, with her back to the camera, she accepts this. Her whole body sags, and the audience immediately knows she has made that decision.

Gestures, in which are included generally body movements as well as facial expressions, use movement of parts of the body to convey meaning. Shaking the head for yes or no, or shrugging the shoulders ("I don't know" or "I'm not sure") are well known in Western society. Some societies reverse the meaning of nodding and shaking the head.

Gesture and body language are particularly irksome to work with, since no really good notation system is available for these forms of communication. The international phonetics alphabet, which allows linguists to transcribe and define virtually any sound in any language, has no real equivalent in any of the other variable areas. Even effort-stress notation or labonotation in dance do not come close. Most dancers feel these are mnemonic devices rather than real transcription systems.

Cross-culturally different body positions and movement can vary enormously. Despite this it is possible to classify communicative movements into five types (Ekman, 1980). These are

1. Emblems: those associated with clear meaning like the circle made with the thumb and index finger in America, with the other three fingers extended meaning "OK." Morris' book *Gestures* (1979) basically deals with emblems. The peculiar stance taken by members of the Japanese underworld and secret handshakes of particular organizations are examples. The most complex variables in this category are the sign languages used by deaf mutes or Native Americans of the Great Plains.

2. Illustrator: movements made mostly by hands and arms that are imitative or that just show some attribute like size, shape, or speed. Somewhat akin to this are the deictic illustrators that point toward objects (their relative position is an attribute). Cultural variation is possible here as well. For example, the Japanese tend to point to their own noses to indicate "I," whereas U.S. Americans generally point at their chests.

3. Body manipulator: the touching of one's own body or an object for no practical purpose. Examples of body manipulators are fidgeting or touching one's clothing. These communication acts are held by Ekman (1980) as being nonintentional. This class of acts is not associated with a specific meaning, but people tend to attribute such acts to certain psychological states such as nervousness, boredom, or anxiety or to personalities.

4. Regulator: largely movements of the eye and the surrounding tissues, which can vary the eye's appearance. Thus frowning, squinting, and eye movement itself are examples. These Ekman (1980) calls regulators because he feels they are involved with regulating the communicative interaction. Even here cross-cultural variation can occur. The eyebrow flick, commonly associated with recognition, is not universal; it is conspicuously absent in Japan (although eyebrow movement in and of itself is sufficiently important that even the traditional Japanese *bunraku* puppets have moveable eyebrows).

5. Facial expression: an expression of external state through use of the musculature

of the face. Ekman (1980) demonstrates that as far as the most fundamental emotions like happiness, sadness, anger, disgust, surprise, and fear are concerned, there is a good deal of universality with little cultural variability. However, there seem to be culture-specific rules to interpret the more subtle aspects of emotional expression.

Touching (Haptics)

Symbolically, touching is used in all cultures, whether it be handshaking, kissing, or some other form of body contact. Montagu (1971) has indicated a psychobiological foundation for touching and noted the importance of tender, loving care. There are a number of case histories of the importance of touch in children, who have literally died from a lack of it.

The variables in this area involve which parts of the body may be touched and with what intensity. Whether one touches softly, slaps, or hits, for example, varies the message dramatically. The range of message in this area is limited, however. Touching generally seems to define or reconfirm the social and emotional relationships between the participants.

Distance and Space (Proxemics)

There seems to be some evidence that overcrowding leads to stress, and so physical distance and space are intimately related with psychobiological variables.

E. Hall (1966) has established four ranges of physical distance that occur between people: intimate, personal, social, and public. Each of these distances serves a particular function, but significantly, the actual distances that define these ranges seem to vary from culture to culture. What North Americans regard as personal distance is regarded in parts of Latin America as public, hence Latin Americans tend to stand closer together when talking than is comfortable to North Americans.

Physical space can also be used symbolically to indicate social distance, status, role, rank, and so on. Consider such problems as occur in trying to create a seating arrangement at an international banquet.

Dress and Body Alteration

The human body can itself be altered or decorated. The ways in which material objects are attached onto the body or the body itself is manipulated can all signal various kinds of meaning. Clothing and accessories require some sort of purchase, and the accessibility of these objects becomes important. The possession of material objects leads to so-called status symbols, which send a meaning to people in a given culture.

The body itself may be temporarily or permanently altered. Humans alter the appearance of their own bodies by applying some objects on it in order to enhance the body's communicative values. Body paint and makeup are good examples of temporary changes made to the body. Within U.S. culture, for example, amount of makeup individuals use changes between peoples of different social status and in different social contexts.

Tattooing, scarring, and piercing represent more permanent change. The mutilation of the body constitutes the most dramatic form of communication in this area. In some societies, knocking out a tooth, circumcision, or cliterodectomy may be used as markers of status.

Actions

The idea that actions carry meanings is hardly new. "Actions speak louder than words" is an old saying in English. Actions usually involve a sender doing something that carries meaning. An act may be something like bringing a gift to someone with whom one is having dinner. The act of gift giving carries with it significant meaning for many cultures. The context in which gifts are presented, the size and nature of the gift, these vary from culture to culture and have to be considered as part of the communicative process in any culture.

Similarly, how people conceive of time and sociability may affect how they act. Whether people show up on time or are late, whether they hold different conversations with several people at once or focus on one conversation with one person, all convey specific messages.

LANGUAGE

Language seems to be the code *par excellence* for specific communication. It is the most commonly used and the most studied form of communication.

It is not uncommon to make several distinctions in dealing with language. The first of these distinctions is the difference between language and speech. Speech is what people actually say, whereas language is the embodiment of the rules for what they say. This distinction is later echoed in Chomsky's (1965) concept of competence (language) versus performance (speech). When talking frequently people often make errors. They backtrack, change their minds in the middle of a sentence, and in the process the sentence loses its grammaticality. People can often recognize grammatical errors in sentences, and in normal speech they may either go back and correct them or let them slide.

A second distinction is between *Language*—written with a capital *L* and not pluralized—as a generalized or universal category, and *language(s)*, the specific forms found in different societies. All human societies have Language, but just which language they have varies. This distinction between the universal and the specific has important ramifications discussed later in this chapter.

The Nature of Language: Phonology, Morphology, and Syntax

Most linguists recognize that languages are made of contrasting units of sound called phonemes. Phonemes are the contrastive units in speech. No speaker need make exactly the same sound each time he or she speaks, as sound spectrograms show, but each speaker does make sounds that fall within acceptable and generally predictable ranges. The significant contrastive units are called phonemes. Sapir (1933) recognized that it was the phoneme, not the actual sound, that had psychological reality for the speakers of a language.

Phonemes merely mark contrasts. They have no individual meaning. The sounds /p/, /i/, and /g/ are simply sounds in English and have no meaning of their own. When meaning is added, the resulting structure is called a morpheme: Generally, a morpheme is the smallest unit of sound with meaning. The separate sounds of *pig* are meaningless, for example, but when they are taken together, they have the meaning they do for English speakers. This feature is known as duality of patterning and is thought by many to be unique to language (Hockett 1960).

The last level of analysis is syntax—the organization of words into phrases and sentences. Morphology, which is the study of the morpheme and their arrangement into words, taken together with syntax, is known as grammar.

Phonology, morphology, and syntax are generally known as "descriptive" or "structural" linguistics. In addition to structural linguistics, linguists have been interested in another area, that of historical or comparative linguistics, which examines language change and the relationships among languages. A third division of linguistics involves the relationship between language and three other areas: social organization (sociolinguistics); culture (ethnolinguistics), and psychology (psycholinguistics). This last area generally deals with cognition, where it has ties to ethnolinguistics, and with language acquisition.

Cognition

When working within a given culture and language, it is possible to come to some understanding or cultural categories through the language itself. The relationship between language and cultural categories is one that has been investigated for many years. Its most popularly discussed formulation is known as the Sapir-Whorf hypothesis (Carroll 1956). An insurance investigator named Benjamin Lee Whorf postulated that certain kinds of accidents were caused by people's lack of understanding of certain linguistic forms, which in turn affected their behavior. The idea that *inflammable* was ambiguous and could be analyzed to mean "not flammable" or "able to inflame" led to the idea that language determined thought and structured reality. Far more complex than this initial postulation, the hypothesis holds that grammatical relationships cause people to perceive the world differently and that the formulation of strict causation seems to vary from place to place.

Today most linguists believe the Sapir-Whorf hypothesis is basically incorrect (see Hudson 1980), at least in most instances, and that rather than being causal, language reflects cultural categories. Popular writing has recently "discovered" the Sapir-Whorf hypothesis, however, and has moved it into the foreground. Many groups believe that by legislating the alteration of linguistic categories, the categories themselves will change. The classic example has been the move to change words like *chairman* into *chairperson*. Supporting the most extreme form of the Sapir-Whorf hypothesis, the argument here is that a change in the language will cause a change in the behavior and the culture. Bendix (1979) has succinctly argued against this contention, claiming that the ability to change the terminology does not cause change; that the ability to cause the linguistic change to happen is an example of growing political power.

Although there are many problems with the Sapir-Whorf hypothesis, outsiders can still gain entrance to the culture through its language. Even if the language itself may not cause the cultural categories to appear, they may well be markers of the existence of at least some categories. Hence understanding a language may require some analysis of its culture.

Many anthropologists believe that by examining the language one can glimpse the underlying categories reflected in the language. In these cases, a "folk taxonomy" structure is sought and the researcher is able to use terms in the language to show a kind of inclusion of terms in some semantic categories. In the same way that biologists would classify living things into different taxons (e.g., humans are kinds of primates, which are kinds of mammals, which are kinds of vertebrates, which are kinds of animals), language may allow for the classification of activities as seen by people in different cultures.

Classic examples of this kind of approach can be seen in Spradley's study of tramps (1968, 1970, 1971) and bars (Spradley & Mann, 1975), where an attempt is made to show how the linguistic categories reflect an underlying conceptualization of the world (see also, for method, Spradley, 1979, 1980).

Spradley is able to discuss, for example, "ways to make a jug" (i.e., ways to get an alcoholic beverage). These can be shown as

Ways to make a jug
    making a run

making the V.A.
bumming
    making a frisco circle
    panhandling
    bumming
cutting in on a jug

In this example, "making a run," "making the V.A.," "bumming," and "cutting in on a jug" are subdivisions of "ways to make a jug" in the same way that birds, reptiles, mammals, and fish are kinds of vertebrates. "Making a frisco circle," "panhandling," and "bumming" are kinds of "bumming" in the same way that cats, dogs, people, and monkeys are kinds of mammals.

The area in which most work has been done is known as *componential analysis*, which involves the analysis of the morphemes of a language to expose the component parts of semantic systems. Much of the early work in componential analysis was done in the area of kinship, where the significance of this kind of analysis has been hotly contested (Burling, 1964; Wallace, 1965; for some criticism of several analytical methods see Beatty, 1980). The basic idea, though, is that the semantics of different languages reveal underlying categories for each culture.

Universals versus Specifics

One of the more formidable tasks in researching the relationship between language and culture has been determining how much of what is known is universal and how much is cultural-specific.

In terms of language acquisition, a major area of research for many linguists has been the way in which people develop linguistic competence. It has been discovered that in any culture children learn their native languages at about the same speed. No language seems any easier or any more difficult than any other. The actual order in which various aspects of language are acquired has received significant attention (Jakobson, 1968). The way in which children acquire significant sounds (phonemes), the specifics of learning regular and irregular verbs, syntactic constructions, and semantics is still under study and doubtless will be studied for many years to come. Considerable universality is evident in certain aspects of language acquisition. Jakobson reports, for example, that children learn front consonants before they learn back ones and that fricatives are acquired only after homorganic stops.

Another area of importance in universals in linguistics is understanding just what patterns may be common to all languages, or which seem to be linked. For example, no language seems to have more nasals (/m/, /n/, etc.) than it has stops (/p/, /t/, /k/). It also appears that by and large languages in which the word order is Subject Verb Object (SVO), like English (e.g., "The man sees the woman"), put relative clauses after the word they modify (e.g., "The man, who is standing on the corner, sees the woman"—literally "man [topic] woman [object] sees"). Those languages that tend toward Subject Object Verb (SOV), like Japanese (e.g., "otoko wa onna wo mimasu"), tend to put the relative clause before the word it modifies (e.g., "kado de tatte iru otoko wa onna wo mimasu"—literally "corner on standing is man [topic] woman [object] sees").

Of particular interest in this area has been the study of Creoles. Creoles in different parts of the world share certain similarities that are difficult to explain by claiming a common ancestor for all of them, since many are "hybrids" of different languages.

Lounsbury's (1964) formal analysis argues that certain universal characteristics can be found in all kin terms that allows for the analysis of kinship systems. For Lounsbury, one need only define eight basic or "primitive" kin types (mother, father, brother, sister, son, daughter, husband, and wife). When different sets of rules are added to these kin, all the kin types will be produced. Hence some radically different kinship systems may vary solely on the basis of a missing rule or two.

In a similar vein, Berlin and Kay (1969) have argued that although a variety of cultures have different numbers of terms for colors, the focus of the colors and the order in which new color terms are added is basically constant.

Adler, Denmark, Miao, Ahmed, Takooshian, Adler, H., & Wesner (1992) have shown that in experimental and laboratory situations, certain schema regarding the distancing of different classes of people (i.e., blood relatives, etc.) remain the same cross-culturally.

The work on universals has been significant in raising questions about why such universals exist. Whether or not scientists opt for a genetic basis for universal behaviors, or whether they are seen as species-typical rather than species-specific (Aronson, Tobach, Rosenblatt, & Lehrman, 1972) has been the focus of much debate in the area. The question of the biological foundation of language and culture is likely to persist for quite some time.

CROSS-CULTURAL VERSUS INTERCULTURAL PROBLEMS

For most researchers working in this area, cross-cultural studies are comparative and involve the analysis of data in different cultures with an eye toward comparing the similarities and differences that occur between cultures. In a sense one can examine the variables used by each culture in communication through verbal and nonverbal means.

Intercultural studies deal with the problems that arise when people from one culture attempt to communicate with people from another. In this area, the variables used by people from different cultures are often not the same, and hence the potential for confusion and misunderstanding increase enormously.

Language and communication can be seen as two areas of human behavior that vary dramatically from culture to culture. Nonetheless, there is at the core of all this variation a certain kind of similarity postulated by some linguists, psychologists, and anthropologists; there is something universal. Without this core, translation from one language to another would be virtually impossible. In effect, by careful analysis of cross-cultural communication, it becomes possible to understand how individuals are able to communicate interculturally. All human languages and cultures seem to share a certain amount of commonality. Specific languages and cultures are variations on this common core, allowing for all cultures to be simultaneously unique yet the same.

5

Cross-Cultural Testing: Borrowing from One Culture and Applying It to Another

Peter F. Merenda

The issues that I am going to discuss are based on observations I have made during the past 23 years as a visiting scholar and research collaborator in a variety of cultures outside the United States. Some of these issues have been addressed in lectures I have delivered and in colloquia I have held at several foreign universities, notably in Iran, Italy, Poland, Portugal, and West Germany. The discussions following these lectures (mainly with university faculty members who were quite knowledgeable with the essentials of psychological testing) have resulted in mutual agreement on positions I have taken on the issues. However, the same ineffective and potentially dangerous practices, as I consider them to be, continue, in general, to the present time. That to which I am referring is the complete or nearly complete transfer of psychological tests from one culture (mainly the United States) to another culture. The medium of transfer is invariably literal translation from the written or spoken American English to the language of the foreign culture, and the simple restandardization of the instrument on local or national samples. Little or no attempt seems to be ever made to revise, modify, or amend the content of these tests to fit the receiving culture. More so and worse still is that the tests and scales are restandardized on representative samples from the populations to be served by these transported psychological assessment devices and techniques without replacing items and rescoring them on the basis of new cultural content and purpose. Finally, but not in the least less serious, the faulty construction and poor psychometric properties of psychological assessment instruments that emanate from the originating culture or subculture, (e.g., the middle- to upper-class white students in normal classrooms in suburban schools in the United States) are retained, naturally, in the transfer. The negative consequences of such transfer are usually twofold: (1) psychological tests and/or other psychological assessment techniques that are presumed to be reliable, valid, and suitable in one culture are naively and erroneously assumed to be quite adaptable to other, rather different cultures; and (2) these same instruments and techniques are quite likely not to be as reliable and valid or even as suitable as they are presumed to be. These two characteristics prevail for even the best-known, most highly respected, and widely used psychological assessment instruments such as the Wechsler or Kaufman scales and the Minnesota Multiphasic Personality Inventory (MMPI) which are also among the most frequently transported from the United States to foreign cultures.

Let me illustrate these points by discussing the MMPI both from the standpoints of its inherent faults and its likely unsuitability for adaption to and adoption by different cultures. Primarily, the major issue is that of literal translation in the language of the inventory—a practice that is more often than not resorted to by the receiving culture.

To begin with let us examine the basic instrument itself. What are its major faults?—and they are many, although we could be led to believe that it is fault-free, considering its worldwide popularity and use (mainly with normal persons—a population for which it was not intended to be used). It is recognized at this point that the MMPI has recently undergone supposedly extensive revision. However, many of the major problems with the inventory remain unresolved, and many—if not most—of the foreign versions currently in use are based on the original inventory developed in the United States more than 50 years ago.

A summary of some of the major faults follows. These are clearly obvious to psychometricians who read the manual, and they have been cited repeatedly by authors of textbooks on psychological testing (e.g., Cronbach, 1960; Anastasi, 1982; as well as reviewers in the Buros Mental Measurement Yearbooks (MMYBs). In fact, some are even cited by the authors themselves in some of their early publications (see Hathaway and McKinley, 1951).

1. The scales are generally unreliable—about half of them are notoriously low, as low as .50 for test-retest coefficients with intervals as short as one day to at most one week.

2. The scales generally lack item homogeneity: split-half coefficients stepped up by the Spearman-Brown Formula are equally low for some scales.

3. The ten "clinical scales" are at best obsolete. As psychiatric scales they have been misleading from the very beginning, and empirical data analyses of items responses (e.g., factor analysis) have continuously produced different clusters than those indicated by the scoring keys.

4. The use of true-false item responses is highly questionable for a number of reasons. The escape category of "?" has in the past presented even further problems from a psychometric point of view.

5. The normative frequency distributions for all ten scales are very severely positively

skewed—an indication that only extremely elevated profiles are legitimately interpretable (especially in light of the exceptionally wide confidence intervals for more than half of the scales).

In addition to the above problems themselves consider the nature of many of the stimulus statements from the standpoint of lack of uniformity across cultures, such items as "The only interesting part of the newspaper is the funnies." "Usually, I would prefer to work with women." "I liked *Alice in Wonderland* by Lewis Carroll." "Women should not be allowed to drink in bars." "I prefer a shower to a bathtub." "I drink unusual amounts of water." "I used to like Drop the Handkerchief."

Consider the MMPI-2, which has now been released for operational use and is certainly likely to begin being adopted soon by cultures outside the United States, perhaps in the same manner that the original version has been introduced in the cultures over the years. While there have been some improvements such as those regarding the restandardization sample but still underrepresentative of minorities, especially Latinos, and rescaling of the basic clinical scales, many of the faults of the original scales remain. For example, the new test booklet contains 567 items; all of the original MMPI items, with certain modifications, are included, and only the first 370 items are used to derive scores for the basic scales.

Another recent example of how an adopting culture can be seriously misled by bodily transferring, through translation alone or even through restandardization of a widely used American test, is the Stanford-Binet Fourth Edition. The scale has recently been redeveloped by Thorndike, Hagen, and Sattler (1986) to ostensibly produce, for the first time in its very long history, four subcategories of intelligence. These areas are Verbal Reasoning, Abstract/Visual Reasoning, Quantitative Reasoning, and Short-term Memory. However, an extensive comprehensive factor analytic study of this version by independent researchers fails to confirm the new authors' claims (Reynolds, Kamphaus, & Rosenthal, 1988). Instead, what the factor analysis results reveal are that the new Binet is still a good measure of "g" as it has been shown to be all these years, which have included practically the entire twentieth century.

What are the positive options to these dilemmas? I would like to submit two major categories of options. First, rather than relying on well-established instruments as models or having them be transferred bodily from one culture to another, foreign psychologists should design and develop their own psychological assessment instruments and techniques (By now I trust that the reader has realized that "well-established" is not necessarily synonomous with "well-developed"). Test constructors in the new culture should borrow the concepts and ideas only, if desirable, from well-established tests and capitalize upon any recognized faults they may possess in order to preclude repeating them. In the past this avenue might have

presented a major obstacle to most "borrowing" cultures for lack of exper-
tise and other resources for self-initiation of test development projects.
However, times have changed and are continuing to change. The United
States, Great Britain, and France, which have been the principal nations
furnishing psychological assessment instruments to other cultures, no longer
have a monopoly in this field. Furthermore, the Division of Psychological
Assessment of the International Association of Applied Psychology and the
International Test Commission are now prepared to render expert assistance
in such enterprises. Although such projects are costly in terms of time,
money, and effort, I am convinced that in the long run, they represent the
only alternative in most instances to borrowing an assessment system that is
either not likely to be effective or, worse still, is likely to lead to disastrous
results.

The second option involves the direct adoption, or at least consideration
of adoption, of psychological tests and assessment devices that are not culturally biased. In this category are those instruments in which language,
either written or oral, is held to a minimum or even eliminated. For example,
the test-taking instructions could—if necessary or desirable—be given
through pantomime. More so, however, the essential feature of these instruments is that they are "culture-saturated." By that is meant that the
stimulus items and response categories present concepts, either concrete or
abstract or both, that are universally understood. To some extent, this has
already been accomplished in a variety of cultures through the rather wide
adoption of the Raven Progressive Matrices; namely, PM 38 and PM 47. I
will illustrate with three other examples that I am offering primarily as examples and not necessarily recommending their direct adoption.

THE RULON SEMANTIC TEST OF INTELLIGENCE

This is an American nonverbal test for assessing a person's conceptual
reasoning ability. The person is taught by pantomime the meaning of certain
related universal symbols, both concrete and abstract.

A combination of figures in plane geometry (e.g., squares, circles, dia-
monds, and triangles) are related to silhouettes of animals in action or in-
action (e.g., jumping or supine stance) (Rulon, 1953). Although the test
that was developed for use in the U.S. Army has never been published in a
civilian edition, examples of the items do appear in Rulon (1953) and Cronbach (1960). Interested parties, I am sure, could receive a complete copy
of one of the forms of the test by writing to the Personnel Research Division
of the Adjutant General's Office, Washington, D.C. However, consistent
with the thesis of this chapter, what is necessary primarily for adoption by
a new receiving culture are the underlying concepts and ideas it conveys.

CALVI'S TEST "G"

This is an Italian nonverbal test for assessing a person's conceptual reasoning ability. It was designed specifically for use in Italy, where dominoes are well known and game sets are quite common in households within the country. Although a verbal set of instructions accompanies the test, it too, like the Semantic Test of Intelligence, can be given in pantomime.

The test consists of series of faces of dominoes each of which represents some inferred logical sequence. The testee is required to choose from among options the correct face that completes the sequence. The test developed in Milan by Gabriele Calvi, a noted Italian psychologist, is currently available along with the Test Manual and technical publications by its author from the publishing house Organizzazioni Speciali, in Florence.

The items in both the Rulon and Calvi tests are spiraled, that is, they are presented to the testee in increasing order of difficulty. Two very easy items are presented early in the sequence of items in each of these tests. The items become increasingly more complex and hence more difficult. In the Rulon test, the format remains essentially the same, that is, black on white silhouettes; in the Calvi test, red dots are quickly added to the black dots.

THE BEDINI TEST OF DISTRIBUTED ATTENTION

This is another nonverbal Italian test. It has been designed to measure a person's ability to focus attention on a task that must be performed very quickly, and then to shift that attention to a reverse task. It is useful in diagnosing possible brain damage or arrest to the nervous system. The color coding of dots and lines is the key factor in test performance. The cultural factors are held constant across various cultures, and the primary deterrents to successful performance are impaired vision and color blindness.

The Bedini Test is currently being extensively researched in the United States for the purpose of producing a version, developed, restandardized, and validated for use in the North American culture.

In summary, what I have attempted to convey in this presentation is the need for precaution against the indiscriminate adoption primarily through the medium of literal translation of tests and other psychological assessment devices or techniques originating in an outside culture. In its place I am strongly recommending the initiation of developmental research directed toward producing within adopting cultures their own instruments, recognizing that the latter practice is time-consuming and expensive. In my own collaborative research projects of this kind I refuse to become involved in or continue the collaborative effort if my foreign colleagues are unable to commit themselves initially and maintain that commitment for a minimum period of five years. It is my firm conviction that only the two options which I have presented here can lead to the successful development of psychological assessment instruments in whatever culture is to be the setting for the application of such instruments.

NOTE

Adapted from a paper read at the Korean Psychological Association International Conference. "Individualism and Collectivism: Psychocultural Perspective from East and West." Academy of Korean Studies, Seoul, Korea, July 9–13, 1990.

Part II

Developmental Aspects in Cross-Cultural Psychology

6

Child Development

Harry W. Gardiner

In a special issue of the *International Journal of Behavioral Development*, Gustav Jahoda (1986) called attention to the fact that cross-cultural studies of human development had been steadily increasing for two decades. He also stated that "developmental psychology has been too parochial in its orientation" (p. 418). In 1983, Berry found the discipline "so culture-bound and culture-blind that . . . it should not be employed as it is" (p. 449). Just a decade ago, a more serious charge was uttered by Schwartz, who declared that "anthropologists had ignored children in culture while developmental psychologists had ignored culture in children" (1981, p. 4).

Such parochialism exists because many developmental theories have not been adequately tested for cross-cultural applicability. A notable exception is the theory of Jean Piaget, which is supported by research literature consisting of thousands of studies in over a hundred different cultures.

INTRODUCTION

Since any attempt to review even a small portion of cross-cultural studies of child development would be futile within the confines of this chapter, we shall focus on some representative areas of interest. These include infancy and childhood, parent-child interaction, Piagetian theory, and mathematical achievement.

For readers desiring a more comprehensive view of cross-cultural development, or for those wanting to explore specific topics in greater depth, several excellent references are available. One might begin with such classics as Urie Bronfenbrenner's *Two Worlds of Childhood: U.S. and U.S.S.R.*

(1970) and the series of books on *Six Cultures* by Whiting (1963), Whiting and Whiting (1975), and Whiting and Edwards (1988).

A requisite source of information is the *Handbook of Cross-Cultural Human Development,* edited by Munroe, Munroe, and Whiting (1981). Its 26 chapters include discussions on universals in human development, behavioral development in infancy, language development, and cognitive consequences of cultural opportunity. Another valuable reference is the *Handbook of Cross-Cultural Psychology,* edited by Triandis and Heron (1981). Volume 4, *Developmental Psychology,* includes chapters on infancy, schooling and the development of cognitive skills, and tests of Piaget's theory.

Supplementing these sources are several excellent review articles, including those by Kağitçibaşi and Berry (1989), Rogoff and Morelli (1989), Jahoda (1986), Segall (1986), Petzold (1983), and members of the Laboratory of Comparative Human Cognition (1979, 1983, 1986).

Before beginning a discussion of specific topics, it seems appropriate to ask, "In what ways can cross-cultural investigations contribute to our understanding of child development?" First, such studies oblige researchers to consider how their cultural beliefs influence the development of their theories and research designs. Nothing will help to reduce ethnocentrism as quickly as looking at behavior in another culture. Second, by conducting cross-cultural investigations, the number of independent and dependent variables can be greatly increased, for example, looking at gender differences, effects of parenting styles on primary school performance, and the measurement of individualism-collectivism. Finally, there is the ability to separate *emics* (culture-specific concepts) from *etics* (universal or culture-general concepts) by testing theories developed in one cultural context in another. The theories of Piaget, Kohlberg, and Freud are examples.

One of the most exciting and promising ideas to emerge from cross-cultural developmental work is the concept of a developmental niche. Based on an extensive series of studies among the Kipsigis-speaking communities in western Kenya, Super and Harkness (1986), a psychologist-anthropologist research team, have provided a way of bringing together and integrating findings from the two disciplines. Since its approach takes the child within his or her sociocultural context as the unit of analysis, it goes a long way toward answering the criticism that "anthropologists had ignored children in culture while developmental psychologists had ignored culture in children" (Schwartz, 1981, p. 4).

The three components of this approach include (1) the physical and social contexts in which a child lives (e.g., nuclear versus extended family), (2) the culturally determined education and child-rearing practices (e.g., informal versus formal schooling and independence versus dependence training), and (3) the psychological characteristics of a child's parents (e.g., developmental expectations). Super and Harkness see these components as interacting and functioning as a coordinated system in which the individual and the developmental niche adapt and influence each other. It is within this new frame-work that a unified account of development is beginning to unfold. It is an approach compatible with the presentation of material in this chapter and one we are certain to hear more about in the future.

INFANCY AND CHILDHOOD

Development during these early years has been extensively discussed in a number of useful sources to which the reader might turn for background information. These include *Human Behavior in Global Perspective* (Segall, Dasen, Berry, & Poortinga, 1990), *Cross-Cultural Research in Human Development* (Adler, 1989), *Human Development and Culture* (Valsiner, 1989), *Childhood Socialization* (Handel, 1988), and *Acquiring Culture: Cross-Cultural Studies in Child Development* (Jahoda & Lewis, 1988). For an excellent review of the nature, quality, and effects of childhood experiences prior to formal schooling, the reader is referred to Olmsted and Weikart's *How Nations Serve Young Children: Profiles of Child Care and Education in 14 Countries* (1989).

Rather than summarize these findings, let us focus attention on several insightful observations made by Werner (1988) in her persuasive article entitled "A Cross-Cultural Perspective on Infancy: Research and Social Issues."

Werner looks at two major issues: (1) the extent to which cross-cultural information about infant behavior and development can be applied in developing countries and (2) the relevancy of such information to social issues being faced by these nations. She suggests that cross-cultural infant research needs to more systematically address issues of demographic constraints, risk factors affecting the survival and quality of life experienced by young children, the changing context in which infant care is delivered, and the consequences of introducing Western intervention programs into cultures of the developing world.

In defense of the cross-cultural method, she states that observations of infant behavior in non-Western countries will result in "a wider range of biological and psychosocial factors that influence the development of infants than in industrialized countries" (p. 96).

At the same time, she supports the idea of universal concepts (etics) by noting that a common core seems to characterize the behavior of infants in different cultural settings. She makes specific reference to Piaget's stages of sensorimotor intelligence and development of such critical social responses as smiling and vocalization.

Werner concludes her article with a plea for "a more systematic linking of cross-cultural, cross-national, and subcultural studies of infant behavior and development, which share a common methodology and test the limits of our favorite developmental models (from attachment theory to Piagetian epistemology)" (p. 110). As we indicate elsewhere in this chapter, researchers are beginning to meet this challenge.

If we continue to carry out the best cross-cultural research we can, one day we may be able to agree with Werner's assertion that such an approach will "help to correct our vision and . . . [give] us a sense of humility about the limits of our present knowledge and a thirst for more . . . [and] it will have served us well" (p. 111).

PARENT-CHILD INTERACTION

The rapid development of cross-cultural research on parent-child interaction stems from much earlier work by Symonds (1939), Minturn and Lambert (1964), Ainsworth (1967), and others. For a comprehensive treatment, the reader is advised to consult a number of major works. For example, *The Family in Social Context* by Leslie and Korman (1985) provides a comparative view of family relationships from a cross-cultural perspective. Family issues are the focus of *Family in Transition* by Skolnick and Skolnick (1989). In *Parent-Child Interaction in Transition,* Kurian (1986) introduces some of the major issues confronting parent-child relationships in multicultural societies. Kurian is to be congratulated for achieving the goal stated in the introduction to the book: "to bring together studies which are otherwise unavailable to the scholar and the general reader to look at parent-child interaction primarily from a cross-cultural perspective" (p. 7).

The most recent contribution to this topic is *Extending Families: The Social Network of Parents and Their Children* by Cochran and his colleagues (1990). This volume provides new insights into the forces that help to shape individuals' behavior, beliefs, and development by analyzing longitudinal data from families living in opposing ecological niches.

The mother's role in this relationship has received attention in a variety of sources. Of particular interest is *Only Mothers Know* by Raphael and Davis (1985). In this book, the authors describe patterns of infant feeding in seven traditional cultures, including an Egyptian village, a Sardinian shepherd mountain community, a Moslem town in Trinidad, and a Mexican family. It is an engrossing narrative, based on women's stories "about hardships and courage and fun and the wisdom of mothers who know—as their own mothers knew—what keeps babies alive" (p. xvii).

A more comprehensive and detailed analysis of the maternal role is presented in *The Different Faces of Motherhood,* edited by Birns and Hay (1988), a collaborative effort by 18 women psychologists, ethologists, scholars, and educators. Among the chapters in this book are those devoted to a description of parent-child relationships in Morocco, China, and the Netherlands.

Whiting and Edwards (1988), in the conclusion of *Children of Different Worlds,* have this to say about similarities in children's development: "These similarities derive from universalities in the nurturing role and from the eliciting power of children. Mothers everywhere must meet predictable needs and wants when caring for children of a given age, and they must teach them socially approved behaviors and train them in age-appropriate skills" (pp. 266–267).

For an understanding of the role of the father, the reader would do well to consult Lamb's book on *The Father's Role: Cross-Cultural Perspectives* (1987), as well as *Fathering Behaviors* by Mackey (1985).

Until fairly recently, studies of parent-child interaction have tended to focus on descriptions within single cultures. Although comparisons among cultures have occasionally been reported, they have frequently produced contradictory results.

Bornstein and his colleagues (1990) have responded to the call for "renewed efforts toward obtaining fresh and expanded observational data . . . by identifying, describing, and comparing mother and infant . . . activities and interactions in Japan and America" (p. 269). For example, these researchers have noted that U.S. babies show more positive exploratory activities than do Japanese babies, whereas Japanese babies tend to vocalize negatively more than U.S. babies. These results confirm earlier findings but also raise questions about the origins of such differences. Additional hypothesis testing is in order, and Bornstein and his colleagues intend to do just this, as noted in this concluding comment: "It will be rewarding in future research to trace the predictive validity and differential developmental course of prominent mother and infant activities already emerging in the first year of life" (p. 283).

PIAGETIAN THEORY: CROSS-CULTURAL FINDINGS

It is Jean Piaget's view that changes in cognitive development result from children's attempts to adapt to the environment and make sense of their experiences. At the center of this work are the basic assumptions that (1) each of the four periods set forth exemplifies a fundamental cognitive structure that applies to all cognitive functions (e.g., perception, memory, and attention) and (2) these periods are universal and invariant (i.e., the sequence and approximate ages at which these structures and their abilities are attained will hold for individuals throughout the world).

Overview

There are a number of excellent reviews of Piagetian research, including the work of Dasen (1982) and Dasen and Heron (1981), who state, "It would certainly have been aesthetically more pleasing if we could now summarize a coherent body of empirical research, either supporting the universality of Piaget's theory or else disproving it. But cross-cultural Piagetian psychology has not yet reached that final stage of equilibrium! . . . Clearly, there is still a lot of work to be done" (p. 335).

Nevertheless, thousands of Piagetian studies have been conducted on hundreds of thousands of children, adolescents, and even adults, from six continents and hundreds of cultures and subcultures. These range from Aborigines in Australia (Dasen, 1977) to Zinacanteco Indians in Mexico (Greenfield & Childs, 1977) and from Eskimos in Alaska (Feldman, Lee, McLean, Pillemer, & Murray, 1974) to school children in Thailand (Gardiner, 1972) and in the Sudan in Africa (Ahmed, 1989).

Sensorimotor Period (Birth–2 Years)

Of all of Piaget's periods, the sensorimotor stage is the one receiving the least cross-cultural attention. A major reason is that observation methods and data-collecting techniques have been developed and standardized only within the last 20 years (Casati & Lezine, 1968; Uzgiris & Hunt, 1975).

The first cross-cultural study of sensorimotor intelligence was conducted in Zambia (Goldberg, 1972). Although minor differences in behavior were noted (a slight advance by African infants over American at 6 months and a slight lag at 9 and 12 months), findings generally supported Piaget's observations. A later study on the Ivory Coast, by Dasen and his colleagues (1978), showed African infants to be advanced in their development of object permanence. In another African study, this one in Nigeria, Mundy-Castle and Okonji (1976) reported that although early manipulation of objects is similar in English and Igbo infants, important differences emerge in later interactions with objects between mothers and infants.

In their review, Dasen and Heron (1981) recognize differences in the ages at which the substages of this period occur. However, they go on to stress that "in emphasizing these cultural differences, we may overlook the amazing commonality reported by all these studies: in fact, the qualitative characteristics of sensori-motor development are identical in all infants studied so far, despite vast differences in their cultural environments" (p. 305). Werner (1979), on the other hand, was led to conclude that "even in the first stage of cognitive development, that of sensorimotor intelligence, culture seems to influence the rate of development to some extent, although the similarity of structure and process is more striking than the differences. Content seems to be of little relevance to the activation of sensorimotor schemata" (p. 216).

Concrete Operational Period (7–11 Years)

The majority of cross-cultural Piagetian studies have focused on the transition from the preoperational to the concrete operational period and the attainment of conservation.

According to Fishbein (1984), the research literature published during the 1960s and early 1970s reported consistently large differences (as much as seven years) in favor of children in Westernized cultures when compared to those from developing cultures. However, Kamara (1971) drew attention to what he felt were three serious faults with most of this work: (1) The study of thinking in both these periods depends heavily on use of language, and most early researchers had little knowledge of either the culture or the language of their subjects. (2) Although Piaget favored use of clinical interviews for gathering information about children's thinking processes, many of these investigators used standardized measures requiring little use of language. (3) Accurate birth dates of subjects were not always available, and attempts to approximate ages were frequently off by as much as two years.

Fishbein cites a study by Nyiti (1982) that varied the languages used and employed three of Piaget's well-known conservation tasks. Subjects were children, aged 10 to 11, from two Canadian cultural groups: Micmac Indians from Cape Breton Island and Europeans (white English-speaking Canadians). The European children were interviewed as one group in English by an English-speaking European, whereas the Indian children were separated into two groups. In Group 1, children were interviewed first in English by an English-speaking European and then in the Micmac language by a Micmac Indian. In Group 2, the order of interviewing was reversed. Performances on the conservation tasks were nearly identical for the white Europeans and the Micmacs tested in their native languages. In addition, their performances were comparable to those of other Canadian, European, and U.S. children. On the other hand, the performance of Micmac Indians tested in English lagged significantly behind the first two groups. Most importantly, nearly twice as many children, at both the 10- and 11-year age level, interviewed in their native language were more capable of solving the three conservation tasks than were Micmac Indian children interviewed in English.

According to Nyiti, "It appears that cognitive structures described by Piaget are universal and represent a necessary condition for any successful acculturation . . . [and] while children in different cultures may have to deal with different realities, they all apply the same operations or processes of thought" (p. 165).

In an extensive review of cross-cultural findings related to performance on conservation tasks, Dasen (1982) found that results could be sorted into four distinct categories, each with a significant number of studies to support its position: (1) those cultural groups in which conservation appears at about the same time as it does in North American and European children (namely, Hong Kong Chinese, Australian Aborigines, Nigerians, Zambians, and Iranians), (2) those groups in which conservation typically develops earlier (notably Asians), (3) those cultures in which conservation appears as much as two to six years later (primarily African and lower-socioeconomic-status Europeans and Americans), and (4) those groups in which some individuals, even during the years of adolescence, fail to engage in concrete operations (Senegalese, Amazon Indians, Nepalese, and Algerians).

What conclusions can we draw from this wealth of cross-cultural data? First, evidence in favor of the universality of the structures or operations underlying the operational period is highly convincing. Second, whether or not these structures become functional and the rate at which this occurs appear to be strongly influenced by culture.

Formal Operational Period (12–   )

In studies among adolescents in New Guinea, using the pendulum problem no subjects performed at this level (Philip & Kelly, 1974; Kelly, 1977). Similarly, few adolescents showed formal operational thought when tested in Rwanda (Laurendeau-Bendavid, 1977). On the other hand, formal operational performance among Chinese children in Hong Kong, who experienced British education, was as good as or better than performance by European or U.S. children (Goodnow & Bethon, 1966), and some formal operational thinking appeared among schoolchildren in New South Wales and Central Java (Philip & Kelly, 1974).

The inability to show universality of formal operational thinking among adolescents and adults is not confined to the cross-cultural area. Studies by Modgil and Modgil (1976) have shown that not all adolescents or adults from Western technological cultures achieve this type of thinking and that they frequently show low levels of success on formal operational tasks. Additional studies conducted by Kohlberg and Gilligan (1971) reported that only 30 percent to 50 percent of subjects in late adolescence perform successfully on such tasks.

Findings such as these persuaded Piaget (1972) to take the position that all adults have the competence for performing at the formal operational level but that such performance may occur only under certain favorable circumstances. It is unclear whether this revised view should be applied only to adults in Western settings, where formal schooling is common, or whether such competence can be viewed as universal (Dasen & Heron, 1981).

Werner (1979) sums up the situation nicely when she states, "Formal-operational thinking might not appear at all or might appear in less-generalized form among cultures and individuals whose experience is limited to one or a few specialized or technical occupations. In other words, survival in a particular culture may not call for, nor be influenced by, formal logical thinking" (p. 224).

In general, research has confirmed the invariance of the sequence and the structural characteristics of the periods proposed by Piaget. However, the pace at which each period develops, and the behavior associated with it, may vary significantly from one individual to another. The achievement of the final period is also open to some question.

While the debate continues, former students and colleagues of Piaget, frequently referred to as neo-Piagetians, are attempting to deal with many of the points just mentioned.

Contributions of the Neo-Piagetians

Shulman and her colleagues (1985) have compiled an overview of research by a group of neo-Piagetians who have shown an interest in issues Piaget either ignored or to which he gave only superficial attention. Some have disproved a number of Piaget's basic theoretical positions (Mounoud & Vinter, 1985), others have provided fresh support (Chipman, 1985; de Ribaupierre, Rieben, & Lautrey, 1985), and still others have generated ideas for new positions (Bullinger, 1985; Doise, 1985).

The work of Schmid-Kitsikis (1985), focusing on social and emotional dimensions of development, provides a greater understanding of the manner in which individuals respond to, interact with, and interpret their environments. For example, she has taken the position that children's cognitive performance is influenced, and to a significant degree determined, by various emotional states.

Bertenthal (1987) concludes that the work of these neo-Piagetians seems to "demonstrate the increasing convergence in contemporary thinking about cognitive development. . . . [and that] the most consistent theme . . . is that new analytic techniques and new theories of development are guiding the current thinking of the neo-Piagetians" (p. 11). It will be interesting to see how their attempts to demonstrate and explain the relationships between cognitive, emotional, and social processes succeed, especially in the arena of cross-cultural research.

MATHEMATICAL ACHIEVEMENT

A contemporary argument states that U.S. school children lag far behind children of other nations in math achievement. It is asserted that Asian children, particularly those in Japan and China, outperform not only those in the United States but those of most other nations as well. What do cross-cultural studies tell us about this topic?

In a recent study of cultural values, parents' beliefs, and children's achievement, Chen and Uttal (1988) conclude that Chinese parents set higher standards and work more with their children on homework than do their U.S. counterparts. It also appears that Chinese cultural values, for example, "human malleability" and self-improvement, help to ensure that children will work "diligently" on assignments. Comparing the performance of students in the United States and Thailand, Gardiner and Gardiner (1991) draw similar conclusions and stress the importance of parents' attitudes toward learning, particularly the concern expressed by mothers.

On the other hand, Bacon and Ichikawa (1988), examining achievement among kindergartners, suggest that high parental expectation does not guarantee high performance. Instead, they point to differences in mothers' teaching styles. For example, Japanese mothers use a style of "patient example" rather than verbal interaction characteristic of U.S. mothers. This supports an earlier finding by Hess et al. (1986) that found Japanese mothers attempt to elicit interest in a subject rather than obtain correct solutions from children, as more frequently happens in U.S. parent-child interactions. White (1987) also noted that whereas Japanese "mothers spend many hours in cooperative games and pursuits with their children, such as drawing, reading storybooks, and playing writing and counting games," U.S. mothers provide their children with games and materials they can enjoy independently (p. 97).

Finally, in a study of the mathematics achievement of Chinese, Japanese, and U.S. children from kindergarten through elementary school, Stevenson and his colleagues (1986) attempted to isolate factors contributing to such differences. They used a variety of learning tasks, interviewed teachers and mothers, and observed children in classrooms. Results indicated that although cognitive abilities were similar, significant differences were present in children's school life, mothers' attitudes and beliefs, and involvement of both parents and children in schoolwork. They conclude that "mathematics and science play a small role in the U.S. conception of elementary education. . . . The poor performance of U.S. children that begins in kindergarten is maintained through the later grades" (p. 698).

What themes emerge from these and other studies? First, there is recognition of the dominant role in this process played by mothers. Second, cross-cultural evidence strongly suggests that an informal teaching style, like that found in many Asian cultures, focused on building interest, is a more effective way to teach very young children a variety of skills, including math. Finally, family size and space between children may also contribute to differences in understanding and performance (Sigel & Parke, 1987).

We need to gain a better understanding of how young children develop mathematical knowledge in the first place. According to Resnick (1989), "there is broad agreement . . . that mathematical knowledge—like all knowledge—is not directly absorbed but is constructed by each individual. This constructivist view is consonant with the theory of Jean Piaget but comes in many varieties and does not necessarily imply either a stage theory or the logical determinism of orthodox Piagetian theory" (p. 162). Resnick concludes that mathematical training in U.S. schools not only "seems not to build on this informal knowledge . . . [but] in some cases, it even suppresses it deliberately" (p. 168). She recommends that elementary school teachers place less stress on computational drill in favor of understanding why arithmetic procedures work. She refers to cross-cultural studies showing that "an elementary school lesson in Japan is likely to consider only two or three problems, discussing them from many angles and exploring underlying principles and implications. A comparable U.S. lesson is likely to spend only a brief time on explaining a procedure and then proceed to have children solve many similar problems, emphasizing accuracy and speed rather than understanding" (p. 168).

The task that lies ahead has been succinctly outlined by Sigel (1988): "What needs to be done now . . . is to move in an interdisciplinary way to link culture to action, as mediated by social institutions such as the family, the school, and the church. The interactions among these institutional settings may help us to understand how the complex networks function similarly and differently in different cultures" (p. 390).

The unique experimental work of David Lancy (1983), who has conducted studies in a very different ecology—Papua New Guinea—represents an exciting new direction for cross-cultural studies of cognition and mathematics. He focuses on what he calls the "co-evolution of culture, cognition, and schooling" and argues that at some point, usually after 16 years of schooling, "the educated individual joins a 'world culture' and has far more in common with his or her similarly educated counterparts on the other side of the globe than with uneducated kinsmen in his or her hometown or village" (p. 195). This is a point not recognized by a large number of researchers.

As the principal research officer in the Curriculum Branch of the Papua New Guinea Department of Education, Lancy's goal was to show how Western-style schooling could be adapted to the cognitive development of children representing ten highly diverse cultural backgrounds within one island society. Using indigenous counting and classification systems, he demonstrated that although the counting system correlated positively with performance on some quantification problems (e.g., Piagetian conservation of length tasks), it was not directly related to mathematics achievement on tests reflecting school curricula.

Lancy's book is filled with exciting hypotheses and speculations certain to inspire future research and is recommended to any serious cross-cultural investigator looking at the relationship between cognitive development and mathematical achievement.

CONCLUDING COMMENTS

This review has revealed a prolific output by investigators from many disciplines. During the past quarter century, data-gathering techniques and research paradigms have been thoughtfully refined and extended. We are seeing a greater emphasis on comparative studies and more attention to careful evaluation of theoretical positions and their applicability (or non-applicability) in diverse cultural settings.

Cross-cultural study of development frequently resembles a confused mosaic of often contradictory findings. Yet therein lies the promise and excitement of future endeavors. Children represent the future, and we need to better understand the factors that contribute to their development in order to provide the best opportunities for healthy biological, psychological, social, and emotional growth. Much more needs to be done, and as the cross-cultural perspective reveals, discovery of similarities and dissimilarities in human behavior will make our understanding both easier and more difficult.

Great challenges and tremendous opportunities lie ahead of us. We can only speculate about what cross-cultural research will tell us during the next quarter century—but, there is little doubt, it should prove most interesting.

7

Preference for Principled Moral Reasoning:
A Developmental and
Cross-Cultural Perspective

Uwe P. Gielen and Diomedes C. Markoulis

The study of moral reasoning and moral judgment constitutes a central concern of social psychology, since moral reasoning provides the norms that regulate social interaction. Earlier theorists in social psychology and anthropology tended to equate morality with conformity to cultural norms. They assumed that the moral development of children and adolescents depends upon the internalization of culturally variable norms through a process of social reinforcement, imitation of culturally structured behavior, and identification with authority figures such as parents. Learning theorists, cultural anthropologists, and psychoanalysts agreed that moral norms are culturally relative and are learned in nonrational ways (Brown, 1965).

During the last three decades the cognitive-developmental theorists Kohlberg (1984), Lind (1986), and Rest (1979) have suggested an alternative vision of what morality is about, how it develops, and how it should be studied. They have emphasized the universal aspects of reasoning about moral problems involving issues of justice. Because they have made quite specific if controversial predictions about the nature of moral reasoning, and because they have developed a variety of challenging research methods, their approaches have in recent years dominated the cross-cultural study of moral reasoning. Using their theoretical and methodological frameworks, empirical studies of moral reasoning have attempted to find out whether moral reasoning in a wide variety of societies develops in a structured, stagelike manner. More than 90 studies have investigated whether development follows a universal trajectory, beginning with a preconventional level of moral reasoning focused on the pragmatic consequences of one's actions, to a conventional level focusing on internalized conventional moral conceptions and expectations, and ending with a principled level emphasizing universalizable conceptions of justice, human solidarity, and dignity. Most cross-cultural studies on moral reasoning have validated the existence and developmental properties of the preconventional and conventional levels of moral reasoning, but the cross-cultural evidence for the postconventional, principled forms of moral reasoning has been weaker (Boyes & Walker, 1988; Eckensberger, 1993; Edwards, 1981, 1986; Gielen, 1991a, 1991b; Moon, 1986; Snarey, 1985; Snarey & Keljo, 1991). Indeed, critics of the cognitive-developmental approach have argued that Kohlberg's and Rest's stages of moral reasoning, and above all the principled stages, include fundamental Western, male, and social-class biases (Gilligan, 1982; Simpson, 1974; Vine, 1986). In the critics' view, Kohlberg's emphasis on moral autonomy as the endpoint of development reflects an ideological, male-oriented preoccupation with the modern Western themes of autonomy and individualism, thus making his theory ethnocentric and sexist.

This chapter focuses on a series of published and unpublished cross-cultural studies, which taken together suggest that principled forms of moral reasoning are recognized and preferred in a considerable variety of Western and East Asian societies. Specifically, the chapter reviews cross-cultural studies employing Rest's Defining Issues Test (DIT), a test that aims at measuring a person's preference hierarchy for moral arguments. After introducing a number of theoretical and methodological issues pertaining to the DIT, the chapter reviews 15 studies based upon the DIT.

It is argued that contrary to the views of critics, the sequence of preconventional, conventional, and principled forms of moral reasoning embodies not a Western and male-oriented ideology of "cold justice" but an evolving, gender-neutral search for more sophisticated and morally valid forms of social cooperation. The claim is made that the results of the studies under review provide support for a multicultural conception of morality while throwing into doubt the more extreme forms of cultural and ethical relativism.

THE QUESTION OF CULTURAL AND ETHICAL RELATIVISM

Cultural relativists emphasize that basic moral values and behaviors differ radically from society to society, and within a society from one cultural group to the next. For the relativist, morality is a concept relative to culture, referring to those values, attitudes, beliefs, and behavior patterns that are prescribed in a given society (Herskovits, 1948). Relativists argue that a belief in universal or universalizable moral conceptions is inherently ethnocentric and frequently reflects a deplorable Western form of "moral imperialism." Ethnocentrism is said to lead to scientific misjudgment and to the morally illicit imposition of the values of one's own society upon the equally valid but different values of another society. In this criticism, cultural relativism—the factual statement that morality *does* vary across societies—is joined to and confused with ethical relativism—the normative statement that one *should not* judge other societies by the standards of one's own society. Various versions of relativism pervade modern social science in the form of social learning theory in psychology, Marxism in political economics, and "culturology" in anthropology (Hatch, 1983). Relativism constitutes the reigning ideology in much of cross-cultural psychology as well.

In contrast to these widely accepted relativistic positions, Kohlberg (1984) has proposed that moral reasoning everywhere follows a sequence of stages that culminates in principled forms of moral reasoning. In his view, the later stages not only are psychologically more advanced but also represent more comprehensive and purer forms of justice. Consequently, his approach to the study of moral reasoning contains two fundamental claims: (1) the scientific or empirical claim that moral conceptions everywhere evolve from less-differentiated toward more-differentiated stages of reasoning and (2) the ethical or normative claim that from a philosophical point of view, the higher stages are superior to the lower stages. The first claim must be investigated empirically, whereas the second claim must be redeemed philosophically. The two claims are separate but intertwined because the empirical and cross-cultural study of moral reasoning can lead us to a more lucid understanding of our own ethical presuppositions.

Kohlberg opposes both cultural relativism and ethical relativism. He claims that cultural relativism is factually incorrect, since reasoning about problems of justice develops in similar ways in both Western and non-Western cultures. In addition, he opposes ethical relativism as being inherently contradictory and thus philosophically unsound: If moral ideas reflect nothing more than internalized cultural norms, are not the theories of the relativists themselves culture-bound and thus devoid of any general validity? Do not the relativists derive prescriptive-normative judgments from descriptive statements, thereby committing the basic logical error identified by philosophers as the "naturalistic fallacy"?

Historical considerations suggest that cultural-ethical relativism develops when rapid social changes in a given society lead to *anomie*, that is, a state of normlessness. Persons lose the conviction that the conventional values and norms of their society possess general validity. Alienation, pronounced individualism, and social disorganization are frequent responses to such a situation. Individuals are thrown back onto themselves but will, under favorable circumstances, develop their own moral principles. It may be said that the development of generally valid moral principles constitutes the "cure" for the "disease" of moral relativism. Implied in this statement is the assumption that moral development proceeds from the preconventional level to the conventional level to a transitional stage incorporating relativistic ideas, to the postconventional-principled level (Gielen, 1986). Kohlberg

(1984) and Rest (1979, 1986b) assume that this progression can be captured by their theory of successive stages of moral reasoning.

STAGES OF MORAL REASONING

Kohlberg (1984) and Rest (1979, 1983, 1986b) have proposed that thinking about interpersonal conflict situations develops in a systematic way. Six stages of moral thinking are assumed to be identifiable in all situations where persons have conflicting moral claims. Each stage of moral reasoning represents a separate and coherent theory of justice attempting to balance the conflicting claims. The six stages as conceptualized by Rest (1983) are depicted in Table 7.1.

When inspecting Table 7.1, it is important to keep several considerations in mind: (1) The stages are concerned with *justifications* that moral actors give for their actions. Persons in all cultures may be asked why they should, or should not, help, steal, lie, kill, or support another person in a specific situation of conflict. It is the answers to such *why* questions that are of crucial importance for Rest's theoretical scheme. (2) Rest's emphasis is upon the *structure* or *form* of the justifications rather than upon the specific and culturally variable *content* of the moral decision-making process. (3) Each stage represents a coherent philosophy of *justice*. Justice is concerned with the balancing of moral claims based upon equality, equity, desert, merit, and special circumstances. Moral situations involving problems of justice are quite varied and may involve competing concerns for human life and welfare, wealth, honor, loyalty, empathy, keeping contracts and one's word, retribution, restitution, and exchange arrangements. (4) The six stages depicted in Table 7.1 focus on the coordination of rules and expectations, schemes for balancing interests, and basic conceptions of rights and duties. Successive stages reformulate these three considerations in more abstract and comprehensive ways. (5) The stages are ordered according to a hierarchy. At the higher stages the range of social cooperation widens, moral considerations are increasingly differentiated from nonmoral considerations, and the divergent interests, needs, and concerns of the various moral actors are better integrated with each other and better balanced. It is assumed that persons tend to prefer the highest stage they can understand because they intuitively realize that the higher stages represent more comprehensive forms of moral problem solving. (6) The stages of moral reasoning apply only to *deontic* reasoning, that is, to reasoning that asks: What should be done in such and such a situation? The stages do not describe metaethical reasoning (reflections on the general nature of morality), reasoning about the good life (What is of value in human lives?); or metaphysical-religious reasoning (What are the ultimate powers of the universe, and how are humans related to them?). The stages do not focus on moral character, personality organization, or mental health; nor are the stage theories of moral reasoning used

Table 7.1
Stages of Moral Development According to Rest

Coordination of Expectations About Actions (How Rules Are Known and Shared)	Schemes of Balancing Interests (How Equilibrium Is Achieved)	Central Concept for Determining Moral Rights and Responsibilities
Stage		
Stage 1 The caretaker makes known certain demands on the child's behavior.	The child does not share in making rules but understands that obedience will bring freedom from punishment.	The morality of obedience: "Do what you're told."
Stage 2 Although each person is understood to have his own interests, an exchange of favors might be mutually decided.	If each party sees something to gain in an exchange, then both want to reciprocate.	The morality of instrumental egoism and simple exchange: "Let's make a deal."
Stage 3 Through reciprocal role taking, individuals attain a mutual understanding about each other and the ongoing pattern of interactions.	Friendship relationships establish a stabilized and enduring scheme of cooperation. Each party anticipates the feelings, needs, and wants of the other and acts in the others's welfare.	The morality of interpersonal concordance: "Be considerate, nice, and kind, and you'll get along with people."

Table 7.1 continued

Coordination of Expectations About Actions (How Rules Are Known and Shared)	Schemes of Balancing Interests (How Equilibrium Is Achieved)	Central Concept for Determining Moral Rights and Responsibilities
Stage		
Stage 4 All members of society know what is expected of them through public institutionalized law.	Unless a society-wide system of cooperation is established and stabilized, no individual can really make plans. Each person should follow the law and do his particular job, anticipating that other people will also fulfill their responsibilities.	The morality of law and duty to the social order: "Everyone in society is obligated and protected by the law."
Stage 5 Formal procedures are institutionalized for making laws, which one anticipates rational people would accept.	Law-making procedures are devised so that they reflect the general will of the people, at the same time insuring certain basic rights to all. With each person having a say in the decision process, each will see that his interests are maximized while at the same time having a basis for making claims on other people.	The morality of societal consensus: You are obligated by whatever arrangements are agreed to by due process procedures.
Stage 6 The logical requirements of nonarbitrary cooperation among rational, equal, and impartial people are taken as ideal criteria for social organization which one anticipates rational people would accept.	A scheme of cooperation that negates or neutralizes all arbitrary distribution of rights and responsibilities is the most equilibrated, for such system is maximizing the simultaneous benefit to each member so that any deviation from these rules would advantage some members at the expense of others.	The morality of nonarbitrary social cooperation: "How rational and impartial people would organize cooperation is moral."

Source: Rest (1983, p. 588). In P. Mussen (Ed.), *Handbook of Child Psychology*, Vol. 4 Copyright 1983. Reprinted by permission of I. Wiley & Sons Inc.

to establish the comparative moral worth of persons or societies. Readers wishing to gain a more detailed understanding of Kohlberg's and Rest's stage theories are referred to Kuhmerker (1991), Kohlberg (1984), and Rest (1979).

PRINCIPLED MORAL REASONING

At the postconventional or principled level of moral reasoning, a person has developed self-chosen, abstract moral principles that tend to focus on respect for individual dignity, benevolence, liberty, equality, human solidarity, and the maintenance of interpersonal trust. The person is able to take an outside-of-society perspective; that is, the person decides moral dilemmas from a point of view that could, ideally speaking, be adopted by any rational and impartial person in the given situation. Moral decision making is expected to be shareable or universalizable, representing an effort to reach consensus based upon nonarbitrary social cooperation.

Moral principles are more broadly conceived than moral rules. Whereas moral rules refer to specific injunctions such as You shall not steal, kill, cheat, lie, or rape, moral principles integrate specific moral rules and give them broader meaning. Moral principles enjoin us never to use another person merely as a means for our own purpose and pleasure, to consistently respect the human dignity of others and the self, and to take an attitude of *jen*— the Chinese virtue of human-heartedness—toward everybody (Roetz, 1990). Throughout the ages principled concerns for justice have been recognized by moral leaders in Western and non-Western societies alike (Vasudev & Hummel, 1987). Sometimes, moral principles are summed up as the Golden Rule or the Silver Rule (Roetz, 1990). The Silver Rule is recognized in India's *Mahabharata* ("This is the sum of duty: Do naught onto others which would cause pain if done to you"), in Chinese Confucianism ("Surely it is the maxim of loving kindness: Do not unto others that you would not have done unto you"), and in the Judaic *Talmud* ("What is hateful to you, do not to your fellow-man. That is the entire Law, all the rest is commentary.") Confucius combines the Golden Rule and the Silver Rule in the following saying attributed to him: "Do to everyman as thou wouldst have him do to thee; and do not unto another what thou wouldst not have him do unto thee." However, the Silver Rule and the Golden Rule must be universalized to all human beings, including women, children, and outgroup members, and to a broad variety of situations involving moral conflict, before they fully express the overriding moral principle of universal justice. In practice, persons as well as cultural traditions consistently fall short of the ideal of universal justice, but they may approximate it to varying degrees. Principled moral thinking is closer to the ideal than is conventional thinking, which in turn surpasses preconventional thinking.

MEASURING MORAL REASONING: THE DEFINING ISSUES TEST

In the cognitive-developmental tradition the two most influential approaches to the measurement of moral reasoning have been Kohlberg's Moral Judgment Interview (MJI) and Rest's Defining Issues Test (DIT). This chapter compares data from studies employing the DIT, which is an objective multiple-choice test that indexes moral development based upon the recognition of, and preference for, 72 moral arguments. The DIT contains six moral and political dilemmas. Two examples are as follows: (1) Should a poor husband (Heinz) steal a drug in order to save the life of his very sick wife if he cannot get the drug in any other way? (2) A man escapes from prison and subsequently leads a model life. Should a neighbor who years later recognizes him report him to the police? In cross-cultural research, culturally inappropriate dilemmas may be deleted and details of the various stories adapted to cultural circumstances.

For each moral dilemma, the DIT provides twelve arguments that can be used to solve the conflict. The arguments reflect different moral stages. Respondents are asked to rate and rank order the moral arguments. Two examples of arguments pertaining to the first dilemma (the Heinz story) are as follows: Stage 3: Isn't it only natural for a loving husband to care so much for his wife that he'd steal? Stage 6: What values are going to be the basis for governing how people act toward each other?

The DIT is objectively scored and provides moral stage scores for Stages 2, 3, 4, 4½(A), 5A, 5B, and 6. Preferences for principled thinking (Stages 5A, 5B, and 6, combined) are expressed by the P%-Score. The P%-Score indicates the percentage of a person's rankings that fall in the principled range. The P%–Score is the most frequently used indicator of moral judgment maturity in the DIT literature; this chapter continues that tradition.

The DIT contains three validity and "consistency" checks to establish whether the person taking the test understands it and is reasonably careful in filling it out. Among the 72 items are a few "meaningless" items (M-items) based upon lofty-sounding but senseless statements. Respondents endorsing a number of the pretentious sounding but meaningless moral arguments are frequently removed from the research sample. A second checking procedure looks for consistency between items *rated* high and items *ranked* high. A third checking procedure determines whether a protocol reflects response sets on the rating task. Should there be too many "inconsistent" respondents in a cross-cultural study, the researcher may suspect a lack of cultural-cognitive fit between the task requirements and/or moral conceptions underlying the DIT and the minds of the respondents.

Rest (1979, 1986a, 1986b) has provided extensive evidence that documents the reliability and validity of the DIT in U.S.-American and selected cross-cultural settings. There now exist more than 600 studies employing the DIT, making it the most frequently used moral judgment test in the scientific literature. Because it is easier to judge moral arguments than to produce them, persons are usually 1–1½ stages "ahead" on the DIT when compared to Kohlberg's Moral Judgement Interview. Adolescents and adults frequently endorse principled moral arguments on the DIT, although they may be unable to construct such arguments in interviews. Just as recognition memory surpasses recall memory, and passive speech develops before active speech, so principled morality may be recognized and intuitively preferred before it can be actively produced in interviews. Therefore, the DIT can be used to establish the degree to which principled moral arguments are preferred over conventional and preconventional arguments in a given society or social group even if most members cannot fully apply moral principles to concrete situations. In addition, cross-cultural studies using the DIT have asked whether preference for principled moral arguments increases as a function of age, gender, social class, educational level, intelligence, and other variables.

COMPARISON OF CROSS-CULTURAL STUDIES USING THE DIT

The following comparisons are based upon a survey of 15 studies employing the DIT in 14 countries. The studies include published and unpublished research projects by Gielen, studies previously surveyed by Moon (1986), and additional studies that have since become available. Research data have been included in the present survey whenever scores for at least three age groups have been reported for a given country.

Moral maturity scores in all studies are expressed by the P%-Score. The P%-Scores have been taken from, or estimated on the basis of, the following studies: Australia (Watson, 1983); Ireland (Kahn, 1982); the United States (Rest, 1986a); Greece (Gielen, Markoulis, & Avellani, 1992); Poland (Frackowiak & Jasinska-Kania, 1991); Belize (Gielen, Cruickshank, Johnston, Swanzey, & Avellani, 1986); Trinidad-Tobago (combination of scores reported by Beddoe, 1980, and Gielen et al., 1986); Hong Kong (Hau, 1983); South Korea (Park & Johnson, 1984); Taiwan (Gielen, Miao, & Avellani, 1990); Sudan (Ahmed, Gielen, & Avellani, 1987); Kuwait (Gielen, Ahmed, & Avellani, 1992); Egypt (El-Shikh, 1985); and Nigeria (Markoulis, submitted). The total number of male and female subjects included in the studies is $N = 8,131$, ranging from 50 subjects for Australia to 4,565 for the United States. All samples except those from Australia, Nigeria, and Belize include at least 240 students. The data for the United States are based upon a composite sample that Rest computed on the basis of numerous individual studies.

Average ages for the various subgroups in the study range from 12 (South Korea) to 22½ years (Greece). The studies typically report data for junior high school, senior high school, and college students. The students' educational background in the various subgroups within the different societies is roughly comparable with respect to number of years of schooling. The age and years of schooling are completely confounded in these studies, but based upon previous research evidence from the United States (Rest, 1979, 1986a, 1986b), Germany, and elsewhere it may be surmised that educational experience rather than age per se is the crucial variable influencing P%-Scores. The 14 countries listed in Table 7.2 represent a variety of Anglo-Saxon countries (Australia, Ireland, and the United States), two European countries (Poland, Greece), two English-speaking countries located in the Caribbean (Belize, which is also a Central American country, and TrinidadTobago), three East Asian countries influenced by Confucian and Buddhist value systems (Hong Kong, South Korea, and Taiwan), three Arab countries (Egypt, Kuwait, and Central Sudan), and one English-speaking country located in sub-Saharan Africa (Nigeria).

Developmental Progression of P%-Scores

Bottom Effect. Except for the Nigerian study, no study reports average P%-Scores for any age group that go much below 18–20 percent. This "bottom effect" probably indicates a situation where a good many students select moral arguments more or less randomly. It may well be that the DIT is too difficult a test for many junior high school students in countries such as Belize, Trinidad-Tobago, and Ireland. This conclusion is strengthened by the fact that the study reporting P%-Scores for Belize and Trinidad-Tobago (Gielen et al., 1986) also reports the exclusion of a high percentage of subjects who failed to pass the various consistency tests.

Developmental Progression of P%-Scores. Apart from the bottom effect, all studies not conducted in Arab countries report that P%-Scores regularly increase with increasing age and educational level. The older, better-educated students endorse the principled arguments more frequently than the younger, less well educated students. Thus, the DIT appears to capture developmental trends in moral reasoning in a considerable variety of Western and non-Western countries.

High P%-Scores for East Asian High School Students. Among high school students the highest scores are reported for Taiwan and South Korea, with Hong Kong not far behind. High school students from the United States (where the DIT originated) receive average scores.

High P%-Scores for Western and East Asian College-University Students. Among college and university students, respondents from North America, Europe, and the East Asian countries receive comparable scores, with the exception of the high-scoring Australian sample. However, the Australian sample is an unusually small sample, and it may not be fully representative of Australian students.

Industrialized versus Third World Countries. Students from Third World countries such as Belize, Trinidad-Tobago, and Nigeria tend to receive lower scores than students from the more industrialized countries located in North

Table 7.2
Average P%-Scores of Students from Different Countries

Country	N	Age/Education	Average P%-Score
Anglo-Saxon Countries			
Australia	50	14.7 years (8th-9th grade)	19.2%
(Watson, 1983)		16.8 years (11th grade)	32.7%
		College/Univ. (Freshmen)	43.8%
		College/Univ. (Juniors)	47.5%
Ireland	508	12-13 years	20.0%
(Kahn, 1982)		15-16 years	20.7%
		18-19 years (College)	34.1%
USA	4565	Junior High	21.9%
(Rest, 1986a)		Senior High	31.8%
		College	42.3%
		(Graduate Students)	53.3%
European Countries			
Greece	353	13-15 years	21.5%
(Gielen, Markoulis,		16-18 years	29.1%
& Avellani, 1992)		19-21 years	40.3%
		22-23 years	43.8%
Poland	286	14 years (8th grade)	23.9%
(Frackowiak, &		15 years (High School Freshmen)	32.0%
Jasinska-Kania, 1991)		18 years (High School Juniors)	32.7%
		19.5 years (College-Freshmen)	39.9%
		22.5 years (College-Sophomores)	37.4%
Caribbean Countries (English Speaking)			
Belize	118	12-14 years	19.9%
(Gielen, et al., 1986)		15-16 years	18.7%
		17-19 years	24.3%
Trinidad-Tobago	292	12-14 years	20.4%
(Beddoe, 1980;		15-16 years	20.8%
Gielen, et al., 1986)		17-19 years	27.4%
		College	28.7%

Table 7.2 continued

Country	N	Age/Education	Average P%-Score
East Asian Countries			
Hong Kong (Hau, 1983)	242	7th-8th grade(Jr. High)	25.2%
		9th-10th grade (Jr. High)	29.3%
		11th-12th grade (Sr. High)	34.5%
		College	37.9%
South Korea (Park, & Johnson, 1984)	240	6th grade	25.0%
		8th grade(Jr. High)	30.2%
		11th grade(Sr. High)	37.4%
		College	41.5%
Taiwan (Gielen, Miao, & Avellani, 1987)	521	Junior High	30.4%
		Senior High	36.8%
		College	41.4%
Arab Countries			
Kuwait (Gielen, Ahmed, & Avellani, 1989)	313	High School (1st-3rd)	27.9%
		College (Fr. and Soph.)	24.6%
		Univ./College (Jr. & Sr.)	28.3%
		(MA level; $N = 2$)	(34.0%)
Sudan (Arab Students) (Ahmed, Gielen, & Avellani, 1987)	253	High School (1st-3rd)	25.1%
		College (Fr. & Soph.)	27.8%
		Univ./College (Jr. & Sr.)	24.5%
		(MA level; $N = 4$)	(39.6%)
Egypt (El-Shikh, 1985)	293	13-15 Intermediate School	21.5%
		15-18 Secondary School	22.0%
		18-21 Univ./College	22.6%
		21-22 One year Postgraduate (Special Diploma)	20.9%
Africa			
Nigeria (Markoulis, 1991)	97	15-16 High School	11.5%
		17-18 High School	18.0%
		19-20 University	30.0%
		21-22 University	32.0%

America, Europe, and East Asia. Thus, the main dividing line for the data is not between Western, Anglo-Saxon, English-speaking countries and non-Western, non-English-speaking countries but between industrialized Western or East Asian countries with demanding educational systems and Third World, less-industrialized countries with less-demanding educational systems.

No Developmental Trends in Arab Societies. The three studies conducted in Egypt, Kuwait, and Sudan do not portray clear developmental trends. In addition, there are signs in these studies that the DIT may not be a satisfactory test of moral reasoning in these societies. In two of the studies more than half of all students failed to pass the consistency check, sometimes ranking and rating the *same* moral arguments quite differently. Even among the students who did pass the consistency tests (their scores are reported in Table 7.2), developmental trends are absent.

Gender Differences. Apart from the Nigerian study (test for gender differences not reported) and the Australian study (number of subjects too small to test reliably for gender differences), tests for gender differences are available for the remaining twelve countries. For six of the countries, namely, Belize, Trinidad-Tobago (study by Gielen et al., 1986), Kuwait, Sudan, Greece, and Poland, nonsignificant gender differences for P%-Scores are reported. In the Hong Kong, South Korea, and Taiwan studies, female students received significantly higher P%-Scores than the male students. Gender differences were small in size, however. In the United States, Thoma (1986) conducted a large-scale meta- and secondary analysis of DIT scores for 56 samples, including more than 6,000 male and female students. Female students at all age levels received slightly but significantly higher average P%-Scores than the male students. Gilligan's (1982) widely publicized claim that Kohlbergian theories and methods downgrade feminine concerns for care and empathy has fared poorly in North American research. It fares equally poorly in the cross-cultural research surveyed here.

Effects of Social Class Background. Several studies report correlations between measures of parental social class (SES) and the students' moral reasoning scores, with age and/or educational level statistically controlled. These studies were conducted in Belize, Greece, Kuwait, Sudan, Taiwan, and Trinidad-Tobago. It should be kept in mind that the studies try to evaluate the effects of social class on the moral reasoning scores of those high school or college/university students who attended the same educational institutions.

Taken together, the studies provide no support for the hypothesis that parental social class is linked in a clear way to the level of moral comprehension of adolescents. Correlations between indicators of social class and moral judgment maturity are very low and frequently statistically insignificant. In no study does social class account for an appreciable amount of the variance in the students' moral reasoning scores.

SUMMARY AND CONCLUSIONS

Kohlberg and Rest have proposed that moral reasoning develops from an initial concern with the practical consequences of one's actions, to an identification with interpersonal and societal expectations, to a level where persons have worked out their own moral principles. The cross-cultural status of the level of moral principles is especially controversial. Critics have argued that Kohlberg's level of moral principles represents a Western, male-oriented, upper-class ideology of individualism that misrepresents the moral experience of non-Westerners, women, and members of the lower social classes. If the critics are right, we should find that samples of male Americans (and other Westerners) from upper-class backgrounds receive much higher scores on Kohlbergian tests of moral reasoning than samples from non-Western countries, especially if the latter include females and students from lower-class backgrounds. We should also find a lack of clear developmental trends in the non-Western studies.

Our review of 15 studies in 14 countries supports Rest's developmental hypotheses in European, North American, and East Asian societies, but the results of the studies conducted in the Arab and Caribbean societies are more ambiguous. Across all studies, gender differences tend to be small and if significant, favor female students. Social-class differences among students attending the same schools have little effect on their moral reasoning scores. Female students from collectivistic East Asian societies such as Taiwan or South Korea are especially likely to prefer principled moral arguments. Given these findings, it must be concluded that the DIT is not biased in favor of individualistic, male-oriented, upper-class, Western conceptions of morality. Notwithstanding this conclusion, the DIT in its present form does not adequately measure the development of moral reasoning in the Arab world, a finding that is discussed more fully in Gielen, Ahmed, and Avellani (1992).

It is one of the main findings of this survey that the students from Third World countries such as Belize and Trinidad-Tobago endorse principled moral arguments much less frequently than the students from industrialized East Asian and Western countries. This finding cannot be explained by theories of Westernization or by the influence of Anglo-Saxon individualism, since the English-speaking Caribbean nations have adopted British educational institutions and are pervasively influenced by North American culture. In contrast, the Republic of China, Taiwan, has kept its native languages and emphasizes "updated" versions of Confucian moral education. It is the overall complexity, modernity, and institutional integration of the East Asian societies, the rigor of their educational systems, and the "developmental pull" of complex ethical systems such as modern adaptations of Confucianism that can help explain the high P%-Scores of East Asian students when compared to the lower scores of the more Westernized but morally more conventional Caribbean students. The moral ethos of Caribbean societies appears to depend on conventional, role-oriented, interpersonal, yet individualistic expectations that are reflected in Stage 3 reasoning. This is especially true for traditional face-to-face relationships in villages and small towns. In contrast, postconventional reasoning is furthered by involvement in tertiary education, active exposure to integrated but competing value systems, and sustained reflection on a widening sociomoral world.

Critics of the cognitive-developmental approach have often confused the concept and ideology of rugged, masculine, rule-oriented individualism with the quite different philosophical idea of moral autonomy. Moral autonomy, as understood by Kohlberg and Rest, refers to an orientation toward internalized, *shareable* moral principles. These principles reflect schemes of cooperation rather than the arbitrary preoccupation with self-expression in the service of individualism. The very purpose of principled moral thinking is to create just solutions to moral problems based upon ideal role taking and shareable moral values. Ideal role taking is usually supportive of so-called feminine concerns for care and empathy. Moral autonomy and a concern for moral principles exist in collectivistic societies (e.g., Taiwan) just as much as in individualistic societies (e.g., the United States) (Gielen, 1990). Moral autonomy and shareable moral principles reflect moral ideals that to some extent transcend culture, gender, and religious ideology. They are not recent Western inventions but may be found in the sayings attributed to the Buddha, Confucius, and Socrates. They are ideals for all time, although they must be reinterpreted and divested of remaining biases as societies change.

Cultural ideals in their most developed forms "fill out" universal intuitions about the nature of moral excellence. Whereas Western secular ideals emphasize the dignity and personhood of individuals, religious Tibetans emphasize the "Buddha-nature" inherent in everyone, Hindus uphold ideals of universal nonviolence (*Ahimsa*), and Confucianists focus on humanistic ideals of human-heartedness (*jen*). These cultural ideals are based upon different metaphysical assumptions, but they all emphasize a concern for human dignity, solidarity, and justice. Moral and cultural relativists have failed to perceive the underlying archetype that unites the moral imaginations of men and women living in different places and at different times. In contrast, Kohlbergian theories and methods are among the first rigorous scientific attempts to capture the inherent nature and development of the age-old human search for justice and solidarity.

NOTE

Uwe P. Gielen is grateful to the H. F. Guggenheim Foundation, St. Francis College, the Pacific Cultural Foundation, and the Columbia University Faculty Seminar on Moral Education for grants supporting his DIT studies. This chapter is dedicated to the memory of our colleague Joseph Avellani.

8

Women and Gender Roles

Leonore Loeb Adler

AN OVERVIEW

The cultural influence on gender roles cannot be overestimated. The effects of gender-appropriate behavior is apparent even before birth; for instance, when the fetus is active, the baby is predicted more likely to be a boy and vice versa, when the fetus is calmer, it is suggested that "it is more likely to be a girl" (Lewis, 1972a). The nurseries, as well as clothing for the babies from birth on, are already sex-stereotyped. In Western countries it is most often light blue for boys and pink for girls. Toys, even at this early age, are frequently oriented toward gender roles, a trend that only increases as the infant grows up. Hyde (1985) pointed out that most infants do not show gender differences; they do, however, experience different physical and social environments. Boy babies receive more rough-housing, for example, whereas girl babies are talked to more (Lewis, 1972b). Whether these patterns of interaction are the causes of differential development and superior language skills in girls are, at best, speculative.

The nature-nurture controversy is still blooming. The sociobiologists, E. O. Wilson (1978) foremost among them, have suggested that the evolutionary process may have predisposed physical traits as well as social behaviors (e.g., males as hunters and females as food gatherers and caregivers of babies). However, Wilson concedes that culture helped shape the genders.

There exists between the sexes a definite dichotomy obvious in terms of reproductive functions. Yet it is the interaction with the cultural environment that essentially shapes the behavior and sets forth the accepted gender roles for males and females. In addition, it is the ethnic upbringing that makes the difference with behaviors such as more frequent smiling by women, who also tolerate being interrupted while speaking (Henley, 1977). Many such behaviors are habits and therefore difficult to eliminate. Yet on observing stereotypical behavior patterns in the media, one may notice subtle changes in behavior that tend to close the gap between sex stereotypes. For example, television anchormen and male newscasters smile as much as women in these occupations.

Some years ago a conference and later its publication dealt with the question: "Does *la différence* make a difference?" (Orasanu, Slater, & Adler, 1979.) In this case " *'la différence'* refers to a popular tagline in Western folklore. A debate among French cabinet ministers about the equality and fraternity [*sic*] of females and males ends with the following celebratory shout '*Vive la différence!*' " (viii). In this volume the editors assembled a group of authors who showed that many gender differences existed in language and speech.

Although enculturation serves to permeate the gender roles, the feminist movement and the psychology of women is attempting to do away with sex-role stereotypes (Denmark, 1977). Especially since now more and more women find employment outside the home, they seek an equal status with men in their professions and on their jobs. There exist an increasing number of women who endeavor to transcend the polarized gender roles and hope in time to eliminate the sex-role concept in the workplace outside the home, as well as, though more difficult, in the domestic domain. Striving for the "perfect" state of transcendence of gender roles means to eliminate or modify gender roles so that all individuals can develop their own potentialities in their own right, unhindered by adherence to the stereotypes of gender roles. In the meantime, David G. Myers (1990) suggests three ways to minimize gender roles. These are that (1) women behave more like men, that is, show assertiveness in social interactions; (2) men show traditional feminine behaviors, such as nurturance and cooperativeness; and (3) both sexes acquire androgynous traits, which include both traditional feminine and masculine traits. Androgyny allows men to pursue "typical" women's professions, such as nursing, and women to take the "traditional" men's jobs, among them those of bus drivers, particularly school bus drivers.

In an informal study during the 1990–91 academic year, the self-perception of male and female college students—were tested by analyzing the responses to Bem's Androgyny Test (Bem, 1974). The results showed that the students' perceptions fell mostly in the androgyny range; this was also the case when others, such as relatives and friends, responded with their perceptions of the same students (Adler, 1990–91, unpublished study). It is not only self-perception and the individual's androgynous behavior but the perceptions by others who accept the equal status that accomplish the acceptance of the lack of gender roles. D. G. Myers (1990) demonstrates this point with an anecdote of Samuel Johnson, a scholar who lived in England during the eighteenth century. Johnson realized that the differences between the sexes were not as great as the variability within genders. His reply to the question: "Who is more intelligent, man or woman?" was simply, "Which man? Which woman?" (p. 180).

ANTECEDENT ACTIVITIES AND
THE FEMINIST MOVEMENT

As a consequence of the draft into military service during World War II, women entered the workforce in great numbers to replace the men who had to vacate their jobs. However, when the men came home, they returned to their prewar positions and the women were retired to resume their domestic roles of raising a family and taking care of the home. Yet many women did not find domestic work as satisfying as following a career and earning money to help upgrade the standards of living for the family. Equality seemed closer at hand—but it was still not reached.

During the 1970s women gathered together in the feminist movement to achieve equal rights with men. Today in most traditional as well as modern countries men continue to occupy a higher status than women. Even though women have made strides toward equality during the twentieth century, particularly after World War II, they are not yet perceived as equals to men either in the family at home or away from home in any of their activities. Of course, industrialization has had a profound effect on women's roles in society. For the importance of the woman's domestic role in the twentieth century has been diminishing (Denmark, Schwartz, & Smith, 1991, p. 2). For example, due to polyester and similar fabrics and the availability of washing machines and dryers in industrialized societies, men as well as women can now take care of laundry chores, which no longer needed the laborious handscrubbing that had always traditionally been performed by women. On the other hand, L. F. Lowenstein and K. Lowenstein (1991) propose that "the pendulum has certainly swung from women being in a very subordinate position in relation to men in society generally to one in which women are, if not equal, approaching equality and, in some cases have usurped the role of the male "totally" (p. 52).

GENDER ROLES IN CROSS-CULTURAL
CONSIDERATION

Almost all over the world women strive for equality with men. The United Nations endorsed the "Decade for Women: 1978–1988," which was launched by the National Commission on the Observance of International Women's Year, Washington, D.C., in March 1978. This was followed by the National Women's Conference in Houston, Texas, in November 1978.

Of course, there are outstanding women of state, such as Prime Ministers

Tunsu Çiller of Turkey and Hanna Suchocka of Poland, Corazon Aquino, past President of the Philippines, as well as the past Prime Minister of France, Madame Edith Cresson. Some years ago, there were the Prime Minister of Israel, Golda Meir, and the Prime Minister of India, Indira Gandhi. The British can point with pride to their Queen Elizabeth II and to Margaret Thatcher, their past Prime Minister, who served in that position for many years. And in the Netherlands there is Queen Beatrice. Yet the two Houses of Parliament can list only 3 percent or 4 percent of their members as women (Lowenstein & Lowenstein, 1991). In the United States of America the situation is not much better: In the 1989 Congress 5 percent of the seats were occupied by women (Boyd, 1988), whereas in Canada 13 percent of the National Parliament were women (Meyers, 1990). From the international scene, more comparisons can be offered. For example, in 1984 there were six women in the Australian House of Representatives (Costello & Taylor, 1991). Yet the women in the former Union of Soviet Socialist Republics (USSR) played a greater part, compared to the countries just mentioned. Women are active in the state administrations and civic life. Lena Zhernova (1991) reports that one-third of all the Supreme Soviet Deputies were women. As compared to men, women continue to play a lesser role in managing the affairs of the state (p. 76). However, after the 1992 elections in Israel, the number of women serving in the Knesset increased to 11 out of 120 members.

Presented here for cross-cultural comparisons are other examples that show the contrary as the "exceptions to the rule." U. Singhal and N. R. Mrinal (1991) report that the women of the Tharu tribe in Northern India run the government. The men of this tribe are dependent and of lower status than women. In their communities the status of a father is enhanced by the birth of a daughter—which, of course, is contrary to the custom in the traditional Hindu families, where the birth of a girl is an unfortunate event. In Western Samoa in the Southern Insular Pacific, by consensus of the adults of each household or family women are appointed to be their chief and to represent them in the village council. The chief is responsible for all household members, overseeing family affairs, directing the use of family land, and assigning tasks according to age and sex of the members. Thus the chief holds great power over individual lives. Nearly 10 percent of the population of 160,500 inhabitants in Western Samoa hold the title of chief, and of these chiefs 400 are women (Muse, 1991).

EDUCATION

Education is one of the most crucial pivotal points for the progress of women's equality with men. Unfortunately, in many Third World countries girls are not favored and their education is frequently nonexistent, inadequate, or too limited in terms of time spent in school.

In most developed and some developing countries school is compulsory for all children. In the United States and Canada, as well as in the countries of Europe and in Australia and New Zealand, elementary and secondary education is considered essential, since about all the countries offer free education and provide free schools to all children. Higher education in colleges and universities is viewed as prestigious, affording the opportunity to secure higher-paying positions. In the United States and Canada 51 percent of the student body are women—roughly the same proportion of the representation of women in the total population in these two countries (Denmark, Schwartz, & Smith, 1991).

It seems that in most countries where the educational level of family members is high, husbands tend to be proud of their wife's achievements in areas other than just their financial contributions to the family income (Lowenstein & Lowenstein, 1991).

A different situation exists in Egypt, where as in other Islamic countries it was in the past believed—and practiced—that formal education was not for girls. When primary schools were finally opened to girls, most people perceived the schools as upper-class institutions. Later, intermediary and secondary schools were opened to girls. However, especially in rural districts the dropout rate of girls has been much higher than that of boys, at a two-to-one ratio. This accounts to a great extent for the illiteracy of the current population (Ahmed, 1991). In addition, Egyptian men often seek wives who are less educated than they are; since Egyptian women are mostly housewives, working inside their homes, and do not take outside jobs, their educational level is not an important issue in Egypt (Minai, 1981). In the Sudan, however, enrollment in school has clearly affected the status of women favorably. Even though the enrollment of girls is increasing, it remains less than that of boys at all three educational levels, especially at the upper levels of education. There is also a smaller enrollment in rural areas, probably because of the dominant tribal values and strong Sudanese traditions against female education (Ahmed, 1991). Sudanese society should comply with the following slogan: "Educating girls may be one of the country's best investments toward future growth and progress" (*Sudanow*, March 1985, p. 7).

The traditions are quite different in India, where both middle-class boys and middle-class girls receive an education. It seems easier for parents to find husbands for their daughters when the daughters are educated, since educated women can find higher-earning jobs—and, in addition, the parents can therefore negotiate for smaller dowries (Kumar, 1991).

Similarly, higher education provides women in Thailand with increased social status within their communities and offers them a chance to move into higher-status occupations. As a result, Thai women gain greater access to legal, political, economic, social, and cultural resources (Gardiner & Sornmoonpin Gardiner, 1991).

The two Chinas—mainland China and Taiwan—have quite different requirements of education. In Taiwan attendance in school is mandatory to the ninth grade, whereas in the People's Republic of China, students are encouraged to attend elementary school, although attendance is not mandatory. Therefore, many women, particularly in rural areas, are illiterate; their families need them to work. It seems a pity that especially for daughters school is one of the lowest priorities of a family that is struggling to survive (Yu & Carpenter, 1991). In Japan, in contrast, the educational level for girls has been raised. After high school almost one-third of all female students go on to higher education, and one-fourth of women students go on to a four-year college or university (Fukada, 1991).

C. J. Muse (1991) reports that in Western Samoa the compulsory attendance laws require children to attend either the village, the district, or the denominational schools from age 5 to age 17. The curricula are similar to those in New Zealand.

MATE SELECTION AND MARRIAGE ARRANGEMENTS

Other important milestones in the life of women are mate selection and the marriage arrangements. In many modern or modernizing countries the young will select their own future spouses. However, in many traditional countries mate selection is handled by the parents or a matchmaker. In the United States and Canada young people tend to choose marriage partners who have a socially similar status, are of the same race or ethnic group, and belong to the same religion (Eckland, 1968). However, among the Alaskan natives marriages are frequently arranged between families in the same community (Fischer, 1991). When an agreement has been reached, the parents of the young girl present the young man with a gift such as a knife, harpoon, or parka; in turn, the young man comes to the girl's family to work for them as his "bride service." This work time may be shortened when the young man catches a seal and presents it to his future parents-in-law. The marriage could be consummated any time during this period, after which the young man and woman are considered married (p. 21).

In South America today mate selection is a matter of choice, no longer an arrangement made by the parents or other relatives. R. Ardila (1991) suggests, that given a choice between becoming a wife and mother or an executive, women would opt for the first choice. Many women combine the two options. However, whereas the wife helps with the family economic support, the husband does not help with the household chores; Ardila (1991) writes that "women have more responsibilities now than they had before; but it appears that they have not been liberated from household duties" (p. 3).

Halina Grzymała-Moszczyńska (1991) reports that in Poland there exists an important age difference between rural and urban customs. Girls in most rural areas marry between the ages of 18 and 22 years, whereas those who live in an urban community marry mostly between 21 and 26 years. Many young farmers face difficulties in finding a prospective bride, since many rural girls "escape" to the city, where they find more freedom and a less strenuous life. Therefore, many young farmers seek the help of a matrimonial agency—although not all are successful, since many young women from the city are afraid to start a life in the country. Today the selection of prospective spouses in the city is done primarily by the young people without parental involvement. Yet the tradition in rural Poland is that the bride bring a dowry to the husband. Usually this dowry includes money and utensils for the future household. In addition—almost obligatory—is a featherbed (comforter), pillows, and kitchen utensils. Of course, "more affluent families can give their daughters houses, some land, and a cow. Even a daughter who lives in the city might bring along a 'symbolic cow' in the form of money from the sale of a real cow" (Grzymała-Moszczyńska, 1991, p. 61).

In the former Soviet Union men and women could marry at 18 years of age, which was also the time of their coming of age. Family relations were legally regulated by Fundamentals of Marriage and Family legislation, which at the same time served, in a sense, as a marriage contract (Zhernova, 1991). In Soviet society it was appropriate for women to marry and have children. As a matter of fact, Soviet leaders awarded the Glory of Motherhood medal to women who gave birth to seven children; when a woman bore ten or more children, she received the title "Mother Heroine" (Takooshian, 1991).

Marrying and having children are considered cultural imperatives in Israel, where the median age for the first marriage is 22.5 years for women and 26.0 years for men. A childless couple is not considered a family. Safir and Izraeli (1991) propose that this may be the explanation why *in vitro* experimentation and services are so well developed in Israel (p. 94).

Islamic societies, including Egypt and the Sudan, among others, have remained strictly marriage oriented. In addition, Islam prohibits premarital relationships between a man and a woman, and instead encourages marriage. It also prohibits celibacy, as Prophet Muhammed decreed that marriage is the only road to virtue (Ahmed, 1991, p. 121). Women in rural areas marry mainly between 16 and 18 years of age, whereas men are between 20 and 25. However, in urban areas young women are usually between 20 and 30 years old when they marry and the young men are usually between 25 and 35 years of age at the time of their wedding. Within the last 20 years matrimonial ads have appeared in Egyptian newspapers, where men and women look for spouses. These individuals are usually well educated and look for spouses in good circumstances (Ahmed, 1991, p. 122). In an unpublished survey, R. A. Ahmed (1984) found that university men "tended to prefer that their future wives be less educated women, either from higher or lower secondary schools or primary schools, or possibly their illiterate village cousins" (Ahmed, 1991, p. 122).

The pattern of mate selection is quite different in India. Kumar (1991) recounts that when a girl reaches puberty her parents will start arranging a match for her. Although at this time she attains a more important status in the family, she is also more restricted in her movements. "Unless she is with a group, interacting freely with boys of her age is prohibited. Male cousins and their friends may or may not be given access to her house." Resorting to "fasting or observing the ritual of tying a cord around the wrist of the young man proclaiming him as an 'adopted' brother are some traditional ways of coping with sexual feelings" (p. 150). The results of an informal study with female college students, related by Parul Dave to Usha Kumar, revealed some interesting views by the women students: They preferred their future spouses to be older, more intelligent, and of higher status and educational level than their own. The women unequivocally opted for marriage as the more desirable lifestyle rather than staying single or cohabitating (150–151). With parents looking for older and better-educated husbands for their daughters, the trend has been for girls to marry earlier. Among Hindus the percentage of single women is almost nil. For marriage bestows on women their socially accepted role. Kumar (1991) also reports an increase of young newly married wives who continue their education, which, she feels, gives impetus to vocational orientation in female education. It appears that the working woman enjoys a higher prestige in India and possesses greater self-esteem.

In Thailand in cities like Bangkok a modernization of the old customs seems to prevail. Many young people reject arranged marriages, preferring to make their own choices. However, in rural areas the traditional patterns of mate selection survive. "College women in Thailand were significantly more egalitarian in their marriage preferences (stress on shared decision-making and female independence) than comparable groups of college women in India and the United States. This finding was attributed to the greater degree of emancipation from traditional role expectations enjoyed by Thai women, as well as even greater acceleration in equality, especially in education and the professions, resulting from contemporary social change" (Gardiner, Singh, & D'Orazio, 1974, pp. 413–415).

In the two Chinas vast progress in modernization has occurred. In 1950 the Marriage Law was passed in the People's Republic of China that freed women from the age-old systems of bondage. They were given free choice of a spouse with monogamy and equal rights for men and women. In the Republic of China, Taiwan, the Marriage Law abolished the feudal marriage system. From then on women could choose their husbands. This law mandated monogamy and assured equal rights for both genders. Women in today's Taiwan retain their family name after marriage. They are allowed to inherit property and keep it and the income in their own name. Lucy C. Yu and Lee Carpenter (1991) describe the procedure of drawing up a contract for a woman to acquire any property; otherwise the husband gets all the belongings that became her property, either from before or during their marriage. On the other hand, women are held responsible for their spouse's debts.

Modernization has also left its mark in Japan by replacing traditional customs with new ones. Although young men and women are free to marry whomever they choose under the new law, parents generally hold on to customs and habits. In general, marriages are arranged by mediators or go-betweens. This procedure is helpful, since the young people may not have adequate opportunities to meet eligible singles (Fukada, 1991).

Whereas in the past in Western Samoa traditionally marriages were arranged, very few, if any, marriages are arranged today. Instead, clandestine rendezvous are arranged by the boy's intermediary. After the formal announcement and engagement period, the wedding follows. However, the bride is only a probationary member of the groom's family until the first baby is born (Muse, 1991, p. 230).

FAMILIES

While the family is being established by the young couple, the woman may have to work outside the home for economic reasons. The traditional role for women is that of a full-time homemaker who takes care of her husband, the children, and their home. However, such circumstances are becoming less and less common in modern times, even though such family constellations still have an aura of being women's first role fulfillment. In the traditional role the husband is the sole breadwinner, which makes the wife and children completely dependent on the man in the house, the husband and father. Of course child care, housework, or farmwork by the wife is never paid—and is unending.

It is therefore not surprising that women in many countries and cultures seek outside, part-time or full-time, work. These situations bring along many benefits, such as more economic security, greater freedom for women, coming close to equality in the workplace, and a greater self-esteem for women. However, these situations also have drawbacks; for instance, the goal of equality for women has not yet been reached. Whereas women have moved into the vocational sphere rather quickly, no such movement has been found for men into the domestic sphere. In most countries where women have joined the workforce outside the home, they have had to accept a dual role. What Halina Grzymała-Moszczyńska (1991) wrote about the Polish woman fits the modern woman in general: "The [Polish] modern woman has had to pay a rather high price for her economic and social independence. This price included the necessity to accept full-time employment and then to respond to demands from both the family and the home, and her employment and the workplace!" (p. 66).

THE LATER YEARS

It was correctly pointed out by Denmark, Schwartz, and Smith (1991) that females were brought up to look attractive in order to find a husband and become a mother; that the aging process is often difficult for some women in the United States and Canada, as well as in other modern countries. The middle-age period in life may be particularly difficult when the grown children leave the home where the woman of the house has had no other major interests than her husband, their children, and the home. Some of these women were identified as having the "empty nest syndrome." However, in a study of 160 women, only 1 showed the typical symptom of depression (Rubins, cited in Greenberg, 1978, p. 75). The other women in this study expressed a "sense of relief," although a few had been ambivalent at the time of their children's departure.

At this time in her life, a woman might take on a part-time or a full-time job to boost the family income. Frequently, when the husband is older than the wife, he may be retired, so that the wife's income maintains most of the household. Not only does this situation increase her self-esteem but often there occurs a change in the perception of gender roles; the elderly couple may have equal status, or because of the wife's job there may be a reversal of gender roles (Hyde, 1985).

Health permitting, during older age women as well as men may pursue hobbies, especially if their financial needs are provided for by family investments or by insurance, such as retirement benefits. In the United States early retirement at 62 years of age, with reduced Social Security benefits, is available; full retirement at age 65 is more or less standard procedure, although these ages will increase by the turn of the century. Mandatory retirement at age 70 is scheduled to be changed in the future in the United States.

Many women spend their last years in widowhood, since the life expectancy for women is generally longer than that of men. In addition, in Western societies men who become widowers frequently remarry, so that most single-family households in the United States are overwhelmingly headed by women. During the past two decades establishments of Golden Age Clubs, or leisure-time centers, have been on the increase in the United States and Britain to fill the free time of older people, left by shorter working hours and labor-saving appliances in the homes.

In other countries and cultures the living arrangements may differ. Ardila (1991) writes that "aging is more positive in Latin America than in many other countries of the First and Second Worlds" (p. 25). Grzymała-Moszczyńska (1991) points out that after retirement, women live fuller and busier lives than men. "A grandmother, retired from professional duties is still the most wanted solution (as a babysitter) for the majority of families in which young adult women, besides being wives and mothers, wish to continue their professional careers" (p. 65).

In the former Soviet Union old-age pensions were given to women who were 55 years of age with a total seniority of no less than 20 years. However, women who gave birth to five or more children received additional pension benefits. They could receive their pensions at age 50 with a total seniority of no less than 15 years. It was also possible in the former Soviet Union to lower pension age by five to ten years, depending on the type of work that was performed and the labor conditions. On the other hand, it must be noted that only few women received pensions large enough to provide a comfortable lifestyle. Most of the women worked even after they reached 55 years (Zhernova, 1991).

A special situation exists in Israel. Whereas elderly women in Israeli cities face conditions similar to those that exist in other Eastern environments, the kibbutzim in Israel present a different ecology. The economic structure of the kibbutz guarantees its members financial security; however, both men and women work as long as they are capable of doing so. Life expectancies of both men and women in the kibbutz are much greater than that of the urban elderly in general. Part of this condition is attributed to the performance of work by all adult members. However, with increasing age, older workers may reduce their work hours and tackle less-exerting tasks (Safir & Izraeli, 1991). In the kibbutz, where social status is greatly influenced by the individual's contribution to the collective, the continued active participation of the elderly seems to be a boost to the kibbutz community.

In Egypt and the Sudan health-care conditions and working environments have improved, which has contributed to the increased number of elderly living there. In addition, the Egyptian Ministry of Social Affairs has established homes for the elderly in Cairo and Alexandria, as well as clubs for senior citizens; and since the 1970s elderly people can receive monthly pensions, which are given to both men and women (Ahmed, 1991).

For a woman of the Yoruba tribe in Nigeria, the death of a husband does not end the marriage unless she so wishes. Okafor (1991) reports that when a man dies, his marital rights go to his junior brother or to his son by another wife (pp. 140–141).

In the Tharu society in India there is always a need for the elderly. Their families are productive units where everybody works together. The aged person is no burden to the family. The elderly women are experts in herbal medicine, which they use to treat a variety of ailments. They perform easier work in general, such as making ropes and cots, as well as drying fish and grain. An old man has the duty to guard the house against wild animals by sleeping at the main gate with a pipe in hand. The oldest members in the Tharu society also enjoy very special rights and privileges (Singhal & Mrinal, 1991).

Japanese *rojin* (old people) are over 65 years of age and can receive a pension from the government. The amount, though, differs based on the individual's circumstances. Many elderly people in Japan prefer not to live with their children, yet about 70 percent of the women and approximately 59 percent of the men do so. In their leisure time they go to clubs and participate in sports; do gardening; enjoy calligraphy, painting, and arts and crafts; or go to lectures on poetry, modern literature, or the classics.

The Japanese elderly who have a superior knowledge or a special ability in any field can register this information with the "Silver Bank," where records are kept. If anybody is in need of consultation, advice, or assistance, he or she can apply for such help and the Silver Bank will send a qualified *rojin* to the applicant. The *rojin* receives remuneration based on the regulations of the bank.

The *rojin* live in cities, towns, and villages, where shelters and rooms are provided for them. However, their most serious problems are financial and health. The suicide rate among the elderly in Japan is continuously increasing, and it is currently the third highest in the world (after Hungary and Austria) (Fukada, 1991).

As in Japan, in Western Samoa the elderly are respected for their knowledge and experience. At times the chief will ask them for advice. Elderly parents are usually taken care of by their sons, who provide them with food and money; the daughters may take them to their own homes to care for them. The elderly have the privilege of being fed first and are given tasks that involve minimal physical labor, such as looking after infant grandchildren or weaving mats or thatch for their houses. The elderly "women continue the traditional making of pigment for tattooing so essential to a young man's preparation for an eventual title. The candle nut burning for tattoo pigment is a ritual taught to younger women by older women, and is similar to the function of old men who meet to discuss the traditional Samoan myths and legends, educating younger men seated nearby" (Muse, 1991, p. 238). Older women are also entrusted with traditional medicines, and their appropriate dispensations and applications (Muse, 1991).

SUMMARY AND CONCLUSIONS

To look at women cross-culturally is to experience similarities and differences. The biological prerogative of giving birth to offspring exists, of course, all over the world. However, women's status in their cultural groups differ, as do their functions and behaviors in the societies and communities in which they reside. In most of these ecologies women follow stereotypical gender-prescribed customs, social conduct, and specific behaviors. Only during the last few decades has a movement toward gender equality been initiated, a movement whose goal has been to give women a more egalitarian existence with their male counterparts. So far that goal of equality between genders remains nebulous. During the process of carving out a niche for their androgynous activities, women have made great progress in vocational and in professional fields in most modern and modernizing countries. However, the domestic spheres are almost solely delegated to women in practically all cultures, whether in developed or developing countries.

By regarding the activities of women in cross-cultural perspective the enormous varieties and great differences in patterns and expressions of gender roles become more apparent (Adler, 1991). To attain a state of transcendence, to eliminate gender roles—where individuals of both genders can function regardless of their sexual determination, yet according to their own capabilities and potentialities—this is the hope and goal of most women cross-culturally.

9

Aging and Old Age in Cross-Cultural Perspective

Cynthia L. Frazier and Anthony P. Glascock

All humans age. Individuals in all cultures grow older. Despite the search for commonalities to describe aging across cultures, older adults defy generalization. "If any generalizations can be made, they point to the great variety of styles and forms of aging in different cultural settings. Here one is struck by diversity rather than uniformity; by variation rather than universality" (Myerhoff, 1978). Fry (1990) explains that older adults become more "different, idiosyncratic, and eccentric" as a result of the length of experience. "The longer they are here the more time they have to experience life and to become increasingly unique physically, psychologically, and culturally."

The process of aging is universal, but the specific behavior of the older adult is determined by the unique interaction between age as a biological factor of physical change with psychological and social (including economic and political) variables. Since one risks stereotyping to classify all older adults as a distinct social category, social scientists have investigated the sociocultural contexts in which people grow older to understand the phenomenon of aging. One strategy for comparing these contexts is to employ a cross-cultural perspective. Information about what is biological or natural must be distinguished from what is shaped by the social and cultural context. The challenge is to collect information that is both valid within a particular cultural setting and comparable with information from another setting.

Simply defining what is considered old illustrates this challenge. Initially, chronological age would appear to be an objective measure of old age until viewed from a cross-cultural perspective. Whereas chronological age as measured by months and years is useful in industrialized societies, time may be conceptualized by seasonal cycles in nonindustrialized cultures. Old age may be determined by the passage of particular social milestones such as retirement, inclusion in a community's council of elders or advisors, or becoming a grandparent or great grandparent. In imperial China, for example, a woman may not bear another child after she has become a grandmother. Retirement in Ladakh begins when the eldest son marries, which also includes all the younger brothers in the customary polyandrous lifestyle marriage. The parents, who are in middle age chronologically, move from the main house into a smaller house nearby to "gradually withdraw from this world of illusion" and "to prepare themselves for a life of prayer and reduced worldly authority" (Adler, 1993; Gielen, 1993). In the United States, retirement from the workforce occurs frequently at age 70, although eligibility for Social Security full benefits begins at the age of 65 and partial benefits at age 62. Among the !Kung in Botswana, all elders by the chronological age of 45 are shown respect by the addition of *na* to their names.

Neugarten, Moore, and Lowe (1965) introduced the concept of an age-norm timetable that is used in societies to specify the expected age for significant life events to occur. Similarly, Kimmel (1980) suggested that individuals develop personal age norms based upon societal norms to conform. Conforming to such norms at the socially appropriate age produces positive outcomes; nonconformity produces negative results.

With increased exchange of information across cultures, creative solutions to problems associated with aging and old age can more readily be found to promote positive adjustment during the last phase of life. As more traditional societies undergo change, they can avoid the trials and errors of more modernized cultures. As Kertzer (1978) stated:

Ways in which societies cope with the problems of assigning different roles to individuals through their life course, and ways in which individuals cope with this experience compose one of the basic problems of social organization. . . . Few are the studies that address the whole aging process in a comprehensive framework, identifying implications for social organization as personal adjustment, identifying sources of strain, sources of change in the system, and the relationship between formal norms and actual behavior. (p. 368)

Since old age cannot be separated from earlier life experiences, transitions through life phases introduce new demands and roles requiring adaptation. As psychologists and gerontologists, our goal is to identify factors that facilitate or interfere with adjustment to current life tasks. The purpose of this chapter, then, is to review the biological, psychological, and social changes during late life that require adaptation and to identify the factors that facilitate positive adjustment to aging from a cross-cultural perspective.

Many studies in gerontology have used measurements of "psychological well being," "quality of life," "life satisfaction," "successful aging," "status," "esteem," and "prestige" to describe positive adjustment (Fry,

1990). These measure concepts cannot be standardized without the risk of losing the cultural validity. Mishler (1986) refers to the use of structured survey instruments as *context stripping*. Likewise, definitions cannot be completely culture-centric without risking the ability to compare data.

Erikson (1963) was one of the first developmental theorists to propose the concept of adaptation, or *psychosocial tasks*, to specific life events. He postulated that the final phase of life was characterized by the psychosocial task of evaluating one's life and accomplishments for meaning. Meaning produces a successful resolution that is experienced as a sense of integrity. The negative resolution of this phase results in a sense of despair. Havighurst (1952) outlined six "developmental tasks" as examples of the types of adjustment required during late life:

1. Adjust to the decreasing physical strength and health

2. Adjust to retirement and reduced income

3. Adjust to death of one's spouse

4. Establish an explicit affiliation with one's age group

5. Adopt and adapt social roles in a flexible way (an expansion in family, community, or hobbies, a slowdown in all activities, etc.)

6. Establish satisfactory physical living arrangements

In responding to life demands, the cross-cultural work of Gutmann (1977) suggested that the *ego mastery style* of the individual changed with age. "Whereas adult males start from a grounding in *active mastery*,[1] and move toward *passive mastery*,[2] women are at first grounded in *passive mastery*, characterized by dependence on and even deference to the husband, but surge in later life toward *active mastery*, including autonomy from and even domination over the husband. Across cultures, and with age, they seem to become more authoritative, more effective, and less willing to trade submission for security." This shift in style represents a role reversal or adaptation necessary for coping with one's changing social obligations. According to Gutmann, these social obligations have traditionally focused on parental responsibilities. He hypothesized that men sacrificed their needs for comfort and emotional expression in the interest of enhancing competitive striving required in their role as breadwinner. Conversely, women sacrificed more aggressive characteristics to prevent alienation of the husbands upon whom they depended and to avert psychological damage to the children.

In addition to psychological adaptation is physical change. As one ages, the human body becomes more susceptible to disease and injury. Aging is often associated with changes in appearance (e.g., graying hair), biological alterations (e.g., menopause), physical illness, and decline in functional capacity. Functional determinants of old age, such as the ability to fetch water or carry wood for cooking, are often used in non-Western societies. The rate of physical disability does increase with old age. However, recent studies have shown that in industrialized countries, chronic disability is being delayed due to advances in medical and social care for the elderly (Fries, 1980; Katz et al., 1983; Barringer, 1993). As disability is deferred, the span of active life is increased, dependence upon others for care and assistance is decreased, and quality of life is improved (Wilder & Gurland, 1989).

Simmons (1960) postulated that old age in traditional societies is divided into a normal stage and a stage characterized by decline to the degree that "further usefulness appears to be over, and the incumbent is regarded as a *living liability.*" In many nonindustrialized cultures, old age is differentiated between the *intact old* and the *decrepit old* (Glascock & Feinman, 1981). The intact old receive supportive behavior including food, shelter, and care. Death-hastening behavior such as withholding food and care, abandonment, or killing, is directed toward the decrepit old, who have become burdens to the social group. Similarly, Neugarten and Neugarten (1986) offered two classifications of *young-old* and *old-old* based upon health and social characteristics rather than chronological age, with the old-old characterized as infirm and in need of special care.

Project A.G.E., sponsored by the National Institute on Aging, investigated the influence of social, cultural, and physical dimensions on the aging process and the elderly in seven locations: among the Zhun/wasi and the Herero of Botswana; in Clifden, County Galway, and Blessington, County Wicklow, in Ireland; in Momence, Illinois, and Swarthmore, Pennsylvania, in the United States; and in four neighborhoods of Hong Kong (Keith, Fry, & Ikels, 1990). The communities were carefully selected to reflect variation in scale, subsistence activities, technology, residential stability, and economy.

Physical status—health and functionality—was found to be an important variable (Keith, Fry, & Ikels, 1990).[3] Ill health threatened the ability to work. Financial security, then, was identified as another important factor in successful aging. Ill health was also linked to the fear of dependence in the U.S. samples. Successful aging was associated with ability to remain independent and self-sufficient. Americans would prefer to live alone or in retirement housing with access to peers or professionals, which does not count as dependence. In Hong Kong, however, subjects were more likely to identify dependence, as opposed to independence, as a factor in well-being.

Interestingly, the more important factor for successful aging according to the Chinese subjects was the ability to get along with relatives, particularly children. Confucian tradition places great emphasis on the parent-child relationship, characterized by filial piety from the son and moral guidance from the father. Subjects reported doing well when relations with children and relatives with whom they lived were stable. Tension was caused by the increasing unwillingness of daughters-in-law to defer to the dominance afforded the mother-in-law by Confucian tradition. According to Yu (1989), daughters are now permitted to assume the duty of caring for elderly parents in the People's Republic of China. Older Chinese, however, preferred living with the son, rather than daughter, as it fulfilled the tradition of filial piety. Both sons and daughters considered it their duty to provide financial support and shelter to their elderly parents.

Marital relations, rather than relations with children, appeared to be the more important factor for predicting successful aging in the American communities studied in Project A.G.E. Being married consistently has been found to be positively related to well-being in the elderly (Gove, Hughes, & Style, 1983; Depner & Ingersoll-Dayton, 1985; House, 1987). According to Lewittes (1982), the ability to develop and maintain relationships with others, family as well as friends, contributed to greater adaptability in old age. Residential stability, aging in a place surrounded by long-time friends and relatives, played a vital role in providing both security and emotional well-being (Keith, Fry, & Ikels, 1990). Butler (1982) suggested that long-term relationships with kin and friends serve as a connection to the past, which enhances a sense of continuity over time. Relationships characterized by intimacy, reciprocity, and assistance have been found to be of greatest support to older women (Lewittes & Mukherji, 1989).

Similar to the results of Project A.G.E., Thomas and Chambers (1989) identified similar themes for successful aging using a hermeneutical approach with older men from England and India.[4] When questioned about the concerns pertaining to aging, the dominant theme for the sample of elderly English men was fear of incapacitation, including fear of helplessness, being useless, a burden, and dependent. Related to this theme was the concern about loss of significant others, particularly the spouse. Life satisfaction was linked to "having made the best of things—of having adjusted to life." In the Indian sample, three interrelated themes emerged: importance of family, salience of religious beliefs, and satisfaction with present life situation. Present life satisfaction was linked to family closeness and fulfillment of religious *dharma*—duty to society and family, particularly children.

Social support, in the form of companionship, services, advice, and financial assistance from family members has been consistently found to act as a buffer against physical and psychological illness (Miller, Ingham, & Davidson, 1976; Dean & Ensel, 1982; Griffin, 1984). Maxwell and Maxwell (1980) found that lack of a family support system was the strongest predictor of poor treatment in old age. For example, elderly living in a kibbutz community in Israel have been found to live longer than those living near a relative (i.e., three additional years for women; six years for men) (Izraeli & Safir, 1993). The social norms of the kibbutz encourage members to work as long as they are able, which is believed to promote the maintenance of a meaningful social role within the community. Physical care is then provided by other members of the community for those who are no longer able to work. In Nigeria, the elderly often return to their native village, where their umbilical cords were buried and the extended family is available to provide necessary support (Kalu & Kalu, 1993).

Imamoglu and Imamoglu (1992) found that even though Turks have more social contacts than Swedes, the Turks felt lonelier and viewed old age more negatively. Thus, older Turks, even with a large number of social contacts with family and friends, are lonely and unhappy. This, the authors suggest, is the result of even higher expectations on the part of older Turks, who anticipated greater social contact and, as a result, a better old age. According to Frazier and Douyon (1989), these findings could be explained by the variable of perception. That is, the perception of social support, rather than actual amount of support, is the best predictor of self-esteem and depression.

Antonucci, Fuhrer, and Jackson (1990) proposed that not all support is beneficial. In an adaptation of the exchange theory, they suggested that one may feel "overbenefitted" if one receives more support than one provides, or conversely, "underbenefitted" if one provides more support than one receives. In a study comparing samples of older adults in the United States and France, the perception of reciprocal social exchanges was associated with higher life satisfaction.

Elderly Americans and Japanese experienced more symptoms of depression when faced with the financial strain associated with living on a fixed income (Krause, Jay, & Liang, 1991). Interestingly, Americans showed an increase in both depressed affect and somatic symptoms of depression. The Japanese manifested depression only somatically. As financial strain increased, older adults in both cultures reported feeling less personal control over the events in their lives and lowered sense of self-worth. Since financial and material success is a major determinant of personal accomplishment and worth in Western cultures, Americans in this sample were particularly prone to experiencing loss of self-esteem associated with financial difficulties (Lee, 1985). According to Lebra (1976), the Japanese view achievement and material success as a moral obligation. Furthermore, financial strain may bring disgrace to significant others due to the cultural subordination of the individual to the group (Marsella, Sartorious, Jablensky, & Fenton, 1985).

While control of tangible resources such as wealth and property is considered an important factor in predicting status for older adults (Simmons, 1945; Amoss & Harrell, 1981), esteem in old age may also be derived from possessing valuable information. For example, a major function of the older adult in Japan is to serve as a senior advisor for family problems. Silverman (1987) found that older adults derived greater esteem if they provided valued "information processing" (including administration, consultation, arbitration, reinforcement of behavior, entertainment, teaching, and instruction) more so than controlling property, having material wealth, or having social or supernatural resources. Thus, it is often not the control of property or resources per se that results in deference and respect for the elderly but, instead, vital knowledge that needs to be both made available to the social group and transferred to younger generations. For example, in the southern area of what was formerly Hungary, elderly women who had developed their craft in weaving were given the title Master of Hungarian Folk Art, along with a monthly stipend, and assigned students to whom to teach their craft.

The value of information of elders may be devalued as modernization advances, thereby diminishing the status of older adults. Cowgill and Holmes (1972) proposed "that the status of the aged in the community is inversely proportional to the degree of modernization of the society." Four aspects of modernization were considered most salient in this devaluation process:

1. Advances in health technology would lead to larger populations and greater longevity, which would generate competition between the young and old, pressuring the old into retirement from valued positions.

2. Advances in economic technology, production, and distribution would create new jobs for younger members of society, making obsolete the traditional skills of the elderly, leading to further pressure to retire.

3. Urbanization leads to the youth migrating to cities, leaving the elderly to maintain a rural way of life considered increasingly undesirable.

4. Extension of mass education provides the young with increasing opportunities to become educated in a modernizing society, which gives them knowledge and skills unavailable to the elderly.

Palmore and Manton (1974) found that the relationship between modernization and status is not linear; instead, status declines in the early stages of modernization from that found in nonindustrialized societies and then rises once again in advanced industrial nations.

Results from the study of Datan, Antonovsky, and Maoz (1985) demonstrated this curvilinear relationship between modernization and psychological well-being. They found that women reporting the highest levels of psychological well-being represented the most traditional subculture (Muslim Arabs) and the most modern subculture (Central European Jews). The lowest levels of well-being were from three subcultures (Turkey, Persia, and North Africa), where greater cultural transition was occurring. In more advanced societies, the status of the elderly has been enhanced rather than lowered by higher education, which is linked to higher income and better health care and nutrition in the elderly (Rogers, Rogers, & Belanger, 1992).

Not only does status in the elderly vary from one culture to the next; it differs by gender. Simmons (1960) found significantly more respect for older men than older women across cultures. Older men received greater prestige in herding and agricultural economies with patrilineal descent. Women received prestige in hunter-gatherer economies where women made a major contribution to subsistence. In a cross-cultural study of deference, Silverman and Maxwell (1978) found that elderly women received similar levels of *service deference*[5] as men in support of basic custodial care, which typically occurred within the immediate family. Men received more *celebrative* or *presentation deference*[6] outside the family.

Older men may be more negatively affected by modernization than older women. Elderly men may lose their position of authority and position of power, whereas women may continue to function as the matriarch in the role of homemaker and caregiver. In contemporary Korean society, for example, the position of authority in making family decisions has shifted from the oldest male family member to the nuclear family (Kim 1993). Interestingly, Brown (1982) found that women experienced three positive changes as they approached middle age and older. These included fewer restrictions related to menstrual taboos and female sexuality, gain in authority to direct labor and make important decisions for younger family members, and new opportunities for achievement and recognition beyond the household, such as participating in governmental affairs. Bart (1969) found that the position of women improved in societies with multigenerational living arrangements. For example, the *abuela* in Mexico receives much respect in her role as grandmother (Diaz-Guerrero & Rodriguez de Diaz, 1993). She cares for the grandchildren so that the mother can work outside the home. The mother-in-law in India makes all decisions about the household and directs the activities of the daughters-in-law residing in the same dwelling (Adler, 1993; Deka, 1993). In Poland (Grzymała-Moszczyńska, 1991) and in Italy (Merenda & Mattioni, 1993) it is the grandmother.

Throughout life each individual faces biological, psychological, and social changes that require adaptation to maintain homeostasis or wellness. In this chapter, the tasks for adjustment in late life have been reviewed from a cross-cultural perspective. Late life is characterized by challenges to the physical body in the form of illness, functional disability, reduction in activity, and physical dependence upon others for care and assistance. Psychologically, the older adult is confronted by emotional reactions to loss (e.g., depression, loss of self-esteem or status, bereavement). Social changes such as retirement require reconsideration of one's role, purpose, living arrangements, and means of financial support. Aging, then, can be best viewed as a complex biopsychosocial process interacting with each unique cultural setting. Successful aging appears to be linked to health and wealth. Resources of wealth include money, property, valued information, and social support. Social support from the spouse, children, and friends is perceived as valuable when it is intimate, reciprocal, and of functional assistance. The maintenance of self-esteem during this final phase of life seems to be a crucial determinant of successful aging. "More than money and material goods, humans hunger for self-esteem, and seeking prestige is the main way to obtain and maintain this sense of self-worth" (Silverman, 1987).

NOTES

1. Persons with an *active mastery ego style* tend to take an active, assertive stance toward their environment. They try to change conditions in the world, rather than change themselves. They pursue their goals aggressively.

2. People with a *passive mastery ego style* are characterized as accommodative. They give in to the situation. Typically, they do not see themselves as being in positions of power. They try to change themselves rather than the situation.

3. The cultures compared in this segment of Project A.G.E included four neighborhoods in Hong Kong; one in Swarthmore, Pennsylvania, a suburb of Philadelphia; and one in Momence, Illinois, a rural community.

4. Rather than being an objective, quantitative, value-neutral analysis, hermeneutical analysis is seen as the result of the interaction of a unique interpreter who draws upon his or her intuitions, assumptions, personal and cultural knowledge to understand a text.

5. *Service deference* refers to any kind of work performed for the benefit of the elderly, such as cooking and housekeeping.

6. *Celebrative deference* refers to any ritual or ceremony that dramatizes the social worth of being an elder. *Presentation deference* refers to any modification of appearance (e.g., wearing modest attire) or bodily position (e.g., kneeling) in the presence of elders.

Part III

Personality and Belief Systems in
Cross-Cultural Psychology

10

Culture and Emotion

David Matsumoto

Kropotkin received the news with what I took to be satisfaction. He too had the inexpressive face and unsmiling eyes which were the Moscow norm. Mobility of features, I supposed, was something one did or didn't learn in childhood from the faces all around; and the fact that they didn't show, didn't conclusively prove that admiration and contempt and hate and glee weren't going on inside. It had become, I dared say, imprudent to show them. The unmoving countenance was the first law of survival.

Dick Francis, *Trial Run* (1978)

INTRODUCTION

Emotions are special events in our lives. The joy we feel with achievement or success, the anger when violated, our sadness at the loss of a friend or loved one, and all the other emotions we experience give life meaning and color. Emotions not only accentuate experience; they also are primary motivators (Tomkins, 1962, 1963), and as such they are central to an understanding of human behavior. Emotions are so important that it is almost impossible to think of life without emotions and feelings.

This chapter is about emotions in cross-cultural context. Most of the discussion here centers on emotional expression because it has been studied the most cross-culturally and because it is the area about which this author knows most. Other aspects of the emotions—what emotion researchers call *components*—such as the subjective feeling of emotion, the antecedents or elicitors of emotion, or the physiology of emotion, are also important, and research needs to continue on them as well (see Matsumoto, Wallbott, & Scherer, 1989, for a review). Yet an analysis of facial expressions brings out the dynamic tensions that have existed in cross-cultural theory and research on the emotions, as well as the major issues that stand before us today in furthering our knowledge of emotion. Studying facial expressions of emotion, particularly in terms of cultural similarities and differences, is also very important to those interested in cross-cultural social interactions in educational, business, or therapeutic settings.

The first part of this chapter describes the cross-cultural research on facial expressions conducted to date and the theoretical knowledge this research has provided us. We will see that although we acknowledge the joint influence of biology and culture in the mechanics of facial expressions, to date there exists no theory that explains exactly what about cultures produces differences in facial expressions, and why. The second part of this chapter offers some speculations about such a theory, reports some preliminary findings that support these speculations, and provides some future directions for further work in this area.

CROSS-CULTURAL RESEARCH ON THE EMOTIONS

Background

Darwin (1872) was the first to suggest that emotional expressions were biologically innate and evolutionary adaptive. Much of Darwin's theorizing, however, was based on anecdotal and observational evidence. For almost 100 years scientists remained unconvinced, arguing whether facial expressions are indeed universal and pancultural, as Darwin suggested, or whether they are specific to each culture, like a language. Those who agreed with Darwin were called universalists (e.g., Tomkins, 1962; Lorenz, 1965; Eibl-Eibesfeldt, 1972), whereas those who disagreed were called cultural relativists (e.g., Birdwhistell, 1970; Klineberg, 1940; LaBarre, 1947; Leach, 1972; Mead, 1975).

Until the late 1960's and early 1970's the prevalent view in psychology was that facial expressions were culture-specific, that no two cultures expressed emotions in the same way. Research from the past 30 years, however, has provided evidence for both universal *and* culture-specific aspects of the expression and perception of emotion.

The Universality of Facial Expressions of Emotion

The universal *recognition* of emotion by literate cultures was documented early in a series of studies by Ekman and Izard (Ekman & Friesen, 1971; Ekman, Sorenson, & Friesen, 1969; Izard, 1971). In these studies photographs depicting a full range of facial expressions of emotion were shown to observers in several different cultures, whose task it was to describe the emotion portrayed. Universality in expression was documented when high agreement was found across 12 literate cultures in the specific emotions attributed to facial expressions. These findings have been replicated in several studies since, with different researchers using different facial expressions (see review in Matsumoto, in press; Matsumoto, Wallbott, & Scherer, 1989).

Some writers argued that these findings were not valid because the only cultures sampled were literate cultures and because a shared visual input, such as the mass media, confounded the research. To answer these criticisms, Ekman and Friesen went to two preliterate tribes in New Guinea and gathered similar judgment data. In this study (reported in Ekman, 1972, 1973), New Guineans were asked to select from three alternatives the photograph that best portrayed the emotion depicted in a series of short stories. Universality was replicated when the New Guineans selected the same photographs as had the members of the literate cultures, answering to a large degree early skepticism.

The universal *expression* of both posed and spontaneous emotions has also been documented. In a separate part of the experiment reported above, Ekman and Friesen read the New Guineans several different situations designed to elicit certain emotions (e.g., "You feel sad because your child died"—cf., Ekman & Friesen, 1971) and asked them to show what they would look like on their face. These expressions were shown to observers in the United States, and universality was demonstrated when the Americans were able to identify correctly which emotional contexts the expressions were intended to portray. This study had unusual import, since the persons displaying the expressions were members of a visually isolated culture in New Guinea and the observers were Americans who had had no previous exposure to New Guineans.

Universality in spontaneous emotional expressions was documented in a study of Japanese and American subjects while they watched stress-inducing films (bodily mutilation) and neutral films (nature scenes). When the subjects were alone viewing the films, a concealed camera recorded their facial expressions. Their facial expressions were measured using the Facial Affect Scoring System (FAST: Ekman, 1972). Universality was shown when virtually the same facial responses of disgust, fear, and sadness were emitted by members of both cultures.

Cultural Differences in Expression and Perception: The Neurocultural Theory of Emotion

Given the overwhelming evidence in favor of universality, it was perplexing why such noted authors as Margaret Mead and Ray Birdwhistell believed that emotions were culture-specific. Ekman and Friesen reasoned that universal expressions may be modified depending on social circumstances and cultural learning, which would lead observers to believe that the expressions were indeed culture-specific. They tested this idea in the American-Japanese study described above. In a second part of the experiment, a scientist was present as the subjects viewed the stress films again. Their facial reactions continued to be filmed using a concealed camera. When the expressions that occurred were measured, Ekman and Friesen found that the Japanese invariably masked their negative emotions with smiles, while the Americans continued to show signs of their negative feelings.

Ekman and Friesen accounted for these findings by positing their neurocultural theory of emotional expression. They suggest that the facial prototypes of each of the universal emotions are stored in a facial affect program that is biologically innate. They also suggest the existence of *display rules,* that is, culturally learned rules for managing emotional expressions depending on social circumstance. This model suggests that the American and Japanese subjects displayed different emotions when the scientist was present because the Japanese had display rules that dictated the suppression of negative emotion in the presence of people of higher status. When they were alone, there was no reason for display rules to modify expressions, thus allowing the display of universal emotion.

Cultures also differ in their *perception* of facial expressions. In a study involving ten different cultures, Ekman et al. (1987) showed observers photos of the universal emotions and asked them to judge which emotion was portrayed and how intensely. Although they expected to find no differences, Ekman and his colleagues found that the cultures did differ in their attributions of intensity. In a later study, Matsumoto and Ekman (1989) replicated these cultural differences in an American-Japanese comparison and found that the attributions are not influenced by the culture or sex of the posers of the photos, nor are they due to lexical differences in the emotion words used in the study. Instead, Matsumoto and Ekman accounted for these differences using the display rule concept, reasoning that people learn to modify their perception of emotion in the same manner that they learn rules for modifying their expressions. That is, display rules in Japan not only may attenuate Japanese expressions of emotion, but may similarly downplay how emotional anyone else is seen.

TOWARD A CROSS-CULTURAL THEORY OF EMOTION

Defining Cultures

Despite the importance of emotional expressions and display rules, our theoretical understanding of emotions in cross-cultural context has not advanced beyond Ekman and Friesen's original formulation of the neurocultural theory. To date there is no study that has examined spontaneous emotional expressions cross-culturally since Friesen's (1972) original study, and there has been only one cross-cultural study of display rules (reported below). Substantial work needs to be done, especially to inform us of exactly *what* about cultures produces differences in expression and *why*.

The absence of research and theory in this area is due in part to our lack of a conceptualization of culture in ways that would help researchers understand and predict similarities and differences. In psychological research, culture is usually operationalized by country, equating culture with nation. Cultures are not geopolitical states, however; they are sociopsychological entities. Most definitions of culture include shared behaviors, beliefs, attitudes, and values communicated from generation to generation via language or some other means (Barnouw, 1985). Cultures transcend national borders and require us to define cultures along meaningful sociopsychological dimensions of variability rather than by physical boundaries. Operationalizing culture by country is theoretically useful only when these dimensions are explicated.

One dimension of cultural variability is known as Individualism-Collectivism (I-C). Several well-known writers, such as Mead (1967), Kluck-hohn and Strodtbeck (1961), and Triandis (1972), have long identified I-C as a primary differentiator of cultures. This dimension refers to the degree to which a culture encourages individual needs, wishes, desires, and values over group and collective ones. Individualistic cultures encourage their members to become unique individuals; hierarchical power and status differences are minimized, whereas equality, despite actual differences in social position, is maximized. Thus, differences between employers and employees, teachers and students, and other vertical relationships are less clearly differentiated.

Collective cultures stress the needs of a group; members identify themselves as individuals through their groups. Hierarchical differences and vertical relationships are emphasized; one's role, status, and appropriate behaviors are more clearly defined by position.

I-C is a key dimension to understanding and predicting cultural differences in emotional expression and display rules. I-C alone, however, cannot account for differences in emotional expression; it is first necessary to specify theoretical differences in social structures, the social meanings of emotion, and the impact of culture on these structures and meanings.

A PROPOSED THEORETICAL FRAMEWORK FOR UNDERSTANDING CULTURAL DIFFERENCES IN DISPLAY RULES

Triandis and his colleagues (Triandis, Bontempo, Villareal, Asai, & Lucca, 1988) have extended our understanding of culture and society by elegantly relating I-C differences to the classic social distinction of ingroups and outgroups (see Brewer & Kramer, 1985; Messick & Mackie, 1989; Tajfel, 1982, for reviews). This distinction is an important one in relation to display rules; self-ingroup and self-outgroup relationships form the most basic distinction for expressing emotion, as emotional displays differ depending on whether one is interacting with ingroup members or outgroup members.

Self-ingroup and self-outgroup relationships become even more complex between cultures because of cultural differences in the meaning of these relationships. According to Triandis et al. (1988), individualistic cultures have more ingroups, and in such cultures people do not feel as attached to any single ingroup, as there are many ingroups to which they can be attached. Ingroups in collectivistic cultures, however, are highly demanding; conformity is required, and sanctions for nonconformity exist. Collective cultures foster a greater degree of cohesion or harmony in their ingroups than do individualistic cultures.

Self-outgroup relationships are also different. Collectivistic cultures emphasize greater distinctions toward outgroups because of the greater degree of harmony required in the ingroups. In individualistic cultures, this difference is not as clear; self-outgroup relationships do not differ from self-ingroup as much, and members of individualistic cultures will not distinguish, or discriminate against, outgroup members as readily as will members of collective cultures.

A cross-cultural theory of emotion also needs to specify the role of emotion in social interaction, especially in potentially meaningful ways that transcend their universality. Kemper (1984) has offered a useful classification, identifying *integrating* and *differentiating* emotions. Integrating emotions serve to foster cohesion among interactants and are important to the maintenance of harmony in self-ingroup relationships. Differentiating emotions serve to foster distinctions among interactants; minimizing these emotions in self-ingroup interactions maintains harmony, whereas expressing these emotions in self-outgroup interactions maintains differences.

Cultural differences in I-C produce differences in the expression of integrating and differentiating emotions because of the degree of cohesion dictated by cultures in relation to self-ingroup and self-outgroup interactions. These specific predictions follow:

1. *Compared to individualistic cultures, members of collective cultures should display more integrating emotions in self-ingroup interactions.* Integrating emotions serve to maintain the cohesion that collective cultures foster.

2. *Compared to individualistic cultures, members of collective cultures should display more differentiating emotions in self-outgroup interactions.* Differentiating emotions will maintain clearer distinctions between ingroups and outgroups in collective cultures.

3. *Compared to collective cultures, members of individualistic cultures should display more differentiating emotions in self-ingroup interactions.* Individualistic cultures tolerate the display of differentiating emotions to a greater extent than collective cultures because of less emphasis on cohesion and group harmony.

Table 10.1
Predicted Cultural Differences in Display Rules

	TYPE OF GROUP	
TYPE OF EMOTION	INGROUPS	OUTGROUPS
Integrating	C>I	I>C
Differentiating	I>C	C>I

Key: C = collectivistic cultures
     I = individualistic cultures

4. *Relative to collective cultures, members of individualistic cultures should display more integrating emotions in self-outgroup interactions.* Individualistic cultures tolerate the display of integrating emotions to outgroups because there is less emphasis on maintaining social distinctions between ingroups and outgroups.

These predictions are summarized in Table 10.1.

An Empirical Test of the Model

A recent study using American and Japanese subjects tested these ideas (Matsumoto, 1990). These two cultures were ideal to test cultural differences in display rules. They differ in both expression (Ekman, 1972; Friesen, 1972) and perception (Ekman et al., 1987; Matsumoto, 1986, in press; Matsumoto & Ekman, 1989). Studies in anthropology and sociology, beginning at least with Benedict (1946), also suggest that Japanese differ from Americans in their understanding of emotion and in the role emotions play in their social interaction (e.g., DeVos, 1986; Doi, 1986; Lebra, 1976).

Hofstede's (1980, 1983) work highlights important I-C differences between the United States and Japan. In his study the United States was ranked 1 on individualism whereas Japan was ranked 22 (39 countries sampled). The Japanese, however, scored higher on Power Distance (another dimension of cultural variability), where differences between individuals' positions, rank, and power are more clearly delineated.

Theoretical works by Doi (1973, 1985) and Nakane (1970) inform us about differences in social structure between the United States and Japan, particularly in relation to ingroups, outgroups, and I-C. Japan is a vertical society (Nakane, 1970) that emphasizes status and position differences among people. As such, differences between ingroups and outgroups are sharply delineated. The United States, however, is a horizontal society that minimizes actual or perceived status, position, or power differences among people. Ingroup-outgroup distinctions are less clear.

In this study, subjects viewed slides of universal facial expressions of emotion (anger, disgust, fear, happiness, sadness, and surprise) and rated the appropriateness of displaying them in seven different social situations (alone,

Table 10.2

American-Japanese Cultural Differences as a Function of Emotion and Group Type

Emotion Type	Emotion		Alone	Social Situation Ingroups	Outgroups	Total
Integrat-	HAPPINESS	US	7.05*	7.74	7.45*	7.45*
ing		JA	5.98	7.67	6.86	6.97
Differen-	ANGER	US	5.46	4.32	1.87**	3.08**
tiating		JA	6.38	5.22	3.01	4.12
	DISGUST	US	5.97	5.21*	2.40	3.71
		JA	5.31	3.99	2.23	3.17
	SADNESS	US	6.72	5.83**	2.97	4.32
		JA	6.73	4.57	2.92	3.93
Unclear	FEAR	US	5.54	4.64*	2.62**	3.62**
		JA	6.18	5.79	4.29	4.99
	SURPRISE	US	5.41	5.71*	3.30**	4.29**
		JA	6.22	6.59	5.18	5.73

$*$ = $p<.05$
$*$ = $p<.01$

in public, with casual acquaintances, with close friends, with family members, with someone of higher status, and with someone of lower status). In a second session, the same subjects viewed a larger set of facial expressions and judged which emotion was portrayed and its intensity.

Based on the predictions provided above, the following hypotheses were tested:

1. that the Japanese would rate anger, disgust, and sadness (differentiating) in outgroup situations more appropriate than Americans

2. that the Japanese would rate happiness (integrating) in ingroup situations more appropriate than Americans

3. that Americans would rate anger, disgust, and sadness in ingroup situations more appropriate than the Japanese

4. that Americans would rate happiness in outgroup situations more appropriate than the Japanese

The data were manipulated to produce separate ratings for three different social groups: Alone (alone), Ingroups (close friends and family), and Outgroups (public, acquaintances, and higher and lower status). An analysis of variance (ANOVA) on the ratings using culture (2), emotion (6), and social group (3) produced a significant three-way interaction. Cultural differences were tested separately for each social group and emotion (see Table 10.2).

The results generally supported the hypotheses. Americans gave higher ratings to happiness (integrating) toward outgroups, and to disgust and sadness (differentiating) toward ingroups. The Japanese gave higher ratings to anger (differentiating) to outgroups. It is also interesting that there were no differences in ratings of Alone for anger, disgust, sadness, fear, or surprise.

There were also some unexpected findings, such as the cultural differences on happiness when alone (Americans > Japanese) and on fear and surprise to ingroups and outgroups (Japanese > Americans). The findings for fear and surprise were particularly perplexing, given that their social meanings are not well established. In general, however, the theoretical model was able to explain quite a wide range of differences.

FUTURE DIRECTIONS: INCORPORATING EMOTIONAL EXPRESSIONS

Although this model is perhaps the most refined statement available about cultural differences in display rules, we still have a long way to go. The most important task facing us now is the incorporation of emotional expressions into this model. As it now stands, the model cannot and does not predict cultural differences in spontaneous emotional expressions well.

Making clear distinctions between display rules and emotional expressions will undoubtedly help. Until now, no cross-cultural study has examined display rules, nor has any theoretical framework advanced our cross-cultural knowledge about them. Although the documentation of the existence of display rules and universal emotions was a breakthrough in our understanding, their overacceptance prevented us from examining these ideas critically.

The findings from the study reported above suggest a major difference between rules and behavior. Even though the Japanese subjects reported that they would be more likely to express negative emotions to outgroups, the Japanese subjects in Friesen's (1972) study smiled to mask their negative feelings in the presence of the experimenter. Behavior can, and at times will, be unlike attitude or belief.

I suggest that researchers and theorists interested in emotions cross-culturally consider display rules as *values* concerning the appropriateness of emotional display that are communicated from one generation to the next via language. People judge the appropriateness of emotional behaviors against the shared consensus of these display rule attitudes in combination with common knowledge about actual behaviors.

I suggest further that an expansion of the definition of display rules be given serious consideration. In the study reported above, display rules were defined simply as the degree of appropriateness of expressing emotions. The findings suggested, however, that display rules are more complex, including not only a dimension of expression appropriateness but also an evaluation of a behavioral response relative to appropriateness. Although the Japanese did rate anger more appropriate than the Americans, it was along with disgust and sadness one of the lowest ratings for the Japanese. Had the subjects told us what they would show on their face if they actually felt those emotions (behavioral response), different results might have been obtained.

Future models predicting cultural differences in emotional expressions need to incorporate these distinctions about display rules. Future models also need to incorporate more refined classifications of the social context of emotional behavior. Although the study reported above did make distinctions between Alone, Ingroups, and Outgroups, future models need to specify exactly whom one was with and to whom the emotions are targeted. Given the importance of I-C in predicting differences, it is only natural that display rules and expressions also differ depending on whether one displays emotion as part of a group or as an individual act.

CONCLUSION

This chapter has described the cross-cultural research on facial expressions conducted to date and the theoretical knowledge this research has provided us. It has offered a theoretical framework to use in understanding and predicting cultural differences in display rules and has reported some preliminary findings that support these speculations.

The original research by Ekman, Friesen, and Izard answered critical questions concerning universality and specificity that were fraught with debate and conflict. Since then, the study of emotion has become well established in social, developmental, personality, and physiological psychology. It now appears that we still have a long way to go in learning about cultures and their effect on emotions. The ideas presented in this chapter are offered to raise new questions and to enlist the help of others in seeking their answers.

NOTE

The writing of this chapter was supported in part by a research grant from the National Institute of Mental Health (MH 42749–01) and by a Faculty Affirmative Action Award and a Faculty Award for Creativity, Research and Scholarship from San Francisco State University. I would like to thank Katia Cattaneo, Andrea Chang, Erika Font, Liz Schloss, Karen Supanich, and Jarrett Tom for their aid to my research program; to Ken Kokka for his editorial assistance; and especially to Masami Kobayashi for her invaluable help in all aspects of my work.

11

Personality Across Cultures

Rogelio Diaz-Guerrero and Rolando Diaz-Loving

INTRODUCTION

June Louin Tapp (1981) is right on at least two counts: A developmental approach is indispensable if we are to understand personality from a cross-cultural point of view, and an all-purpose and conclusive enlightenment of such a theme would require her elephant research strategy (ERS). In her painstaking study, besides carefully delineating the six conceptual elements of ERS, she conscientiously reviews cultural, anthropological, and psychological antecedents. Like Tapp, the authors of this chapter believe that, indeed, the most promising and useful road to advance the topic is the developmental, particularly if it is based on an ecological, ecosystemic approach (Diaz-Guerrero, 1989a; Diaz-Guerrero & Diaz-Loving, in press).

What is happening in the field of personality, particularly in the United States, is very far from this pronouncement, however. Instead of writing a chapter reviewing the literature yet again, we felt it would be more striking and currently critical to compare at least one important development in the North American psychology of personality with one in the cross-cultural literature and one in Mexico. Interestingly, it is in Mexico where many younger psychologists are discovering that the personality of the Mexicans is quite idiosyncratic.

To complete the chapter we ask: Are there indeed universal personality dimensions? Here we try to compare the results of the two, more similar approaches arriving at what appear to be pertinent statements. The nature of the comparison forces what may be a useful insight about the nature of personality study on its own and across cultures and about the limitation and illimitation of personality measurement.

AMERICAN PSYCHOLOGY AND THE BIG FIVE

It is probably a good guess to state that between 80 percent and 90 percent of everything that has ever been written about the psychology of personality and the development of tests of personality is the work of American psychologists. As commonly used, the term *American* is inaccurate. Geographically it would be far more correct to speak of Meso–North American psychology. North America includes Canada, the United States, and Mexico. Nevertheless, beginning about mid-century, after 50 years of productivity and enthusiasm, came a period of close to 30 years in which there proliferated negative criticism and scepticism about psychology's capacity to measure personality traits. It is during these years that Skinnerianism grew strongly. Among Skinnerianism's positive aspects could be found a negative one, namely, the denial of the existence of anything that could be called personality. In contrast, beginning in the 1980s, enthusiasm began growing about the measurement of persistent traits of personality and the scientific conviction that this would prove useful for understanding and prediction in every field of applied psychology.

In his chapter on personality for the *1989 Annual Review of Psychology,* Carson (1989) dedicated only a small section to the "so-called person-situation controversy," feeling that this was a closed issue and pointing out that even Mischel (1973) abandoned his radical situationist point of view in favor of what appeared to be a frankly interactionist perspective. In the third section of his chapter, Carson speaks of the problem of identifying "the elements or dimensional units comprising personality." Indeed, beginning in the 1980s (Goldberg, 1981, 1982), many U.S. personologists became preoccupied with determining, not to what extent the traits measured by personality inventories consistently predicted the behavior of individuals, but if there were a limited number of basic, universal dimensions that described personality. This was what researchers like McCrae and Costa (1985, 1986, 1987), Costa and McCrae (1985, 1988), and Digman and Inouye (1986), as well as numerous collaborators and colleagues, have been highlighting. These researchers have published a number of studies using various methods and different sources of data and applying varied factorial analyses in their effort to demonstrate that within the enormous literature dealing with traits and within personality inventories, such as Cattel's or Eysenck's there existed only five dimensions. These, they argue, were the only basic, universal dimensions of personality. Such a preoccupation with finding universals was remindful of Osgood's efforts (Osgood, May, & Miron, 1975; Osgood, Suci, & Tannenbaum, 1967) leading to the demonstration that there were only three essential and universal factors for the subjective meaning of concepts and the efforts of psychometricians to ascertain a fixed number of abilities in the structure of intelligence.

It is in this vein that Digman and Inouye (1986) confidently state that previous studies of personality trait organization have frequently suggested that a five-factor model not only would be sufficient to account for the observed correlations in many studies but also would stand the test of replicability. In order to further specify the five robust factors of personality, they provided teachers with 43 adjectival scales to rate 499 Hawaiian children. Each mentor had to rate between 20 and 30 children. So that the teachers would master the psychological meaning of the scales, every concept in the scales was defined for them. Thus, for instance, the scale concept *considerate* was defined as "thoughtful of others; sensitive to others' feelings; cannot do things which hurt others' feelings; sympathetic when others are in trouble and tries to help" (p. 120). The factor analyses of the results of this research end up supporting the five-factor model. The authors actually obtain seven minimum factors, but the sixth and seventh are explained away and there remain, but five, albeit strong, factors. The authors labeled the factors, combining the definitions provided by Norman (1963) with their own.

Factor 1. Surgency, which the authors call extraversion and define according to the following adjectival scales: talkative-silent; sociable-reclusive; adventurous-cautious.

Factor 2. Agreeableness. Here the authors agree with Norman's label. This is defined by the following scales: good natured–irritable; mild, gentle–headstrong; cooperative-negativistic; not jealous–jealous.

Factor 3. Conscientiousness. The authors again agree with Norman's label. This is defined by responsible-undependable; persevering–quitting, fickle; fussy, tidy–careless; scrupulous-unscrupulous.

Factor 4. Emotional stability, which the authors call neuroticism. This is defined by the following scales: calm-anxious; composed-excitable; nonhypochondriacal-hypochondriacal; poised–nervous, tense.

Factor 5. Culture. This the authors call openness or intellectuality. Defining scales are imaginative–simple, direct; artistically sensitive–insensitive; intellectual–nonreflective, narrow; polished, refined–boorish.

All these investigators show the strong implicit assumption that these five dimensions of personality are universal. The first column of Table 11.1 presents these five factors—which may well be the key only to an English lexical structure of personality—in order to compare them with other scales regarding the dimensions of human behavior.

To get an idea of the heuristics that this type of research has stimulated, consider the questions that Digman and Inouye ask and the way they answer them. First they ask: What are these factors? How are they to be interpreted? Some researchers, the authors do point out, are weary of seeing these factors as anything other than five classes of connotative adjectives. However, they assert, others have attempted to relate these big five to personality theory.

Table 11.1
Are There Basic Universal Dimensions of Personality? A Cross-Cultural Comparison

Hofstede's Universal Factorial Dimensions	The Five Robust North-American Factors	La Rosa's & Diaz-Loving's Nine Factors of the Self-concept in the Mexican University Student
Power Distance (extent to which the masses accept that power is distributed unequally)	Factor 1 Surgency or Extraversion (talkative-silent, sociable-reclusive, adventurous-cautious)	1. Social Affiliative (courteous-noncourteous, well brought up-badly brought up, amiable-rude)
Uncertainty Avoidance (degree of threat of ambiguous situations and creation of beliefs and institutions to avoid it)	Factor 2 Agreeableness (good natured-irritable, cooperative-negativistic, not jealous-jealous)	2. First Emotional (happy-sad, depressed-joyous, bitter-jovial, frustrated-realized)
Individualism-Collectivism (the self-concept as "I" or as "We")	Factor 3 Conscientiousness (responsible-undependable, persevering-quitting, tidy-careless, scrupulous-unscrupulous)	3. Social Expressive (quiet-communicative, introverted-extroverted, reserved-expressive)
Masculinity-Femininity (Masculine values: success, money, possessions. Feminine values: caring for others and the quality of life)		4. Emotional Interpersonal (romantic-indifferent, affectionate-cold, tender-rude)

Factor 4

Emotional Stability or Neuroticism
(calm-anxious, composed-excitable,
poised-nervous, tense)

Factor 5

Culture or Openness
(imaginative-simple, direct, artistically
sensitive-insensitive intellectual-
nonreflective, narrow, polished, refined-
boorish)

5. Occupational
(responsible-irresponsible, punctual-
unpunctual, keeps promises-does not
keep promises)

6. Third Emotional
(impulsive-reflexive, temperamental-
calm, aggressive-peace loving)

7. Ethical Factor
(honest-dishonest, loyal-disloyal,
truthful-liar)

8. Initiative
(active-passive, fearful-risk taking, slow-
fast)

9. Accessibility
(accessible-inaccessible, treatable-
untreatable, understanding-
nonunderstanding)

129

Digman and Inouye cite as an example Digman and Takemoto-Chock (1981), who are of the opinion that these five factors are at the very least personality constructs that have been in the personality literature for a long time. The authors also refer to Hogan (1983), who made an ambitious effort to utilize the five factors in framing personality from a sociobiological frame of reference.

What is fascinating is that Digman and Inouye consider no other way of interpreting these five robust factors of personality. Not even their insistence that these factors have been found again and again in personality constructs from research in the United States leads them to say that the five-factor model may be a U.S. culture–bound phenomenon,[1] bound, at least, to the "culture" created by personality researchers. This "culture" defends the proper ways to elucidate the fundamental characteristics of personality. In the early days of research, professional needs as well as a knowledge about human psychology led personality researchers to design personality inventories. In contrast, today researchers of the big five appear to follow the psycholexical tradition initiated by Allport and Odbert (1936) and strongly revived by Norman (1963) with his "adequate taxonomy" of personality attributes. In this tradition, despite utilizing diverse sources of data from diverse groups in the United States, these researchers have continued to find these five basic factors. Yet they fail to consider the possible alternative, nor do they cite any author who contemplates that alternative, namely, that these five basic measures, and their relative importance according to the amount of variance for which they account may be diagnostic of the basic dimensions of personality present specifically in North American culture. In this connection let us advance the hypothesis that although some of those dimensions may be universal, we will find that their importance, that is, their variance, is different from one culture to another. Granting also that the basic dimensions across cultures remain around five, it is quite possible that only some will be universal, whereas others will be what cross-cultural psychologists call emic, or idiosyncratic, for a given culture, group, nation, or habitat.

The second question contemplated by Digman and Inouye asks: Are the five factors sufficient? Do they account for the observed relationships, or are additional factors necessary? Here the authors conclude: "The big five robust factors then, are not necessarily the verities of personality description. They represent the degree of complexity, the *dimensionality* of the personality rating process. These five dimensions also provide us with a quite stable framework within which we propose all verbal descriptions of personality are likely to be found" (p. 120).

The third and perhaps most interesting question is stated by the authors as follows: If the number of factors in this domain is five, what are the reasons for this? They consider the possibility that the five traits may indicate not actual behavior but only the raters' perceptions of behavior. That trait ratings have been correlated highly with behavior, .85 in one case

(Small, Zeldin, & Savin-Williams, 1981), and are also correlated with other independent measures makes it unlikely that the traits are only perceptions of behavior rather than the behavior itself. However, something remains impressed in the minds of human beings. The authors have this to say: "Consider the teacher-raters of the study reported here. Faced with the prospect of getting to know 20–30 children, a teacher-rater forms some mnemonic *impression* of a given child to differentiate him or her from the other children. We suggest that this impression has five (at most 6) aspects to it and that this number is related to limits in our capacity for information processing (Mandler, 1967; Miller, 1956)" (p. 120).

In a later study, Botwin and Buss (1989) recaptured the five-factor model of personality utilizing a behavioral methodology for the structure of act-report data. However, their discussion of the meaning of these five dimensions remains not only ethnocentric but extremely specialized. How much of ethnocentrism is exclusively a matter of excessive specialization and the complexity of the subject with which one is dealing? This would be very difficult to decide. What is unequivocal, though, is that this degree of specialization together with the assumption that what is discovered in North American subjects is universal is clearly shown in all of these studies. The lack of reference to work other than U.S. work is why this chapter is dedicated to bringing together a comparison of dimensions of behavior obtained by different methods in different ecosystems. This approach will undoubtedly, in some cases, show a certain degree of cross-validation of the five-factor model and, in others, provide the opportunity to understand behavior in a broader, perhaps ethnopsychological and universal, frame of reference.

HOFSTEDE'S FOUR UNIVERSAL CULTURAL DIMENSIONS

As Leung and Bond (1989) point out, the approach employed by personality psychologists intent on identifying basic dimensions of personality is not directly applicable to the specification of cultural dimensions. Among the methods they consider valid for identifying dimensions of cultural variation they include the work of Hofstede. The comparative study of work-related values by Hofstede (1979, 1980, 1982, 1983), which consists of a set of well-matched samples of employees of different subsidiaries of the same multinational business corporation, is unique. Hofstede worked with the responses in 117,000 individual protocols from subjects in 50 countries. Carrying out a factor analysis of country averages for his value measures, he identified three cultural dimensions, one of which was later split into two components, finally producing four dimensions on which all countries covered could be given a score.

Hofstede labeled the first dimension "power distance." He defines this dimension as the extent to which the less-powerful members of institutions and organizations accept that power in every realm is distributed unequally. He points out that the basic anthropological-societal issue related to this factor is social inequality and the amount of authority one person holds over others. The second dimension he calls "uncertainty avoidance." This dimension is defined as the extent to which people feel threatened by ambiguous situations and have created beliefs and institutions to try to avoid the uncertainty. Thus, the way a given society utilizes beliefs and institutions to deal with conflicts and aggression and with life and death is, according to Hofstede, the basic anthropological-societal issue to which this dimension is related.

Hofstede identifies the third dimension as "individualism versus collectivism." Interestingly, Hui and Triandis (1986), Marin and Triandis (1985), and Triandis (1988) have reported a great deal of work with a very similar dimension also called individualism-collectivism, a dimension that defined after Hui and Triandis (1986) carried out a study in which the sample was a group of cross-cultural researchers. Marin and Triandis (1985) have found that this dimension permits researchers to comprehend amply a number of differences that exist among Anglo-Americans, Latin-Americans, and Hispanics. Hofstede feels that this dimension reflects a culture's position on a bipolar continuum. One of the poles, individualism, is defined as a situation in which people are supposed to look after themselves and their immediate families only; the opposite pole, collectivism, is defined as a situation in which people belong to ingroups or collectivities that are supposed to look after its members in exchange for loyalty. The anthropological-societal issue related to this dimension is the individual's dependence on the group, his or her self-concept as I or we. It is of interest that Hofstede (1980) found correlations of as much as .80 between the rank of a country in his individualism score and the gross national product per capita; that is, as people become affluent, they become financially and, apparently, emotionally independent from their ingroups.

The fourth dimension has been labeled "masculinity versus femininity." This dimension has been extensively studied in the United States by Spence and Helmreich (1978), and more recently Diaz-Loving, Diaz-Guerrero, Helmreich, and Spence (1981) have shown that with certain modifications it works also for Mexicans. However, Hofstede's dimension is broader, thus masculinity is defined as a situation in which the dominant values in society are success, money, and material possessions; in contrast, femininity is defined as a situation in which the dominant values in society are caring for others and for the quality of life. The important issues to which this dimension relates, according to Hofstede, are the choice of social sex roles and the effects of these roles on people's self-concept.

In column 2 of Table 11.1 are enumerated Hofstede's four universal cultural dimensions to compare with the five basic factors of personality in the United States. Even though personality studies are usually carried out with

college students and Hofstede's study was done with employees of a multinational corporation, we invite readers to consider the differences in the
dimensions, particularly when reading the following excerpt taken from
Triandis (1988):

Rodrigues (1982), working in Brazil, replicated several classic social psychological
experiments. Amir and Sharon (1987), working in Israel, replicated a systematic sample of studies published in the best social psychological journals. In both cases the
results have been alarming. About half of the Brazilian studies did not replicate North
American results. In the case of the Israeli replications 34 results out of a total of 64
(more than 50%) did not replicate. . . . I claim that these results are alarming because
both Brazil and Israel are relatively similar to Europe and North America (Hofstede,
1980). (p. 1)

THE RISE OF AN ETHNOPSYCHOLOGY
OF PERSONALITY

" 'Information is knowledge. Knowledge is power.' More than ever, this
saying is acquiring compelling force. . . . But with the extension of relationships with societies, this maxim of Auguste Comte becomes even more pertinent. Those who lack knowledge see their fate shaped by others in the
light of their own interests. . . . Millions of human beings are subjected to
oppressive forms of domination, both covert and overt, because they lack
access to knowledge" (Schwendler, 1984, p. 3).

It was primarily with the financial support from UNESCO's project on
the exchange of knowledge for endogenous development that the International Union of Psychological Science called for a special conference to be
held in conjunction with the Twentieth International Congress of Applied
Psychology in Edinburg, Scotland, on July 24–26, 1982. The goal of the
small international working group brought together by congress was, in the
words of the organizers, "to document and evaluate the transfer of psychological knowledge and its impact on traditional thinking patterns and value
systems in the Third World" (Sinha & Holtzman, 1984, p. 1). It was likely
that in this conference, attended by distinguished scientists and scholars
mostly drawn from the Third World, the terms *indigenous psychology* and
indigenous concepts were utilized for the first time, with greater or lesser
import, by several of the participants.

The International Association for Cross-Cultural Psychology (IACCP), at
first interested in testing cross-cultural differences of what were thought to
be universal theories and concepts and aware of the growing evidence for
idiosyncratic characteristics of the people of different cultures, in 1986 organized its Seventh International Congress of the IACCP, a symposium
entitled "Indigenous Psychologies." The symposium's success prompted its

coordinators, John Berry and Uichol Kim, to edit a book with the same title (1993).

For a number of highly debated historical reasons, including the extensive mixing of blood and culture between Spaniards and native Indians in Mexico, interest in the psychology of the Mexican has been aroused ever since the beginning of this century. It is following this tradition that Diaz-Guerrero (1971) declared, "The psychologist in a developing country must therefore dedicate his attention to his own culture; paralleling the empirical constructs developed in the Anglo-American culture, he must pore over the peculiarities of his own people and develop concepts that will fit their specific and idiosyncratic nature. . . . He must think about how he can construct tests that are valid totally and specifically to the mental characteristics of his own people" (p. 13). The blueprint was there. The first dimension typical of the Mexican culture was reported a year later (Diaz-Guerrero, 1972). The article was titled "A Factorial Scale of Historico-sociocultural Premises of the Mexican Family" (translated from the Spanish). By 1977 a number of indigenous studies permitted Diaz-Guerrero to say, "The universality— not the scientific character of psychology—is challenged by data suggesting the need for a sociocultural psychology of personality" (1977b, p. 934).

The story ever since has been long, but it has ended in the need to start developing a new discipline, an ethnopsychology. At the heart of this effort is the concept of the historico-sociocultural premise (HSCP). It is pointed out that the most significant part of the human subjective world is given in generalized statements that are defended by an operational majority or a psychologically significant minority of the people of a given culture, generalizations that govern the thinking, the feeling, and, if the situation permits, the behavior of individuals of a given culture.

Several papers (Diaz-Guerrero, 1982, 1986a, 1987; Diaz-Guerrero & Iscoe, 1984) have described 13 preliminary factorial dimensions of HSCPs so far discovered in the Mexican culture. Among them is *machismo,* defined by items supporting the superiority of males over females and the attitude that submissive women are the best. Another is *virginity,* defined by beliefs such as these: "To be a virgin is of much importance for single women," and "A woman should be a virgin until she marries." Besides prescriptive dimensions, others deal with preferred styles of coping with stress, among them *affiliative obedience versus self-assertion.* These coping dimensions derive from generalized HSCPs that command the appropriate way of dealing with problems. One of the conclusions of the vast longitudinal cross-cultural study of child development by Holtzman, Diaz-Guerrero, and Swartz (1975) was that

Americans tend to be more active than Mexicans in their style of coping with life's problems and challenges. . . . An active style of coping, with all its cognitive and behavioral implications, involves perceiving problems as existing in the physical and social environment. The best way to resolve such a problem is to modify the environment. A passive pattern of coping assumes that, while problems may be posed by the environment, the best way to cope with them is by changing oneself to adapt to circumstances. . . . Many of the cross-cultural differences in the present study can be understood in terms of this general dimension of active versus passive coping style. (p. 339)

A proper ethnopsychology, it is proposed (Diaz-Guerrero, 1986b; 1989b), must show that the factorial cultural dimensions discovered for a given community must relate significantly and meaningfully to independent measures of cognitive, personality, and moral development; to vocational interests; and to consequential sociological and economic variables measured in the same subjects. In the cited papers there are several tables with data obtained in earlier studies confirming various aspects of this assertion. An ethnopsychological approach demands that the studies be carried out to discover the crucial dimensions for every culture. The methods to be followed are not as important as the fact that the discovered dimensions are cogent, valid, and will bear meaningful relationships to psychological and other social science constructs in the given culture.

It is in this ethnopsychological context that La Rosa (1986) and La Rosa and Diaz-Loving (1988) decided to approach the problem of the dimensions in the self-concept of the Mexican. This was done with a methodology different to the historico-sociocultural premises approach. Their procedure is also different from what was utilized in the work dealing with the five fundamental dimensions, the "big five." It is valuable to present it step by step.

La Rosa and Diaz-Loving defined the self-concept in abstract terms and then carried out several brainstorming sessions in which samples of Mexican senior high and university students of both sexes (N = 118) participated. In this way they identified five dimensions of the self-concept: *physical* (appearance and functioning); *occupational* (role and functioning in any type of work); *emotional* (intraindividual feelings and interpersonal interactions); *social* (satisfaction and dissatisfaction in social interactions); and *ethical* (congruence or incongruence with personal and cultural values). Next, using these extracted dimensions of the self-concept, they applied a questionnaire soliciting all the adjectives, positive and negative, that came to the minds of a more heterogeneous sample of 358 students of both sexes from the senior high and university levels. From the several thousand adjectives that resulted, those with highest frequencies and least synonymic overlap were selected (35 to 40) for each of the dimensions. Next were two pilot studies with 200 subjects each, heterogeneous samples of students from high school to university level, in order to determine the most adequate antonyms for the adjectives. In one case the antonyms selected were those most frequently chosen by the students; and in the other, those with the highest negative correlation with their opposites (provided that they were psychologically significant). Then, with a semantic differential (SD) format and the concept *I am,* 418 students, again from heterogeneous samples, responded to 54 scales of selected pairs of adjectives resulting from the previous steps. A factor analysis was carried out to verify the construct validity. From 13 factors, 8 explained 59 percent of the total variance; being conceptually congruent, these 8 were selected. The pairs of adjectives for the physical dimension, which were rather heterogeneous, did not produce any physical factor. There were three emotional, two social, two ethical, and one occupational factor.

After careful psychological analysis of this pilot study and the addition of congruent adjectival scales of the self-concept, a questionnaire containing 72 adjectival scales on an SD format were administered to the most heterogeneous sample, containing 1,083 students of both sexes. These had a mean age of 21 and a standard deviation of 4.32. From the factor analyses that followed there resulted 9 congruent factors explaining 49 percent of the variance.

Factor 1 turned out to be a social affiliative factor with high loadings on courteous-discourteous; well brought up–badly brought up; amiable-rude.

Factor 2 was one of three emotional factors with highest loadings in happy-sad; depressed-contented; bitter-jovial; frustrated-realized. This was labeled intraindividual emotions or mood states.

Factor 3 was a social expressive factor with highest loadings in quiet-communicative; introverted-extroverted; reserved-expressive.

Factor 4 turned out to be an emotional interindividual factor. Its determinants were romantic-indifferent; affectionate-cold.

Factor 5, an occupational factor, had as its determinants responsible-irresponsible; punctual-unpunctual.

Factor 6, the third emotional factor, had as its determinants impulsive-reflexive; temperamental-calm.

Factor 7 was an ethical factor, its determinants were honest-dishonest; loyal-disloyal.

Factor 8 was considered to be an initiative factor. Its determinants were apathetic-dynamic; slow-fast.

Factor 9 was the third social factor, defined by accessible-inaccessible; understanding-nonunderstanding (*comprensivo-incomprensivo*).

Importantly, La Rosa and Diaz-Loving (1988) connect these nine factors not only with the results of most previous ethnopsychological work but, cogently, with ordinary, quotidian personal and particularly social behavior of Mexicans. It is difficult not to conclude that hidden in these nine factors are the Mexican big five.

It is interesting to add that La Rosa (1986), among other studies, included a correlation with Diaz-Guerrero's (1972) original scale of HSCPs of the Mexican family. All but one of the factors in his self-concept correlated significantly with affiliative obedience, but the first two correlated highly with Factor 6.

ARE THERE UNIVERSAL PERSONALITY DIMENSIONS?

We have purposely selected three obviously different research approximations to the understanding of human behavior. Personality, remember Allport (1937), can be defined in at least 50 different ways. James (1968) spoke of a social self and advanced that each individual has many a social self, each appearing in relation to different social groups. We feel that the big five in any culture may represent the modal quotidian behavior. We are convinced, however, that although this everyday behavior may approach universality, the five fundamental dimensions will be ordered differently in different cultures. Thus, for example, as clear in Table 11.1, Factor 1, socially affiliative, of the Mexicans may correspond with Factor 2 of the Americans, though with a different tonality, and there is little doubt that Factor 3 in the Mexican study is Factor 1 of the big five.

In one case exploring intracultural variation of the pathological correlates of sadness, and in the other comparing clinical patterns of depression with Holtzman Inkblot scores across Mexican and U.S. students, Diaz-Guerrero (1984, 1985) concludes that depression should be more prevalent in Mexico and anxiety in the United States. The only psychopathological factor among the big five is Factor 4, calm-anxious. The only factor resembling it among the nine Mexican factors is Factor 2, sad-happy, depressed-joyous. Here there is not only a different tonality but the implication of a different etiology for possible pathological manifestations.

United States Factor 3 and Mexican Factor 5 have as their first determinant the adjectival scale responsible-irresponsible, with the interesting possibility that Mexican Factor 9 represents U.S. Factor 5. Readers will undoubtedly realize that in spite of these similarities, the Mexican patterning with two social and three emotional dimensions is interestingly idiosyncratic.

There is no overlap between Hofstede's cultural dimensions and either the big five or the nine Mexican factors. Masculinity-femininity has appeared in the studies of the big five as a sixth or seventh factor. The conceptualization, procedures, and subjects in the cross-cultural study are very different from the other two.

It is the strong impression of the authors of this chapter that apart from the five factors that so well describe the quotidiannes of personality, the dimensions that critically intervene in specific human habitats like home, school, church, business, industry, and government vary. One of the insights that can be gained from the present comparison across cultures is that clinical, educational, industrial, criminal, and social as well as other specialized psychologists must develop appropriate inventories that permit quantification of the behavioral dimensions functional in their respective realms. Thus, Hofstede's four universal dimensions plausibly best relate to the ordinary behavior of employees in a multinational corporation, whereas the big five factors of personality and the nine Mexican factors of the self-concept aptly summarize expected ordinary, everyday personal and social behavior. The big five appear more useful to clinicians; the nine Mexican, to educational and industrial psychologists.

To detect and properly quantify universal traits across cultures requires a rigorous methodology, even if the order of factors, and thus their cross-cultural variance, obviously differs. In addition to maintaining a consistent focus and procedure and conforming to the usual requirements of the cross-cultural endeavor, one should clearly define and enumerate the critical functions and behaviors typical of the ecosystems and/or habitats selected.

NOTE

1. This in spite of the fact that Bond, Nakasato, and Shiraishi (1975) in an early study dealing with the results of the administration of a translation of Norman's (1963) 20 original scales to Japanese and Philippine students and comparing their results with Norman's, conclude that Factors 4 and 5 are construed in culturally specific ways.

12

Beliefs and Cultural Social Psychology

Albert Pepitone

The study of human history leaves little doubt about the importance of beliefs in the affairs of our species. We need only recall the accounts of the Holy Crusades, the witch trials, the strange concoctions that are said to cure cancer, the reading of horoscopes to foretell the future, the searches for elixirs of love, to realize that much of our cultural evolution over the past fifty thousand years may aptly be described as social behavior organized around beliefs. Despite their importance in the social life of human beings, however, the literature of social psychology contains little theory and research on the subject.

The neglect derives, to some degree, from the natural science "ideology" widely adopted by psychology in general and experimental social psychology in particular. The basic prescription of the ideology is that theoretical statements must be general across content domains and universal across cultural samples (Pepitone & Triandis, 1987). Accordingly, the processes and structures that constitute major theories of mainstream social psychology are assumed to hold whatever the content of the independent and dependent variables may be. Such theories are also viewed as universal; they hold in whatever culture the sample of subjects is embedded.

There is another related characteristic of contemporary social psychology that inhibits the study of beliefs—its "individuocentrism." Most theoretical processes and structures are conceived to operate in the autonomous individual mind (Pepitone, 1976, 1981). The structures and dynamics that exist in groups such as status hierarchies and shared culture play only a minor role in theories of social psychology or are ignored altogether.

Although content generality is a desideratum of theory, it is not easy to suppose that a meaningful theory of beliefs could be absolutely content-free.

Indeed, the content of beliefs is what appears to be of major theoretical interest. Thus, we would like to answer precisely such questions as why some people believe that illnesses are caused by the evil eye, whereas other people believe that the same illnesses are the wages of sin. To consider all beliefs as theoretically equivalent precludes the hypothesis that different beliefs serve different functions.

Finally, there is an ontological premise in contemporary social psychology—again derived from the natural science paradigm—that generates a disincentive to study beliefs. Many beliefs—for example, the belief in witches, in the soul, in angels—refer to entities that are not real in terms of any measurable material existence. Therefore, it is argued, beliefs are beyond the bounds of legitimate scientific inquiry! The crucial point missed in this "argument" is simply that people hold such beliefs. Whether or not the referents of the beliefs exist in an objective material order does not alter the reality that people believe in their existence. It is not merely the phenomenological reality for the believer that makes beliefs a legitimate subject of scientific study but the objective reality of their effects. It is relevant to note here that the large number of experiments in psychology on extrasensory perception (ESP) and other paranormal phenomena have been designed to refute the claim that extraordinary, unnatural psychic powers exist and rarely to show how and why people believe in such powers (Alcock, 1981).

Although the concept of belief is not entirely absent from the literature of social psychology, it has few if any distinctive conceptual properties and is connected only vaguely if at all to the phenomena of everyday life such as prayer, superstition, and fate. For example, in the field of decision making, belief refers to the individual's view of the "state of the world," specifically, the probability and the "payoff" (valence) of the possible outcomes. In social psychology proper, beliefs represent the cognitive dimensions of an object, the probability of its existence (Fishbein & Raven, 1962). In this meaning, beliefs have to be taken into account as a necessary variable in predicting behavior from attitudes.

THE DEFINITION AND CLASSIFICATION OF BELIEFS

The idea of the existence of things captures the essential meaning of beliefs and brings us to a working definition: Beliefs are relatively stable cognitive structures that represent what exists for the individual in domains beyond direct perception or inference from observed facts. More particularly, beliefs are concepts about the nature, the causes, and the consequences of things, persons, events, and processes. Such concepts are more accurately described as social constructions that are part of a culture and have guided the socialization of those who share that culture. In this definition, beliefs are conceived as cognitive structures that are more or less adopted from what is already there in the culture rather than entities formed from the raw

Table 12.1
A Classified Sample of Important Beliefs

SUPERNATURAL	
Religious	god(s), human soul, resurrection, reincarnation, angels, devils, holy shrines, faith healing
Secular	fate/destiny, good or bad luck, superstition, witchcraft, evil eye
Paranormal	telepathy, precognition, psychokinesis, animal magnetism, orgone
Personality	ability to control life events, genius, sexuality, characterology
Society	origins of class structure, economic systems
Culture	ethnicity, race
Moral Justice	distribution of resources, punishment of bad deeds and reward of good deeds

material of social perception, inferred through empirical observations, or deduced via a system of logic from premises and assumptions. We would have to add an obvious feature of valuation to this essentially cognitive definition. To "believe in" means to endorse, to favor, to be committed to, and so on. The conflation is not always the case, however, and there is a necessary conceptual distinction to be made between the belief about "what is" and the value "what should be." Finally, consistent with the cultural origin of beliefs, we may observe that beliefs are exclusively human; no orangutan believes in witchcraft or in the Second Coming of the Messiah.

The task for the cultural psychologist is to construct empirically based theories that support general propositions about the structure of beliefs, their origins, and their psychological functions in individuals and groups. As in the study of other psychological phenomena, the first order of business is to organize and classify the phenomena. In a field that is as yet so uncultivated, there are several options in undertaking this first step. One provisional classification—which can be elaborated and corrected as knowledge accumulates—can be seen in abbreviated form in Table 12.1. Arguably, included in the principal categories and subcategories are the most important beliefs in the human repertoire, beliefs that have had the greatest influence in the history of the species. Although the categories in Table 12.1 are neither exhaustive nor independent of one another, they have a common denominator: The objects, agents, processes, powers, and so on, to which the beliefs in these categories refer are nonmaterial and not verifiable by the logic and methods of physical or social science. They contrast with the vast body of material beliefs about the natural world of physics and biology. The distinction is not always clear-cut, but we may set aside the boundary issue in order to pursue the analysis of nonmaterial beliefs.

The plan of this chapter is to survey a number of important beliefs and their essential properties, to specify research and theoretical issues, and to present some recent research findings that bear on such theory, specifically on the functions of beliefs.

RELIGIOUS BELIEFS

Besides the variety of deities, holy spirits, angels, the soul, and other divine agents and powers, the large category of religious beliefs includes sacred objects, places, and supernatural processes such as resurrection and reincarnation. Religious beliefs have a special quality that beliefs in the other categories lack, an awesome and mystical quality connoted by the terms *holy*, *sacred*, and *divine*. In the cognitive structures of the members of most religious groups, the beliefs—in divine laws, in the efficacy of prayer, in life after death, and in holy objects, places, and events—tend to exist together in organized structures. At the center of such structures is the belief in a God or Gods who are thought to be more or less omniscient and omnipotent spiritual agents, and the belief in the soul, the spiritual center of the person. Also in this more or less organized structure are beliefs about the functional relations among beliefs—belief theories. For example, through prayer, sacrifice, propitiation, and obedience to God's laws, the soul may be purified and qualify for salvation and admittance to an eternal afterlife or higher spiritual order of reincarnated existence.

A psychological question of deep interest is how such religious beliefs, built as they are on intangible beings, powers, and insubstantive spirits utterly outside the material realm, can be so widely diffused in the world and so resistent to extinction. How can people continue to believe when what they believe in cannot be perceived or empirically demonstrated in terms of objective criteria? One observation relates to the definition of beliefs given previously: The maintenance of a belief or of faith in general (faith may be regarded as a metabelief in the truth of beliefs) does not depend in any simple way on empirical evidence. What is called religious experience—for example, feeling the presence of God or seeing tears in the eyes of statues—may reinforce beliefs and may convert predisposed individuals into full-strength believers, but no such sensory events are necessary to maintain the belief that God and saints exist. Indeed, according to dissonance theory, beliefs about God and salvation can be strengthened following an objective disconfirmation of the latter's existence (Festinger, Schachter, & Riecken, 1958). Nevertheless, from a theoretical perspective, one can assume that beliefs are maintained because they serve functions for individual and group. A key objective for theory and research is the specification of such belief functions.

SECULAR SUPERNATURAL BELIEFS

Compared with religious beliefs, the supernatural beliefs classed as secular are less a part of organized, differentiated structures; typically, they are relatively simple structures independent of one another. Secular supernatural beliefs also lack the special qualities of holiness, sacredness, and so on. However, the secular-religious distinction is not always consistent. In one culture, a belief may be secular whereas in another the same belief is religious. We will briefly examine some important secular beliefs and their properties.

FATE

Fate is probably one of the oldest and most influential beliefs in the human repertoire. Its relationship with systems of religious beliefs is not uniform. In the Islamic religion, fate is that which is ordained by Allah. More generally, fate is an impersonal power that is part of a cosmic belief system; hence the close link to astral movements. In many cultures certain life events and outcomes are normatively and ritually believed to be determined more or less by fate: when and how one will die, who one will marry, whether there will be children, and so on. Whether actual life events of such kind are attributed to fate appears to depend on their characteristics. Everyday observations suggest that the life events interpreted as products of fate are unexpected and perceived as coincidences with uniquely meaningful outcomes for those affected, outcomes that are particularly relevant to their past experience ("uncanny") or contrary to what might reasonably be expected ("perverse" and "ironic") and, therefore, apparently purposive and predestined. Generally, such "meant to be" outcomes could not have been avoided or controlled. In regard to future events (destiny), however, horoscopes and various forms of divination may help to find out what fate has in store and so provide some possibility for avoiding or, in the case of positive outcomes, facilitating the occurrence of the event. At the concrete cultural level, one finds varieties of fate-beliefs. In the Hindu belief system important conditions of life such as one's caste position, chronic illness, or state of poverty are functions of one's Karma, a metaphysical index of the individual's spiritual purity based on past deeds. Karma is an inexorable law of fate; one reaps what one has sown. With respect to one's future existence, the form of one's reincarnated life outcome is determined by the Karma that one is creating by the deeds of the present. The belief in Karma is thus both a belief in fate and a belief in individual control.

We may note that many important and unexpected events of life are attributed to a purposive God rather than to fate, including illnesses, accidents, failures, and successes, even when those who experience such outcomes are in no way deserving, when it is not a matter of divine justice; that is, when it is not God's punishment or reward. It is commonly believed that "God moves in mysterious ways." In most such instances it is a powerful and absolute belief in God that constrains this preferential interpretation. We would not be surprised to find, however, that characteristics of the outcome have an influence. Thus, for example, God is chosen over fate when the unexpected outcome makes no connection to past experience, or when it is not an ironic coincidence, thus precluding the idea that it was predestined.

WITCHCRAFT

The belief in witches including varieties of "satanism" still flourishes in many parts of the world, and there is evidence that it was an element in the culture of our Cro-Magnon ancestors. In its essential form, witchcraft refers to supernatural powers employed by extraordinary persons through incantations, curses, trances, and other "black magic" for the purpose of harming persons or damaging their property. Unlike fate and God, conceived as supernatural agencies, witchcraft is practiced by real human beings, albeit "special" ones. Like the belief in fate, the belief in witches is sometimes connected to religious beliefs. Thus, in the period of the European witch trials, from the fifteenth to the seventeenth centuries, the witch was believed to be the creation of the Devil (Trevor-Roper, 1967), and as such, a threat to the Church. It was symptomatic of the evil of Manicheanism, which placed the Devil on a par with God in a titanic struggle for the human soul. Although such diabolism has declined and the Church no longer holds inquisitions, there are today priests who specialize in exorcising witches and other evil corrupters. African types of witchcraft, on the other hand, do not involve diabolism and are not connected with institutional religion.

The belief in the evil eye—in the power of the eye to harm—may be included in the category of secular supernaturalism. The evil eye is a concept similar to that of witches in that it is a supernatural power exercised by human beings against human beings with harmful consequences. Whereas witches operate in many modalities and have a special talent for evil that makes them extraordinary persons, the evil eye operates only through the visual medium, and the carrier or launcher of the eye is no one special. Those who have the eye are not easy to identify; indeed, those who have it may not know it. There are as many varieties of the beliefs about how to avoid the eye or minimize its effects as there are about who possesses the eye, what causes it, and who are its favorite targets (Maloney, 1976).

LUCK

The most common secular supernatural belief, which in one form or another is widely diffused throughout the world, is the belief in luck, a mysterious power that affects outcomes favorably or unfavorably, over and beyond the influence of ability, motivation, and chance. The power of luck is implicit in the great store of superstitions that make up a culture's folklore. If X happens (a mirror breaks, a black cat crosses your path, and so on), then an unspecified misfortune will befall you. The agent of fortune or misfortune is rarely identified or is conceived to be semihuman, an organism with some humanoid features, yet of a distinct species such as elves or fairies. The belief in luck plays a prominent role in gambling contexts, where outcomes are determined by objective laws of chance. In such contexts, the deliverer or witholder of luck is often personalized, as are the ways designed to invite positive interventions. Thus, bigtime gamblers make "side bets" of only respectful size and magically importune the favors of the mysterious Lady Luck by, for example, blowing on dice or wearing a lucky article of clothing. It is also commonly believed that luck is bestowed upon certain individuals like an endowment. When we say, "She is a lucky person," we imply that she is characteristically favored by the agent of good fortune. Omens, auguries, and auspicious signs are beliefs about mysterious powers that are of the same type as luck. Luck tends to be attributed to life events and outcomes that are inexplicable in terms of chance ("against the odds"), to ability (a case of "dumb luck"), or to drive ("I wasn't even trying hard"). Moreover, luck is not usually attributed to the most tragic misfortunes of life. The unexplained death of a child, for example, would rarely be blamed on an unlucky day or on the mischief of an evil elf. Further, the attribution to luck is not necessarily symmetrical between negative and positive outcomes. Although a major tragedy is not likely to be a matter of bad luck, winning $10 million in the state lottery could be assigned to luck. Such a gratuitous outcome would hardly seem to be the work of God.

CHANCE

In everyday discourse *luck* and *chance* are often used interchangeably; even the dictionary defines one in terms of the other. As beliefs, however, the two concepts are different. When we consider the belief in chance, we leave the realm of the supernatural, although psychologically we do not necessarily enter the material realm of science. The ordinary believer does not internalize statistical inference theory or the probabilistic laws of quantum theory. To the believer in chance, there are no personal or impersonal agencies responsible for the outcome; the characteristics of the person affected by a chance outcome cannot have had anything to do with the outcome. Only at a given point in time did random and independent elements concatenate to produce the outcome. Before or after the outcome, the random assembly would have been different. Finally, the belief in chance does *not* usually refer to life events that are extremely improbable and extremely important. Even in the domain of natural events like earthquakes and volcanic eruptions, the belief that chance is the exclusive cause is rare among the numerous attributions that people spontaneously make.

PSYCHOSOCIAL BELIEFS

The psychosocial category encompasses a large variety of beliefs that refer to individual abilities and the structure and dynamics of groups, crowds, and institutions, as well as to culture (beliefs that people hold about their own cultural traits and those of other groups). Psychological beliefs most commonly refer to mental or personality processes or underlying structures that enhance existing abilities or create special and unique ones. In addition to beliefs in so-called paranormal abilities, the category includes the ability to induce trances in oneself or others and to circumvent, or break down, another's will. Historically, the belief in animal magnetism, Mesmer, Svengali, and Rasputin illustrate the psychological genre. Beliefs in phrenology and similar concepts about the structure of the mind are also assignable to this category. More generally, the belief that self and others in certain ways and in certain areas have the ability to control to some degree life events and outcomes, including one's ultimate destiny, properly belongs to the psychosocial category of beliefs. It is understood, of course, that such events and outcomes—a successful career, a long and healthy life, a durable marriage and devoted children, and so on—are judged to be the result of multiple agents of control such as political and social support, fate, biological assets, or God's help. It is quite common to observe that when measured against objective criteria, the attribution of the source of control as well as the amount of control is distorted, sometimes either extremely exaggerated or underestimated. In such cases we may talk of "illusory" control (Langer, 1975). A distinction should be made, however, between such distortions and beliefs that are wholly supernatural. The latter are based on insubstantive and unmeasurable psychic energies, abilities, and powers, either indigenous or accessible from external sources, such as beliefs about "will power," "mind over matter," or therapeutic crystal. The distinction is relevant to the recent explosion of beliefs about diet, exercise, and health, particularly in the United States, which may be described as a revolution of consciousness in which people believe that they have almost unlimited control over their bodies, health, and longevity. Although such beliefs may have some validity, they are often illusory, some even falling frankly into the category of magic, alongside beliefs about fountains of youth, the rejuvenating effects of ground rhinocerous horns, and the cancer-curing properties of apricot pits.

Beliefs about society abound, including beliefs about the origins of class and caste system, economics, organized religion, conflict between groups, and political power dynamics. Beliefs about culture include beliefs about the "kind of people" we or they are—how good, how intelligent, how much control they have over specific life events, and so on.

MORAL BELIEFS

In general, moral beliefs are concerned with states of goodness and rightness, and the ways to achieve those states. One prominent set of beliefs or values in the moral domain relates to justice. Justice is not a unitary concept; there are several quite distinct states to which this belief refers, including, for instance, the alleviation of political oppression, equal treatment in juridical judgments about criminal penalties, and the distribution of resources in proportion to merit. In the context of religion and ethical philosophy, justice may refer to a moral order in which the good are rewarded and the bad punished. Such concepts are often connected directly or indirectly with beliefs in God. Justice in all human affairs is believed to be a major preoccupation of the Judeo-Christian and Muslim God. God not only is just but also believed to have more or less control over the world to bring about justice.

METHODOLOGY, THEORY AND RESEARCH

The beliefs described in the foregoing survey have to be seen as part of normative prescriptive systems that evolve and function in cultural and subcultural groups. This view that beliefs are shared norms that operate in groups raises an important question about whether universal theories are possible. If the beliefs of any culture are unique, are we not locking ourselves into a cultural relativism in all things? It is true that the social psychologist who adopts the position that beliefs are cultural products of groups cannot assume a priori that belief theories are universal, but it would be equally fallacious to rule out the possibility of universality (Pepitone, 1986). For one thing, inasmuch as culture is created to address basic biological needs, there is the presumption that at some deep level cultures are the same. Second, it must be kept in mind that theory is an abstract representation of phenomena. Even though beliefs may vary in many aspects across cultures, theories may be stated in terms of more abstract universals such as belief categories used in the present analysis or belief functions. Finally, there is ethnographic evidence that religious, magical, and other supernatural beliefs exist everywhere in the cultural atlas (Murdock, 1945). In any case, it is a premise of cultural social psychology that cross-cultural research is necessary to formulate hypotheses and to determine empirically the degree of their generality. The final section of this chapter discusses research that focuses on the functions of beliefs.

THE PSYCHOLOGICAL FUNCTIONS OF BELIEFS

As with beliefs themselves, there are many ways to classify their functions. Four functions may be specified in simple propositional form.

1. Emotional: Beliefs serve directly to reduce emotional pain or stress associated with fear, hope, anger, awe, uncertainty, and so on. For example, the belief in the efficacy of prayer provides a feeling of security.
2. Cognitive: Beliefs provide cognitive structure that gives a sense of control over life events. Thus, as Evans-Pritchard (1937) has hypothesized, the belief in witches provides an explanation of misfortunes.
3. Moral: Beliefs function to create a sense of moral order and certainty, the impression that goodness begets good effects and badness has bad effects; they also function to reduce moral "pain" through regulating the allocation of moral responsibility between self and others. For example, the belief that a misfortune was caused by fate allows the believer to disclaim responsibility for it.
4. Group: Beliefs serve to enhance group solidarity by providing people with a common identity. Emil Durkheim's (1912/1915) analysis of ancient totemic religions concluded that totem worship was the symbolic expression of societal identity and power. In modern society, social affiliations are often based explicitly on religious creed and practice.

Research on Belief Functions

The direct emotional stress–reducing function of beliefs is perhaps the most intuitively obvious—especially in the case of religious beliefs. Beliefs in God, saints, faith-healing, and life after death are indeed explicitly recommended by spiritual leaders for the lifting of hopes and the relief of despair and suffering. Surprisingly, there has not been much empirical documentation of this commonly supposed function in the research literature. A recent experiment, however, allows for the inference that religious beliefs have an anxiety-reducing function. Shrimali and Broota (1987) studied two groups of patients in a Delhi clinic—those awaiting what doctors classified as major surgery, and those awaiting minor surgery. A third sample of subjects was randomly selected from among healthy nonhospitalized persons. Questionnaire items selected from a standardized religiosity scale were administered before and after the surgery (successful in all cases) to measure the strength of belief in God, prayer, and so on. In addition, part of an anxiety scale was administered before and after the surgery. Shrimali and Broota found that preoperatively, those patients expecting major interventions scored significantly higher on religiosity than those about to have minor surgery and the healthy subjects. After surgery, however, their religiosity was no different from that of the other samples. The pattern of mean scores on the anxiety scale was parallel; that is, the patients awaiting major surgery were significantly more anxious than the other samples, whereas after surgery their level of anxiety was no different.

The compelling and straightforward interpretation of these results is that the patients in the sample subjected to the strongest life threat most strongly affirmed their religiosity. When the threat passed, the belief weakened and returned to baseline.

Although this functional interpretation is intuitive, there is what appears to be an inconsistent effect commonly observed. After avoiding an almost certain injury or death in an accident—after a "close call" or "near miss"— it is sometimes observed that religious beliefs often become *stronger*—at least for the period immediately after the threat has passed. There is no inconsistency here, however. In contrast to successful surgery that in most cases did away with the medical problem once and for all, avoidance of injury and death in what are classed as accidents does not necessarily preclude future dangers, particularly when they are created by others. The Shrimali and Broota research, of course, has to be repeated in a way that rules out demand characteristics; but if their findings hold up, they would be consistent with other common observations that when people reach old age and begin to contemplate the nearness of death, especially if they suffer from infirmity or progressively debilitating disease, they become more religious. That the religious impulse is felt when people face serious danger can be observed in a wide range of situations—prayer for the desperately ill, by those on a sinking ship, and on the battlefield.

Of deeper theoretical significance than the conclusion that beliefs are functional is the proposition that beliefs are *selectively* functional. The idea comes from an evolutionary perspective. In the beginning of human history, shared beliefs about animistic and naturistic powers, as well as magic, served to reduce the emotional stress of our primitive ancestors and provided cognitive structure about the large domain beyond perception about which there was complete ignorance. Further, such prescriptive belief norms that evolved from primitive religion and magic were retained and modified on the basis of their effectiveness in increasing the welfare of groups or important members of groups. Finally, we assume that like tools, beliefs became increasingly specialized to deal with the important events of life around which ignorance flourished. In a recent experiment, Saffiotti (1990) tested the hypothesis that for people who share a culture, beliefs function selectively to provide cognitive structure about life events, that a selective correspondence exists between certain kinds of events and beliefs. Members of a culture do not themselves have to believe in a given agent or power to know the normative functions of the belief and define the kinds of events for which the beliefs are functional.

Saffiotti presented to her sample of more than a hundred middle- and lower-middle-class college students a set of audiotaped descriptions of life events that the subject was to imagine happened to him or to her. (We ignore here other conditions of the experiment). There were two variations of each of eight types of life events, for which, on the basis of pilot research and common observation, certain beliefs were hypothesized to be most effective in providing cognitive structure. After hearing each event, subjects were asked to comment, to "interpret" what had happened. These open-ended comments were then reliably analyzed and coded into categories representing explanations and theories as to why the event occurred, attributions of responsibility for the event, evaluations of the event in moral or material terms, and other cognitive structure. More specifically coded in such categories were agents, powers, and processes such as God, fate, luck, chance, and laws of moral justice. Before presenting some of Saffiotti's results, it will be useful to highlight some of the hypothesized properties of beliefs and the corresponding kinds of events for which such beliefs selectively provide cognitive structure. It should be understood that the properties specified are not exhaustive, nor are they stated in their final, most precise form. It is also important to note that Saffiotti's results are based on a culturally diffuse North American sample. Preliminary results from West European studies, however, are on the whole consistent with Saffiotti's basic hypothesis. (Studies conducted in the Netherlands and Italy confirm the hypothesis that beliefs function selectively to provide explanations, but show variation in the beliefs used in Saffiotti's life event cases.)

God. For most believers, even if they are not strong believers, God would be the agency selected to explain sudden recovery from a fatal illness that cannot be explained in medical, material terms—miracles. For instance, cases of spontaneous remission of tumors that are medically inexplicable are typically attributed to God's intervention.

Fate. Fate-determined events are those that are perceived to be predestined and purposive. The attribution to fate is likely when important events are unexpected but meaningful so that they can be interpreted as meant to be. For instance, when long-lost brothers meet in a place where neither has been before, attribution to fate is likely.

Luck. Events for which luck is the normative interpretation are against the odds or beyond chance, and yet not the result of ability, motivation, or social agency. Winning nine out of ten consecutive card games is what the power of luck would explain to a player with only average skill.

Chance. The belief in chance selects for events that are not "against the odds," not of world-shaking significance—for example, winter colds, accidents on roads during rush hour, or where alternatives to an event are few (e.g., the roulette wheel stopping on black) and appear to have no determinative agent behind them.

Justice. Events that are interpreted by beliefs in justice are those associated with definitely positive (morally attractive) or negative (morally unattractive) character or behavior on the part of the person who is affected by the event. Thus, a "positive" law of justice is attributed to an unexpected, ad hoc event

Table 12.2
Percentage of Subjects (n = 103) Who Select Given Beliefs in Interpreting
Given Life Events

Life Event	God	Fate	Luck	Chance	Justice (neg)	Justice (pos)
miracle recovery	49.5	2.9	4.9	0.0	0.0	3.9
contrary to expectation	11.7	31.1	12.6	18.4	0.0	1.9
against odds	4.9	10.7	53.4	6.8	0.0	0.0
casual meeting	1.9	1.0	2.9	45.6	0.0	0.0
embezzler has losses	1.0	1.9	8.7	4.9	66.0	0.0
good person is rewarded	3.9	5.8	13.6	5.8	0.0	52.4

Note: To simplify the exposition of the theory, 7 additional belief categories used to interpret the 16 general kinds of events have been left out of the table, as have 2 kinds of events. The table includes the most frequent belief categories used in response to one each of 6 kinds of events. For full details see Saffiotti (1990).

that results in a large benefit to a person with a positive character or history of positive deeds. A "negative" law of justice is cited when an event is punishing or causes losses to a person with negative moral standing. Justice is sometimes mediated by transcendental impersonal agencies similar to fate or by God.

Table 12.2 presents the percentage of subjects whose comments on each of six life events were coded as the primary or only explanation or causal attribution that explicitly mentioned God, fate, luck, or the laws of justice. Because of space limitations, omitted are descriptions of the events that select for the belief in material causation and the belief that moral transgression can lead to self-destruction. The results are consistent with what is presented in the table.

If one inspects the diagonal of Table 12.2, a clear correspondence is seen between the life events listed in the left column and the beliefs selected by subjects to explain or otherwise provide cognitive structure about them. The beliefs predicted to provide what was hypothesized to be the normatively appropriate explanations and other cognitive structure for given life events, which we have described above, were in fact selected for this purpose more often than other beliefs. Indeed, Saffiotti found such selective correspondence—when the modal frequency of subjects mention the normatively appropriate belief—in all but two of the sixteen life events presented to the subjects for interpretation.

CONCLUDING COMMENT

This chapter has specified some of the properties of a small number of the most important beliefs in the human repertoire, from the diverse cate-

gories of the supernatural, secular, psychological, and moral. It has emphasized the view that beliefs are norms, shared concepts about agents, powers,
events, psychological processes, and states of goodness and rightness. It has
also described some research findings that lend support to the theory that
beliefs are selectively functional. This chapter, of course, is only the beginning of an analysis of belief systems. Much needs to be explained; but first
much more needs to be observed.

Part IV

Applications for Cross-Cultural Psychology

13

Multinational Enterprises

Justin P. Carey

The bird of time has but a little way
To flutter—and the bird is on the wing.
> Omar Khayyám, *Rubáiyát* (c. 1100),
> trans. by Edward Fitzgerald, 1857

These are the times that try men's souls.
> Thomas Paine, *The American Crisis*, 1776

Plus ça change, plus c'est la même chose.
> French proverb

Mandarin Chinese does not have a single ideograph to express the concept written in English as *crisis*; instead, it uses two: *wei gee*, translated as "dangerous opportunity." As psychologists confront the dual crisis of growing bureaucratization and politicalization of our profession, the *wei* aspect of our situation is obvious. It is the *gee* to which this chapter is dedicated.

A GLOBAL PHENOMENON

The current opportunity for psychologists is the Multinational Enterprise, or MNE, with positions opening now and benefits predicted to continue well into the twenty-first century. The MNE is a cyclical occurrence, rising, growing, maturing, and dying, throughout recorded history. Consider the ancient Phoenician traders and the more recent British East India Trading Company (1600). The modern phenomenon is the exponential growth rate in the number of organizations entering the MNE category, from relatively few companies at the end of World War II to an extrapolation of close to 100 percent by the beginning of the third millennium.

MNEs may be any type of organization: for profit, nonprofit, private, governmental, manufacturing, distributing, servicing, and so on. All share the characteristic of conducting business across national borders. Wherever the home office is located, one or more host countries will be involved in production or marketing of goods and/or services. An increasing number of MNEs are moving into the upper range of "multinational" and are becoming truly *global* in their scope.

MANAGEMENT PROBLEMS AND PSYCHOLOGICAL SOLUTIONS

As an MNE adds more nations to its enterprise, management problems develop, not by arithmetic but by geometric progression. This is so because management is essentially the task of managers getting things done through other people, and the behavioral performance of those other people is going to be influenced by their culture. As the MNE interacts with multiple cultures, it becomes aware that the reliable and validated operational procedures standardized for successful business in the home country are not working as projected. If management is not culturally sensitive, it may not become aware of the cultural basis of the problem in time to create an effective solution.

This problem area of cross-cultural conflict is built into the nature and concept of the MNE. The relevance of effective resolutions and solutions to success or failure of the enterprise in a given host nation is receiving increasing emphasis in business school curricula. The objective is to train managers who are aware of cultural diversity, who respect those whose culture is different from their own, and who seek solutions that are compatible with both the demands of the host culture and the legitimate needs of the MNE.

Business schools are not training cross-cultural psychologists—that mission belongs to psychology—but they are educating MNE managers to the need for expert advice and guidance on cross-cultural matters to safeguard their operations across cultural borders. This opens the door to countless opportunities for a professional position with an MNE as staff officer or consultant for cultural relations, for psychologists who are competent in cross-cultural psychology by virtue of training, knowledge, and experience. Responsive departments of psychology will offer courses in cross-cultural psychology to their undergraduate and graduate students.

Students of cross-cultural psychology who are interested in affiliation with an MNE will be well advised to take, at a minimum, an undergraduate introduction to management course and either the undergraduate or graduate course in international management. Practical work experience in business or industry, domestic or foreign, will be helpful. A minor in management to accompany the major in psychology is valuable. It is realistic to say that some business background will significantly improve the MNE interviewer's perception of you not only as a cross-cultural expert but as a colleague who can speak the language of management and who has an appreciation of the needs and objectives of the organization.

CROSS-CULTURAL BUSINESS

Even before crossing national borders, when we consider the composition of the contemporary workforce in the United States, we should appreciate the importance of cultural sensitivity on the part of those responsible in purely domestic enterprises for moving workers along the path of achieving organizational objectives. No country today has as heterogeneous a workforce as does the United States. At the other extreme, with maximum homogeneity, is Japan. It is interesting to note that with little need for cross-cultural sensitivity at home, Japan is among the world-class leaders in multinational enterprises.

The cross-cultural psychologist has opportunities for an MNE position both abroad and at home. Just as U.S. organizations are becoming MNEs, or expanding their MNE operations to additional countries, so foreign corporations are becoming MNEs, or expanding, by crossing the national boundary of the United States to carry out their business operations. There is equal need for the skills of the cross-cultural psychologist on the part of both the U.S. MNE and the foreign MNE.

THE ROAD TO MNE

Why does an organization adopt as a corporate strategic objective the goal of acquiring (or expanding) MNE status? Cross-cultural psychologists seeking affiliation with an MNE should first do some research on the specific company; convenient sources are the business reference section of your local library, stockbroker offices, or the firm's annual report by request to the public relations department. These sources may answer the above question on strategy for a given corporation but should be preceded by acquisition of background knowledge on the nature, birth, and growth of MNEs in general; seeking to build a multinational career track should be preceded by a survey of the road MNEs follow in their various operations, its pitfalls, barriers, and detours, all of significance to the affiliated cross-cultural psychologist. The basic characteristics of this sequence will be highlighted as we examine the major phases of operation a business implements as it travels along the road to being a multinational enterprise.

The decision to engage in business across one or more national borders is part of the organization's strategic plan, rooted in necessity: to defend, to maintain, or to expand when confronted by threats and/or opportunities. The threats to present profits may be either foreign or domestic and may be found in the decisions of our own or other governments, of competitors or labor unions, of consumers or suppliers. Opportunities may also arise as a consequence of changes in any of these same areas. The organization with "smart" management is prepared to take advantage of the opportunities and to neutralize or compensate for the threats. This includes utilization of cross-cultural psychologists as a component for effective multinational moves.

The type of business action decided upon will determine the need and extent of cross-cultural orientation required. Modern MNE actions go beyond the traditional roles of importer or exporter. They include, for example,

- building or buying a foreign manufacturing plant
- creating or acquiring a foreign distribution system for exported products
- developing a joint venture with one or more host country partners and/or with other MNEs
- licensing arrangements whereby the licensor grants the licensee the right to use something possessed by the licensor (e.g., management skills or cultural expertise)
- management contracts to provide specific managerial skills to one party for an agreed fee (e.g., in the special functions of personnel or purchasing)
- manufacturing contracts with a host country manufacturer to produce or assemble parts in compliance with MNE specifications
- franchising to market and sell goods or services already well-developed by the MNE (e.g., McDonald's Big Mac in Belgrade, Serbia)

Most psychologists are not aware of the fully potential for employment of cross-cultural consultants by MNEs implementing any of these strategic actions. The cost of such a consultant may be seen as an insurance premium to cover a real business risk at the interface of different cultures. Psychologists should also know that the volume of international trade, for 1991 estimated to be over $3 *trillion,* is still growing. Consider the continuing growth of MNE activity in the Pacific Rim, the fully operational impact of the European Economic Community in 1992, and the move to a market economy, free enterprise, and entrepreneurship of the newly liberated countries of Eastern Europe. All these events comprise strategic career opportunities for cross-cultural psychologists with an interest in the applied aspects of their specialty. It is perhaps easier for the applied practitioner of cross-cultural psychology to perform research as an incident of their practice than for the researcher to move into practice, and this chapter is mainly addressed to those with a primary interest in practice.

GEOCENTRIC ORIENTATION

The best recommendation to the MNE cross-cultural psychologist is to understand, accept, and endorse the *geocentric* orientation for human resource management by the MNE. The most accomplished MNEs have adopted this policy position as a comprehensive management perspective. Geocentric means world-centered; when applied to personnel, as in calls for a vacancy to be filled by the best-qualified available person, it means considering job candidates wherever in the world they may be.

The majority of MNEs do not yet have this global approach, but the cross-cultural psychologist may serve as a facilitator in encouraging its adoption. Even though the logic of the geocentric view may be appreciated by management for its rationality, for it to be successfully applied, management is required to have an international information system that may be costly to acquire and is difficult for managers to master.

What are the more popular, but not better, perspectives?

The *polycentric* orientation is held by MNE managements whose perspective has not moved to the geocentric or who reject it as too difficult or impossible for their managers. In fact, they regard the culture of any foreign (host) country as too difficult for home country managers to understand and apply in business decision making. The practice under polycentrism is for MNE operations in each host country to be managed and staffed to the maximum extent by nationals of that host country. The rationale is that local people know the local culture, workforce, customers, and so on, best. The polycentric approach has some advantages under its premises, but there are also disadvantages: All host nationals are not equally and interchangeably expert in local culture, and for local managers career development and advancement is automatically limited to opportunities arising inside their own national borders. MNE management with a polycentric orientation is a prime candidate for the services of a cross-cultural psychologist, whose job it would be to evaluate and select the best host nationals under polycentrism and to educate management toward at least a limited geocentric perspective.

The *ethnocentric* orientation is deservedly in last place. Executives with the ethnocentric philosophy of management assume as a basic premise that the way management is practiced in the home office in the home country is beyond criticism because it is obviously the best and only right way to conduct a business. A corollary of this position is that only home country managers will be competent to conduct MNE affairs in any other country. The fallacies in ethnocentrism are clear to a cross-cultural psychologist, but the MNE management that holds them as truths may not be interested in your bid to educate them to reality until the MNE has suffered a major financial loss directly traced to an ignored cross-cultural variable. The more successful the MNE has been as a domestic enterprise, the greater the temptation to transfer the self-image of national champion to world-class know-

:r & Gamble (P&G), for example. In the domestic U.S. ndustry, P&G expertise was the standard by which others ent. This was a valid reputation, believed and appreciated es, since they knew it all, including consumer psychology on of consumer research to product marketing. When an aign worked well, there was no need to fix it, even when transferred to another culture.

Philosophical premises die hard, particularly those of an ethnocentric nature. It took 13 years and losses estimated at a quarter of a billion dollars for P&G to learn that cultural variables in Japan are not necessarily the same as those in Europe. Where was the cross-cultural psychologist as insurance against that loss? Actually, a Japanese employee warned of the cultural conflict, but P&G knew better, as reported by J. A. Trachtenberg in *Forbes*, 15 December 1986, 168–169 ("They Didn't Listen to Anybody").

SELECTION AND TRAINING FUNCTIONS

The skilled cross-cultural psychologist should from the beginning have a role in selecting MNE managers to be stationed in other than their own home country. This includes the preselection determination of recruitment policies—deciding what sources will be used in recruiting suitable candidates for actual selection. Such policy decisions will be seen to reflect top management's orientation: ethnocentric, polycentric, or geocentric.

Working closely with the MNE human resource department, the cross-cultural psychologist will have been told what kind of positions need to be filled and where in the world they are located. He or she will review the *job description*, a comprehensive statement of the details comprising the work to be performed in the position; also provided will be the *job specification*, listing the qualifications (education, experience, skills, etc.) required for the person holding the position to perform at an acceptable level.

Decisions to be made include the use of sources that are internal or external to the organization: there are advantages and disadvantages to each. The source country to use for a particular position must be chosen. When a foreign source is used, recruitment itself becomes an international operation subject to all the cross-cultural complications and conflicts potential to routine business in an MNE. Newspaper ads and employment agencies are common sources, but the cross-cultural psychologist might recommend recruiting international management trainees from the graduating students of business schools in the MNE home country who are nationals of foreign countries where the MNE is planning operations. A supplement to this source would be graduates of foreign business schools, especially in countries where the MNE already has a presence.

Women are significantly underrepresented and underutilized in the ranks of international management. The cross-cultural psychologist can recom-

mend taking advantage of this source of high-quality manag
skills and also use his or her own psychological skills to ove
and neutralize the prejudice frequently found in MNEs regarc.
ment and selection of female managers for foreign assignment.

The failure, turnover, and replacement rate for expatriate employees is
higher than for any other employee category, ranging from 30 percent to
70 percent, depending on the cultural distance between the employee's
home country and the host country to which he or she is assigned. Since
MNEs by their complex and costly nature usually originate in developed
countries, the higher failure rates are found with MNE home office employees who are dispatched to lesser-developed countries, thereby experiencing relatively greater culture shock—a stress reaction stimulated by an
individual's perception of unfamiliar, strange, and different cultural components: people, places, customs, values, and so on.

High turnover rates equal high costs for relocation and replacement ex-
penses, which reduce profits, plus additional significant losses in business
and possibly customer satisfaction engendered by the usually deteriorating
quality of performance and service by the unhappy and dissatisfied expatriate
employee. Again, the solution for the MNE is found in the services of a
competent cross-cultural psychologist who will practice psychologically
sound selection procedures to prevent, or at least minimize, the usually high
degree of job dissatisfaction.

Higher culture shock and expatriate dissatisfaction correlate with lower
ratings for adaptability, tolerance, and understanding. The pattern of these
variables provides an initial basis for screening applicants or nominees for
foreign assignment. Cross-cultural sensitivity is a prime requisite for the satisfied expatriate. When eligibility for further consideration has been determined by application of the above general criteria, specific information
should be provided to the candidate, using the comprehensive job analysis
plus up-to-date research on the particular country and culture relevant to
the vacant position. As more and more specific data are disclosed to the
candidate, his or her responses are continually monitored by the psychologist for evidence to support a valid negative judgment that would preclude
further screening and orientation. Although skill in the local language is a
big positive factor, its absence should not exclude the candidate. What
would be sought is skill in any other language or interest in learning the
local language, as indicators of cultural sensitivity.

Assuming the applicant's candidacy has survived the above screening hur-
dles, most MNEs would consider the person ready for transportation to the
foreign culture. Some MNEs have an additional phase in the eligible candidate's orientation that would call for explicit participation by the cross-
cultural psychologist. Managers with prior experience in the country relevant
for the candidate make presentations and answer questions to give a picture
of what may be expected from a cultural viewpoint; this may be supple-

mented by invited nationals from the host country, obtained from within the MNE, from diplomatic and industrial missions, from universities, and so on.

The goal of the cross-cultural psychologist is to do what is necessary to have the MNE provide a *realistic* job preview for the applicant as the final step before the official assignment. It would probably prove to be long-term cost-effective to send the successful candidate on a temporary trial assignment in the country as the final screen *by the candidate* before he or she accepts the company's offer.

FAMILY ADJUSTMENTS

Most MNE assignments to foreign countries are for a term of years. For the married manager under consideration for such a position, all that has been stated regarding the screening variables applied to the employee is equally valid and relevant for the candidate's family. The family usually accompanies or shortly follows the new expatriate employee to the host country. When the employee fails and has to be repatriated, the probable causes of low adaptability, tolerance, and cultural sensitivity very frequently originate in one or more of the other family members.

For the cross-cultural psychologist, the solution to this problem is clear: bring the family of the applicant in for screening regarding the culture shock potential of the new environment; in addition, evaluate the family for personality characteristics compatible with good adjustment to strange people, language, customs, and so on. The solution, however, has a problem: Family members are not MNE employees, and if required to undergo screening and psychological evaluation, some will protest it as an invasion of privacy.

The psychologist as problem solver neutralizes this problem by altering the requirement to a persuasive invitation, acceptance being truly optional, but with the valid benefits to all parties—employee, family, and MNE—being spelled out in detail. It is assumed that the employee is technically competent to do the job. Therefore, the thrust of the screening, the information provided, the in-depth interviews, the testing, the presentations and previews, is to minimize the probability of an outcome assignment that will result in a failing employee and an unhappy, dissatisfied, even frightened family. Conversely, the procedure may result in an eager, interested, enthusiastic family group, fascinated by the opportunity to make new adjustments, learn new words, know new people, and understand new cultural behaviors.

The cross-cultural psychologist who has not had personal experience with the candidate's proposed host country should make every effort to borrow a repatriate from that country to participate in the interviews. The orientation for the family members should include videotapes giving an approximation of a *realistic culture preview,* not a traditional travel tape to entice tourists. This should also be given or loaned for home use as a basis for private family discussion and decision. The psychologist knows and should emphasize that a supportive, satisfied family is essential for the expatriate employee to succeed—and the MNE should know that the cross-cultural psychologist is a key person to help the MNE to succeed.

14

Pathological and Clinical Aspects

Juris G. Draguns

How much do abnormal patterns of behavior and experience vary across cultures? Are the differences in these manifestations of psychological disturbance basic or trivial? Moreover, what, if anything, about mental disorder can be realistically compared across culture lines? And are these differences relevant for the practical tasks of intervention and treatment across culture lines?

This chapter attempts to provide answers to the above questions on the basis of the current state of knowledge on the cultural variations and constancies in abnormal behavior. In the process, the weight of cultural factors in some of the major mental disorders, such as schizophrenia and depression, will be addressed. The chapter will also concern itself with cultural influences upon such social phenomena relevant to adjustment and disturbance as alcohol and substance abuse, suicide, borderline personality disorder, and anorexia. Of necessity, coverage will be selective rather than comprehensive; the topics chosen correspond to the foci of both curiosity and investigation in this young, yet rapidly growing field.

The term *culture* as used in this chapter and throughout the text has two distinct yet related referents. It pertains to the ways of life or the human-made environment, in Herskovits's (1948) famous phrase, of people linguistically, historically, and sometimes racially distinct whose habitats are geographically removed. In this sense, we speak of the Japanese, Brazilian, or Swedish culture. In the United States and, increasingly, in many other countries around the world, including Australia, Israel, India, Singapore, and Canada, we encounter the situation of several culturally distinct groups of people living side by side. Cultural diversity, then, evokes remote and exotic locations, yet in many parts of the world it is part and parcel of daily life and is observable around the block. This chapter addresses cultural diversity near and far. The practical implication of its existence not only in remote locations but in our neighborhoods is that the interplay of culture and abnormal psychology is relevant to the activities and techniques of the members of the mental health professions.

CULTURE AND SCHIZOPHRENIA: CONSTANCY AND VARIATIONS

Perhaps the most serious and challenging mental disorder is schizophrenia. Its causes are multiple and complex; it does not predictably yield to any single mode of treatment, although it is helped by a wide range of modes of intervention; and theories about its origin, manifestations, course, and outcome abound. In reference to culture, one might speculate whether this disorder is unique to or at least characteristic of the cultures of Western Europe and North America, where it was originally described and named. Conversely, if it is a biological disorder with disruptive psychological manifestations, as an influential current of contemporary professional opinion maintains, does that leave room for culture to shape or influence its manifestations, and if so, to what degree?

A series of studies sponsored by the World Health Organization (WHO) provide empirically grounded answers to these questions (World Health Organization, 1973, 1979; Sartorius, Jablensky, Korten, & Ernberg, 1986). The WHO research team applied a standardized diagnostic schedule in nine countries designed to maximize the cultural and historical contrast and to encompass the major existing political and economic systems. Specifically, the following cultures were included in this investigation: China (Taiwan), Columbia, Czechoslovakia, Denmark, India, Nigeria, the Soviet Union, the United Kingdom, and the United States. The principal result of this unique research project was the identification of a core syndrome of schizophrenia that was in existence at all sites of investigation. This common pattern was characterized by a restricted range of affective expression, inadequate insight, thinking aloud, poor rapport, incoherent speech, unrealistic information, and delusions with bizarre and/or nihilistic features. This finding left open the question of any variation of schizophrenic symptoms across the nine research centers. It solidly substantiated, however, the notion that the same symptoms were observed in a large proportion of schizophrenics at all the participating research locations. The initial research report did not inquire into any cultural differences, although such differences were identified in the subsequent publications of the WHO project (World Health Organization, 1979; Sartorius, et al., 1986). First, somewhat counterintuitively, the WHO researchers reported that the outcome of schizophrenia was more favorable in the three centers in developing countries, Colombia, India, and Nigeria, as opposed to the other six, located in more industrialized and prosperous settings. A variety of interpretations can be advanced for this unexpected finding. However, this positive result does not stand alone (e.g., Murphy & Raman, 1971), even though there have also been a few refutations (cf. Westermeyer, 1989). The second result by the WHO team reverses one of the most solidly established conclusions based on research in the Western world: that schizophrenics' prognosis is inversely proportionate to their educational and occupational level (Dohrenwend & Dohrenwend, 1969). In the WHO study, it was the poorer and less-educated patients in the developing countries, exemplified by India and Nigeria, who recovered more rapidly and readily. Thus the series of WHO studies reinforce the notion that schizophrenia occurs in a substantially similar form across a wide range of countries. Yet the same project also contributed information on the cultural shaping of the disorder. In this respect, the WHO report does not stand alone; there is a wealth of comparisons, observations, and reports that testify to an impressive variety of schizophrenic manifestations across cultures (cf. Draguns, 1973, 1980, 1986). Later in the chapter, the meaning and nature of these differences will be addressed.

The feature that is allegedly identical around the world is the incidence rate of schizophrenia, provided that this disorder is objectively, cautiously, and conservatively diagnosed. Upon the application of such precautions, the allegedly constant rate of schizophrenia amounts to 0.3 percent (Odejide, 1979). This conclusion would accord well with the currently prevailing majority opinion in the field according to which the sources of schizophrenia are fundamentally biochemical rather than psychological or social. Murphy (1982), however, questions the validity of these conclusions and points to a number of cultural groups, large and small, that have been shown to have high or low rates of schizophrenia. In the former category, he includes western Ireland and the Istria peninsula in northwestern Croatia. To the latter category he assigns the Hutterites, a Pacifist sect found in western Canada, and the Tongas of the South Pacific. He even identified two additional tribal groups in which the incidence of schizophrenia changed from low to high in the course of a generation. On the basis of a searching analysis of all of these groups, Murphy (1982) concluded that the claim of worldwide constancy of rates of schizophrenia was premature. Moreover, he tentatively identified a social pattern of influence that was likely to be responsible for cultural variations in the incidence of schizophrenia. According to Murphy (1982), the few regions characterized by a high rate of schizophrenia exhibited social ambivalence toward its inhabitants, on the one hand pushing them to succeed and emigrate while, on the other hand, reproaching them for any lapse in loyalty toward their home region. A parallel to the well-known dynamic of double-bind within the schizophrenic's parental family is readily recognizable. Murphy's contribution has been to transpose the double-bind from the family to the culture. Since the original double-bind formulation has not fared well in light of systematic empirical research, skepticism is warranted concerning Murphy's novel and promising formulation. So far, however, it has been the only explanation advanced to account for any cultural variations in schizophrenia.

To conclude, there is an impressive amount of evidence pointing to the existence of schizophrenia, the constancy of some of its basic features, and its tendency toward occurrence at about the same rate at a great many sites around the world. None of these conclusions can negate the cultural influences upon this disorder, especially in its manifestations, course, and outcome. These influences have been established by means of increasingly systematic and objective investigations; it is unlikely that their results will prove to be artifacts. The degree and meaning of cultural shaping of schizophrenia, however, continue to be subjects of debate and controversy.

DEPRESSION AND CULTURE: A COMPLEX PATTERN OF INTERACTION

On an intuitive basis, most professional observers would probably argue for a greater weight of cultural factors in depression than in schizophrenia. The available research evidence generally supports this judgment. However, worldwide, or at least widely encountered, features of depression have also been identified. Studies by means of a variety of methods converge in suggesting that depression is not the exclusive property of Judeo-Christian cultures, even though such cultures are especially susceptible to the experience of guilt, (Binitie, 1975; Diop, 1967; German, 1972; Zeldine et al., 1975). The more basic and universal components of depression are the vegetative and related symptoms that occur at the interface of psychological and organismic experience such as lack of energy, inability to concentrate, loss of enjoyment (World Health Organization, 1983), fatigue, loss of sexual interest, and reduced appetite with or without the resulting weight loss (Murphy, Wittkower, & Chance, 1967). Sad affect and feelings of worthlessness should be added to this list of depressive symptoms found in cultural milieus as different as those of Canada, Switzerland, Iran, and Japan (Jablensky, Sartorius, Gulbinat, & Ernberg, 1981; World Health Organization, 1983). Guilt, however, has shown a great deal of cross-cultural variation in the comparison of these four cultures, and in many other cross-cultural studies. The pivotal role assigned to guilt feelings in a number of influential Western conceptualizations of depression may be called into question on the basis of cross-cultural data. So far, the cross-cultural study of depression has not yet progressed to the point of being able to pinpoint the worldwide invariant manifestations of depression. Moreover, depression has both an elusive core and fuzzy boundaries. Both of these features raise the question of depressive equivalents in a cross-cultural perspective. Kleinman's (1982) extensive observations of depression in China have led him to conclude that a pattern of fatigue, discouragement, and weakness constitutes the contemporary Chinese mode of depressive manifestations in mainland China. Other observers (e.g., Skultans, 1991) call this equivalence into question and advocate a more emic or indigenous classification of expressions of distress that would bypass the search for the cultural idiom of depression, which remains historically a Western concept. Its application beyond the range of interrelated cultures in which it originated remains residually controversial.

China is not the only country in which somatization has been identified as a prominent avenue of experiencing and communicating personal unhappiness and psychological distress. It is widespread in other East Asian cultures such as Japan and Korea and has also been identified among various African and Latin-American groups. It is also frequently encountered among patients in the United States, even though because of the psychodynamic orientation of a great many North American mental health professionals, it is not highly valued. All these observations have caused Kirmayer (1984) to conclude that "at present there are insufficient data to support the claim that some cultures are more prone to somatization than others" (p. 170). At the same time, he concedes that "the nature and meaning of somatic symptoms vary widely across cultures" (p. 170). Among other features, bodily symptoms of depression may vary across cultures in prominence and visibility. While the bias of numerous North American clinicians would be in favor of psychological manifestations of distress, as opposed to psychological ones, Kirmayer (1984, p. 170) cautions that "the other face of somatization is psychologization, the tendency to perceive distress in psychological terms and to seek psychological treatment. Just as both interpersonal and intrapsychic problems can be expressed through bodily complaints, so somatic disease and social conflict can be cloaked in psychological guise." These considerations may forestall an ethnocentric, deficiency-oriented explanation of the somatic experience of depression and other modes of distress. The Chinese depressives and other depressives who voice physical complaints may be genuinely more perceptive of negative bodily sensations that accompany depression than are their Euro-American counterparts.

Like many other psychopathological phenomena, depression may be construed as a transaction (Kleinman, 1986; Wiener, 1989). In such a view, the social perception and communication of depression assumes prominence. Moreover, these social components of depression are subject to cultural shaping. Thus it has been demonstrated that affective symptoms are often missed by diagnosticians in patients who are members of a different cultural group (e.g., De Hoyos & De Hoyos, 1965; Kiesling, 1981). This finding is often cited in connection with the demonstrated tendency to label members of other cultural groups schizophrenic or to assign them to the various personality disorders. Some observers (e.g., Fernando, 1988; King, 1978) have ascribed this phenomenon to prejudice, rejection, or racism. A more cautious explanation (Draguns, 1990a) posits that the subtle clues that are indispensable for the perception of depressive experience in another person are easy to miss across a cultural gulf. Moreover, empathy does not travel well across culture lines (Draguns, 1973). In the face of behaviors that are both strange and disturbed, clinicians fall easily into the trap of opting for the most disturbed and deviant category, which in psychiatry is schizophrenia. Recognizing genuine distress despite the obtrusive trappings in which it is cloaked and experiencing its affective reverberations is a challenge to clinicians who work in culturally pluralistic settings. Speculatively, the lag that transcultural investigators experienced in acknowledging depression in Africa, South and East Asia, and other locations may be traceable in discerning depressive affect in culturally alien contexts. By this time, it is generally recognized that some aspects of depressive experience are encountered over a wide range of cultures and that no major region of the world is free of its manifestations. It would be premature to assert, however, that depression is a human universal that is present in all cultural groups. Such a statement not only would gloss over the complexity of pinning down the essential features of depression but would also be vulnerable to refutation by a single well-documented negative instance. At this point, I am not aware of such a refutation so that one can say that depression has so far been found wherever it was studied.

Subject to these complexities, it can be stated on the basis of the available evidence that the incidence rates of depression are subject to cultural variations. Depression, though present, occurs less frequently and, according to some observers, is expressed less elaborately in various regions such as the Far East and south of the Sahara in Africa (Kleinman, 1982; Yap, 1965; German, 1972). Its mode of presentation and the nature of its experience have less to do with self-castigation than with total and overwhelming distress.

Less can be said of the opposite extreme of the affective spectrum: abnormal excitement, mania, and euphoria. In the Euro-American cultures these phenomena occur within the context of bipolar affective disorder. This pattern of disturbance has seen little systematic cross-cultural study. What can be said is that manic disturbances do occur in a variety of cultural settings. In the case of the Pennsylvania Amish, Egeland, Hofstetter, and Eshleman (1983) have documented the tendency of the local psychiatrists to misdiagnose the manics in their midst as schizophrenics, another instance of using schizophrenia to cover instances of extreme deviance in people who are generally "different" and little understood.

SUICIDE: A CENTURY OF COMPARING RATES

Emil Durkheim (1951), the great sociological theorist, is usually credited with having inaugurated the international comparison of official suicide statistics. Moreover, he proposed an explanation of differences in suicide rates across countries that remains viable, though not uncontested, to this day. What Durkheim proposed was that social cohesion counteracted suicidal tendencies and that social isolation, loneliness, and alienation promoted suicidal tendencies. A prominent variant of suicide was traced to anomie, a condition in which human behavior is ineffectively regulated and insufficiently integrated into a social setting. Anomie as a social condition has proved to be exceedingly difficult to assess, so that it is more often invoked post hoc than predicted as a determinant of high suicide rates. Durkheim's idea that Protestant countries would have higher suicide rates than Catholic ones, presumably because of the difference in the levels of anomie, did not lead to clear-cut positive results, although several Catholic countries, such as Ireland and Spain, showed extremely low suicide rates, and a number of Protestant countries, such as Denmark and Sweden, had high suicide rates. At this time, close to a century after Durkheim's formulations, the generalization is even less valid. Consider three countries with some of the highest suicide rates in the world: Austria, Czechoslovakia, and Hungary, all of which have a substantial majority of Catholics, even though the influence of the Church over the lives of the people in these three states has experienced a considerable decline over the last few decades. Obviously, the nominal religious affiliation of the majority of the inhabitants is, at best, a very uncertain guide to the social cohesion of their country, and the degree of social integration is, at most, only one of the factors that determine the frequency of suicide. Other characteristics come into play, such as the proportion of aged and/or unattached persons in the population, which in turn is related to a country's birthrate. Old people are at risk for suicide, especially if they live alone. Another vulnerable segment of the population is composed of young people, and observations in the recent decades have generated a lot of concern with the increase in the suicide rate of adolescents and young adults. According to Jilek-Aal (1988), this is an international trend, observable in the same time span in cultures as different as those of Norway and Japan, and of the Indians and Inuit of northwestern Canada. Paris (1991) has gone further and linked these recent age-specific increases to social disintegration within the family. As social cohesion has broken down, there has according to Paris, been a virtual epidemic of behavioral and affective turbulence among young people, which in North America is typically diagnosed as borderline personality disorder. These personality patterns are associated with an increased proportion of suicide attempts. As the family environment restabilizes, Paris (1991) predicts, the rash of impulsive suicide attempts mainly occurring among the young will also subside, and some tentative indication of a decline of suicide rates in this age group have been observed in Canada and the United States in the last few years. Paris cites Tseng and McDermott (1981), who have concluded that the rates of completed suicide for the entire population of a country reflect enduring cultural factors and are typically subject to little change over time. By contrast, rates of attempted suicide are much more sensitive to disruptive and discontinuous social change.

Suicide rates, then, are an index of several coalescing cultural characteristics. It is generally recognized that they are an imperfect indicator contaminated by the distortions of suicidal statistics that are brought out by embarrassment, concern for the survivors, or sheer administrative and clerical sloppiness. It should be added, however, that much progress has been made since Durkheim and others blazed the trail in using suicide statistics as a social indicator. The available statistics are used with a sophisticated awareness of their imperfection.

ANXIETY DISORDERS IN OTHER CULTURES: THE CASE OF JAPAN

On the whole, a disproportionate share of cross-cultural information on abnormal behavior is focused upon the most disabling disorders: major depression and schizophrenia. Ironically, these disorders may be among the ones least susceptible to cultural shaping. This is especially true of schizophrenia. The urgency of studying and understanding these debilitating states is probably a major reason for their prominence in the transcultural research literature. The other reason, more down to earth, is the availability of hospitalized patients for international comparison. By the same token, anxiety states, which are with few exceptions ambulatory, have been relatively neglected, at least in major comparative international studies. There is just no research parallel to the WHO international comparisons of depression and schizophrenia. What multinational studies have been conducted (Lynn, 1971, 1973, 1975; Lynn & Hampson, 1975, 1977) are based on indirect, ingenious, but arguable indicators of anxiety in the general population. For these reasons, the relevance of this research for the understanding of the interplay of cultural factors and clinical disturbance is not clear. The descriptive literature on the culturally distinctive manifestations of some of the anxiety disorders is well worth noting. In Japan, for example, psychiatrists have described the syndrome of *taijin-kyofushu* (Russell, 1989; Tanaka-Matsumi, 1979), a variant of social anxiety that typically occurs in young men who are insecure about social status. Transitions from adolescence to adulthood, or changes in job or residence, are among the conditions that precipitate this disorder. Its principal manifestations include extreme self-consciousness often accompanied by negative concerns or beliefs about one's physical appearance and bodily odor. Sometimes these convictions reach a delusional elaboration and intensity. In reference to the official diagnostic manual used in the United States, the DSM-IIIR (American Psychiatric Association, 1987), this disorder is rather difficult to classify. Four components of it have been empirically established (Kirmayer, 1991). They range from a relatively simple stress-related anxiety state, through a social phobia of varying severity, to a clearly psychotic delusional state that would be diagnosed as paranoid schizophrenia by Western clinicians. What these observations suggest is that the current official U.S. catalogue of mental disorders can accommodate a prominent disorder from another culture only with difficulty. Perhaps this conclusion is both obvious and trivial, but it does point to the range of cultural plasticity in expressions of distress. Social anxiety is experienced in both North America and Japan; its respective expressions show more than a culture tinge.

In this connection, the general problem of culture-bound reactive syndromes may be addressed briefly. Over a century or more, reports of indigenous manifestations of psychological disturbances from remote and exotic lands have been accumulating (Murphy, 1982; Prince, 1985). Such behavior patterns as *amok* and *latah* have been identified. Without describing any one of these syndromes in detail, what can be said is that many of their manifestations are dramatic and conspicuous. Their onset is sudden, and the symptoms of the disorder are often dangerous to self and others. The immediate need is for restraint. If the person is protected from his or her frenzy, the disturbance quickly subsides. Chronicity is rare. Such is the case with *amok*, which can be described as a combination of excitement and fury, often set off by a relatively mild interpersonal slight or disappointment. The apparent disturbance is extreme, but this impression is belied by the quick disappearance of its symptoms. Moreover, it is not clear whether all the culture-bound syndromes really belong within the rubric of abnormal behavior as the term is commonly understood. In same cases, they constitute ritualized and consciously controlled responses, usually to a stressful situation (e.g., Salisbury, 1966). In other instances, there are serious doubts whether the behavior in question, such as *Windigo,* a cannibalistic frenzy among Ojibwa Indians, ever actually occurred (Marano, 1982). The alternative construction, supported by copious evidence and persuasive argument, is that a mythical belief and an observable behavior pattern were confounded.

The challenge to Western observers is to find for these syndromes appropriate and flexible slots in their diagnostic system, which originated at a point in space and time yet aspires to comprehensiveness and universality. This effort has recently gathered strength (Kirmayer, 1991; Prince, 1985) connected with the objective of making the next edition of the DSM-IV, the U.S. diagnostic manual, more culturally flexible and sensitive. Subject to the conditional nature of this effort, most of the experts on the subject recognize that these culturally distinct syndromes are not entities *sui generis* but, rather, slightly to moderately different variants that can be fitted into the existing slots of the diagnostic system. Often they are psychotic in appearance but upon more thorough observation and analysis have closer affinity to anxiety and/or stress disorders. The flip side of the coin is the emerging recognition that some of the disorders in the DSM-IIIR may be the culture-bound conditions of their place and time. Among the candidates for such status are some of the prominently diagnosed syndromes of contemporary North America such as the borderline personality disorder and anorexia nervosa.

THE CULTURAL FACTORS IN EATING DISORDERS

In the 1970s and 1980s, speculations were voiced about the cultural sources of the dramatic burgeoning of the incidence of self-induced starvation, or *anorexia nervosa*. Why did this disorder mushroom and spread across the United States and Canada, a phenomenon apparently paralleled in other economically developed countries (DiNicola, 1990)? Prince (1985) was among the first to recognize the potential role of the culture in the development of this syndrome, although data on ethnic differences within the United States and other pluralistic cultures remain inconclusive, as do also the results of international comparisons. Selvini Palazzoli (1985) identified anorexia nervosa as the syndrome of the affluent society, and DiNicola (1990) was able to confirm this association in a searching review of the pertinent evidence. In his words, "Anorexia nervosa shows a developmental gradient across cultures, with predominance in industrialized, developed countries. . . . Both the social class and cultural bias of anorexia nervosa share an association with affluence" (DiNicola, 1990, p. 286).

VARIATIONS IN ALCOHOL ABUSE AND THEIR CULTURAL MEANING

Ethnic and cultural differences in alcohol consumption and in the rates of alcohol-related disorders are well-established topics of cross-cultural study. Over the years, much information has been collected on the cultures that produce a disproportionate amount of alcohol abuse. Cultures that are characterized by low percentage of problem drinkers have also been investigated. In the latter category are Jews, Chinese, and Italians, both in their countries of origin as well as in the United States and other New World locations. The former category includes the Irish (Stivers, 1976) and several Native American (Mail & McDonald, 1980) groups. The differences between these two types of culture pertain to the manner in which alcohol consumption is socialized and controlled (MacAndrew & Edgerton, 1969). Contrary to what one might expect on a common-sense basis, the typical child in the Jewish, Italian, or Chinese family is introduced to alcoholic beverages early in life. This, however, usually occurs in a ritualized, festive context at which the amount of alcohol consumed is at most moderate (Synder, 1958). By contrast, alcohol in many other ethnic groups, including those with a reputation for excessive consumption, is first tasted in secret, outside of the family setting, and often in the context of rebellious assertion of adulthood and/or masculinity. Alcohol in low-consumption cultures is regarded as food, in those characterized by heavy use it is viewed as akin to a drug, designed to produce changes in mood and consciousness. In more extreme cases, alcohol becomes a general antidote against frustration, as a universal means to drown out sorrow. If such an attitude is widespread within an ethnic group and if, moreover, it is transmitted by explicit instruction or implicit modeling, its members are likely to be at risk for alcohol abuse. Other factors no doubt play a role, such as the perceived uselessness and the resulting low self-esteem of many Native American and black young men, deprived and cut off from their traditional male roles. Alienation fosters heavy drinking: Aboriginal alcoholics, removed from their customary habitats yet not integrated into modern, Australian urban life, come to mind in this connection.

And yet it would be a mistake to conclude that all the pieces in the above picture fall neatly into place. Above all, it is easy to succumb to the stereotype of the alcohol-prone Irish and of the Jews or Chinese who are immune to this problem. Historical research has shown that the Irish reputation for heavy drinking originated in the eighteenth century (Stivers, 1976). The contemporary Irish-American figures for alcohol consumption approach the national average. Conversely, as Jewish family life in the United States loses its distinctive traditional characteristics and approximates the general norm, some of the built-in safeguards against heavy alcohol consumption are likely to weaken. Indeed, there are some tentative indications that the alcoholism rate among the Jews in North America is gradually rising.

Finally, there are unsolved problems and unanswered questions. Let me limit myself to one. Volumes have been written about the major alcoholism problem in France (e.g., Sadoun, Lolli, & Silverman, 1965) and about the low number of alcoholics in Italy (Lolli, 1958)—both countries that are Latin, Catholic, wine producing. There is a need for analyses and comparisons that would shed light on the hidden, yet crucial difference between these two countries.

FROM FINDINGS TO EXPLANATIONS: THE MEANING OF CROSS-CULTURAL DIFFERENCES IN PSYCHOPATHOLOGY

This chapter's cursory survey of cross-cultural differences is now complete. It has hit some of the highlights but omitted a lot of the details. The time has come to explain these findings. What general principles would account for the data just summarized? If possible, the nature of the relationship between culture and psychological disturbance should be identified and the differences in abnormal behavior traced to their corresponding cultural features.

In reference to the first objective, one possible link between modal and abnormal behavior within a culture is that the latter represents an inappropriate exaggeration of the former. Typical and adaptive patterns of behavior are applied at the wrong place and time or in the wrong way. They become a reduction to absurdity or a caricature of culturally prevalent modes of coping. One example will suffice. Diaz-Guerrero (1967, 1970) identified passive versus active responses as the characteristic modes of coping with stress in Latin-American and Anglo-American milieus respectively. Numerous comparisons of Latin-American and North American psychiatric patients have demonstrated that passive symptoms are prevalent among the former, active symptoms among the latter (Draguns, 1990b).

As far as the second objective is concerned, progress in this field has for a long time been stymied by the absence of empirically based dimensions on which various cultures could be placed. This need has been met by the well-known major study by Hofstede (1980) in which four such dimensions were identified. This was done by means of multivariate statistical procedures applied to the analysis of responses of several thousand subjects from over 40 countries of all regions of the world. The four dimensions derived in this manner were individualism-collectivism, uncertainty avoidance, power distance, and masculinity. A recent attempt was undertaken to extend these four variables to the domain of abnormal psychology (Draguns, 1990a). Individualistic cultures, as exemplified by the United States and the countries of Western and Northern Europe, were found to be characterized by internalization of distress, experience of guilt, chronicity in schizophrenia, and predominance of cognitive symptoms. In collectivistic cultures, such as Japan, China, and several Latin-American cultures, psychiatric symptoms revolved around specific human relationships. If guilt was felt, it occurred in the context of such relationships, rather than in reference to violations of absolute and abstract principles (Kimura, 1965). Uncertainty avoidance was discovered to be associated with manifestations of anxiety, whereas masculine cultures tended to promote catastrophic responses to failure, for example, in the form of suicide. These leads are at this point few and isolated, but they should be extended if research is initiated to test explicitly the relationships between Hofstede's four dimensions and the features of psychological disturbance.

At the same time, a start has been made toward connecting these four basic variables with the culturally distinctive components of psychotherapeutic intervention (Draguns, 1990a). That psychotherapy differs across cultures has been solidly established (cf. Prince, 1980), even as the cross-culturally constant ingredients of psychotherapy have been identified. The interplay of the cultural and the universal transactions in the psychotherapeutic encounter is sometimes conspicuous and at other times subtle and barely perceptible. It has been proposed but as yet not demonstrated that psychotherapeutic intervention in individualistic cultures would emphasize self-understanding and insight, together with themes of guilt, alienation, and loneliness (Draguns, 1990a). In collectivistic cultures, in contrast, a more expressive and close relationship between the therapist and client would be promoted, with the goal of enhancing well-being rather than festering self-understanding. Cultures with a high need for uncertainty reduction would stress scientific and objective explanations, whereas in low uncertainty-avoidance cultures, variety and spontaneity in psychotherapy would prevail and immediate experience would be prized. Power distance in a culture would be characterized by emphasis upon the therapist's expertise; low power distance would go hand in hand with egalitarianism, confrontation, and improvisation in the conduct of psychotherapy. In masculine cultures, the therapist would facilitate the client's adjustment to the culture. By contrast, therapists in feminine cultures would foster the client's self-realization and self-expression in preference to the culture's rules and concerns. These expectations have as yet not been systematically tested, even though they are compatible with descriptive accounts of psychotherapy in various cultural settings characterized by low or high placement on the above four dimensions.

CONCLUSIONS

The investigation of the interplay between culture and mental disorder is a young but rapidly developing area of investigation. Much progress has been achieved in the past 25 years, and these advances are reflected in the preceding pages. The extent and limits of cultural influences upon the manifestations of abnormal behavior have been identified, and a much clearer panoramic picture has emerged of the manner in which these influences operate. Certainly gaps and ambiguities remain, but an agenda for the systematic exploration of the field is being implemented. It will keep investigators active for decades to come.

15

Mental Health Treatment and Service Delivery in Cross-Cultural Perspective

Harriet P. Lefley

In most societies the form and content of mental health service delivery has been based on a constellation of cultural variables and socioeconomic realities. Belief systems, values and value-orientations, religious and medical practices, family structure, economic organization and resources, and societal needs for protection and order have all affected both identification and treatment of persons defined as needing mental health treatment. In some countries the political philosophies of persons in power have also had a significant impact on the structure of mental health service delivery.

Across cultures, practitioners differ in their explanatory models of disorder or illness, their diagnostic practices and treatment technologies, and often in the types of patients their particular specialty is designed to serve. Although in many traditional cultures the priest and healer are one, most distinguish between religious practitioners and herb doctors. The latter, however, functioning on the principle of mind-body unity, can usually cure afflictions of the spirit as well as physical illness or disability. Almost all cultures in the world, from tribal units to nation-states, acknowledge an officially sanctioned Western medical system as well as a traditional healing system. They also recognize the types of cases their respective practitioners are trained to serve. In cases of persistent behavioral deviance, or psychotic behavior, indigenous healers typically recognize when Western medicine is indicated and make appropriate referrals (See Lefley, 1984; Ruiz & Langrod, 1976).

Paradoxically, the training of mental health professionals in Western industrialized nations has often been less specialized and more diffuse. There is greater reliance on a core body of etiological theories and standardized diagnostic procedures rather than, as in native healing, on specific precipitants and correlative cures for individual cases. In Western education, although psychotropic medications are in the purview of those who are medically specialized—psychiatrists and psychiatric nurses—all core professions have been trained in psychotherapies oriented toward treating persons with ordinary problems in living or impediments to self-actualization. In many programs there is a far greater training emphasis on this clientele than on treatment and rehabilitation of persons with serious mental disorders (National Institute of Mental Health, 1990). In developing countries with scarcer resources the tendency is to orient both training and services toward the most needful populations and to integrate these services with primary health care at the village level (see Nagaswami, 1990; Yucun, Changhui, Weixi, Tingming, & Yunhua, 1990).

The treatment techniques of indigenous and Western healers inevitably differ, although both will use medications and somatic therapies as needed. In healing disorders of the mind/spirit, native healers look to supernatural causality or external malevolence, focus on immediate precipitants, and help afflicted individuals direct their behavior toward propitiating gods, performing requisite rituals, or balancing unequal forces. Western healers look to internal causality and individual history or behavioral patterns. They focus on eliciting verbalization, abreaction, insight, and/or behavioral or cognitive change. Western psychodynamic therapies have often been lengthy, costly, and elitist, and except for the affluent and educated few, are not frequently practiced in non-Western societies. In these cultures Western psychopharmacologic and rehabilitative technologies are usually directed toward those people whose psychotic symptoms and incapacity for self-care have overtly identified their need for professional intervention.

In Chapter 14 of this book, Juris Draguns has spoken of cultural concepts of psychopathology and correlative issues of diagnosis. It is evident from a proliferating body of biological research that certain core diagnostic entities such as schizophrenia appear to be found in all human groups. However, problems of differential diagnosis continue to abound. There is a very large literature on cultural aspects of diagnosis such as those relating to the use of assessment instruments and interviewing techniques, language and psycholinguistics, understanding culturally normative and deviant behavior, and other issues involving social distance between clinicians and patients (Lefley, 1990a, 1991). Diagnostic clarity may be confounded by cultural differences in behavioral manifestations of psychosis (Chu, Sallach, Zakena, et al., 1985; Fabrega, Mezzich, & Ulrich, 1988; Katz, Marsella, Dube, et al., 1988; Mukherjee, Shukla & Woodle, et al., 1983). This is why such studies as the International Pilot Study of Schizophrenia are so important, since they develop mechanisms for diagnostic uniformity across cultures (See Sartorius, Jablensky, Korten, et al., 1986).

This chapter deals primarily with the structures that cultures have developed to deal with the mental health needs of their populations. It discusses the development and interface of community and institutional mental health systems, as well as the interface between Western medicine and indigenous healing systems. Commonalities of traditional and modern cultures are described.

Differences in approach derive from differing world view and belief systems, kinship structure and caregiving roles, and cultural attitudes toward dependency and disability. Enculturation within the matrix of sociocentric versus individualistic societies affects both self-perception and the way society treats persons perceived as behaviorally deviant or as mentally ill (Lefley, 1990a). Social structure and world view also affect care-giving roles and family-professional relationships—particularly the manner in which professionals perceive and interact with their patients' kinship networks. Longitudinal changes in the Western world and cross-sectional changes as nations begin to modernize are linked in projecting the cultural context of future mental health systems throughout the world.

COMMUNITY MENTAL HEALTH IN DEVELOPING COUNTRIES

In 1975 the World Health Organization (WHO) began a collaborative study on strategies for extending community-based mental health care in developing countries. Services were to be offered by primary health care workers in pilot study areas in selected countries as part of general medical care. The study found that these primary health care workers could indeed deliver mental health care at the community level. According to the major investigators, the research itself was a catalyst that "has served to change attitudes toward disease and health in general as well as toward mental illness; it has served to sensitize workers to important wider psychosocial issues" (Sartorius & Harding, 1983, p. 1462). Further collaborative research has continued with respect to optimal dosage and duration of psychotropic medications, effectiveness of psychosocial interventions at the primary care level, management of common psychiatric problems of patients visiting primary health care facilities, home management of the mentally retarded, and factors that influence help seeking and attitudes of health personnel toward mental health problems (Sartorius & Harding, 1983).

In most countries of the world, mental health and health care are merged, long predating the "linkage model" that became popular in the United States in the 1970s and continues today in health maintenance organizations and other types of managed care. Private mental health care in the United States, however, is oriented toward acute hospitalization and time-limited interventions. It does not address the needs of chronic patients, who are largely handled in the public sector. In most settings, medical and psychiatric services continue to be segregated both conceptually and physically. On the other hand, integrated medical, mental health, and case management services have long been incorporated in the more fluid and less-compartmentalized systems of the developing countries. Presently there is an initiative to include psychosocial rehabilitation in the national health care programs of developing countries (Nagaswami, 1990).

Despite the relative advantages of Western nations in funding, facilities, and professional personnel, several areas of relative strength are apparent in the service delivery systems of developing nations. First is the more efficient utilization of scarce resources, with providers often offering home services that are typically unavailable in the clinic-based systems of industrialized countries. Second, culturally syntonic diagnostic and treatment procedures merge indigenous healing systems with scientific modalities. Third, and extremely important, is the inclination of most practitioners in the developing world to welcome and integrate their patients' families, their natural support systems, into the treatment process. In fact, in a series of mental health program descriptions in various developing countries, not one fails to mention that families are viewed as the central supportive resource in care giving and treatment (Lefley, 1990b).

The planning process and training of skilled paraprofessionals facilitate some efforts from which Western systems could learn a great deal. For example, a few trained primary health workers doing a field survey for a "community mental health care net" in a district in China with 190,000 population—about the size of a community mental health center catchment area in the United States—were able to identify all individuals needing help for severe psychiatric problems. This is certainly more direct and efficient than our customary needs assessments. With far greater resources, U.S. systems target estimated percentages of at-risk populations, rather than identified individuals in need of mental health care, and would consider direct case finding an extraordinary luxury.

In contrast, also, to our earlier conceptualization of community development as "primary prevention" (see Lefley & Bestman, 1991), in developing nations this is a means of providing tertiary rehabilitative care for persons already identified as mentally ill. Dunlap (1990) has described activities and programs that operate at the interface of community development, rehabilitation services, and community reintegration of mentally ill persons in countries as diverse as India, Micronesia, and Australia. Here community resource development is "conducted for the purpose of making normative roles of living, working, socializing available to persons with mental illness that is of a disabling nature" (p. 67).

The Italian Experiment

One of the most intriguing developments in modern community mental health is the experiment of Italian deinstitutionalization. In 1978, under the leadership of Italian psychiatrist Franco Basaglia, Italy passed Law 180, which banned all new admissions to public mental hospitals, converted all inmates to voluntary status, and decreed that in place of state hospitals, psychiatric units of 15 beds per 150,000 population would be established in all general hospitals (figures considerably below the need established in the United States, where there are 130 psychiatric beds per 100,000 population). In the United States, deinstitutionalization was endorsed by an unlikely alliance of civil libertarians and fiscal conservatives. In Italy, Law 180 was pushed through by left-wingers who merged antipsychiatry with Marxism, in consort with right-wing Christian Democrats who viewed deinstitutionalization as a money-saving measure.

Community mental health services have since developed very unevenly, with great disparity in the resources available in northern and southern Italy. Of the estimated 55,000 patients who were in the public hospitals at the time Law 180 was passed, approximately 35,000 have remained. Conditions in the public mental hospitals have been described as "appalling," with minimal staff, great use of restraints, no ward activities, and patients forbidden to work because this may exploit them (Jones & Poletti, 1985). In some parts of the country the formerly government run hospitals have been taken over by the Catholic Church, so that deinstitutionalization has in effect not occurred. However, new patients are rarely admitted. In many parts of Italy families are greatly burdened with a major care-giving role and inadequate clinical supports to deal with grossly psychotic behavior. In the south, Jones and Poletti (1985) have found that community support services are virtually nonexistent.

In northern Italy, however, in Trieste, Brescia, and Verona, resources are on the cutting edge of optimal psychiatric rehabilitation. There are almost 100 cooperative industries for people with mental disabilities, which started in the early 1970s even before the reform law was passed. In order to break the barrier of stigma and marginalization of mentally ill persons, it was felt that these industries would have to function at a superior level. Boston University's Marianne Farkas, an international trainer in psychiatric rehabilitation (Farkas & Anthony, 1989), frequently visits these industries and reports that their products are of excellent quality, with "gorgeous, Madison Avenue type publicity" and enthusiastic patronage (Farkas, 1992, personal communication). Examples are a fine costume jewelry shop, a handbag factory and shop ("Gucci quality"), and a moving company. There is a food division that has its own farm, food-processing plant, grocery store, and four-star restaurant. There is a landscaping company and architecture firm. Their arts division has a radio station, a video company, a computer center, a publishing house, and an industry that reconditions old manuscripts and books.

The industries have been so profitable that they jointly bought a sloop to take their patient-workers on vacation cruises. They are also organizing a travel agency that will offer a low-cost travel package designed for people with psychiatric disabilities. They have been able to obtain individual support persons to travel with each patient when this is necessary.

The specialized industries are developed by experts and are run jointly by patients and staff proficient in that industry. The radio station has an "intellectual hour" that recruits top-flight people to donate one hour a month to the enterprise. From this outreach they have developed a pool of expert consultants who help with product design, advertising, training, and marketing.

Two items are readily apparent in the northern Italian experiment. First, patients work in first-class industries of which they can be proud. Second, they work under conditions that are optimal for mentally ill persons. All businesses are small—no more than 15–20 people. Since psychiatric patients have difficulty tolerating overstimulating or high-demand environments (see Lefley, 1992), here they can work without excessive interpersonal stimulation and at their own pace.

The ease with which experts are enlisted attests to the sociocentric, group-oriented emphasis in many European countries (the cooperative model is currently being replicated in Geneva, Switzerland). Cooperatives have long been favored in Italy and are consonant with a culture that is oriented more toward the family and group than toward the individual. In the individualistic culture of the United States, for example, there is currently a movement away from congregate living for the mentally ill and an emphasis on scattered-site individual housing with occasional visits from case managers. In Italy scattered housing is seen as punishment. We will speak more of how conceptual differences among sociocentric and individualistic cultures have impacted mental health service delivery.

INDIGENOUS HEALING AND WESTERN MEDICINE

In many countries there is a respectful acceptance of dual and sometimes mutually referring modern and traditional medical/mental health systems. In hospitals in the People's Republic of China a pharmacopoeia of herbal remedies coexists with the latest in psychotropic medications. A center for Ayurvedic medicine is found among the buildings at the National Institute of Mental Health and Neurosciences in Bangalore, India, an important modern training center for psychiatrists and other mental health disciplines. In many African countries, indigenous healing is integrated with modern psychiatry. Nigerian psychiatrists have described how the two major orientations in contemporary Nigerian psychiatry utilize folk beliefs. In the "culture-bound" approach there is a deliberate reinforcement of the healing process through joint roles of native healers and Western-oriented psychiatrists. The "non-culture-bound" approach simply incorporates discussion of herbs and rituals in group psychotherapy. For most patients, group therapy is seen to entail accepted rituals that are meant to placate or destroy diabolical spiritual forces.

The ARO village system in Nigeria was started by World Health Organization psychiatrist Lambo (1978) and has since been extended to Senegal and other African countries. Here, after treatment in a Western mental hospital or clinic, psychiatric patients live with a relative in a traditional village close to the mental health facility. Treatment is organically related to village life, combining native healing rituals with psychotropic medication and group therapy. Asuni (1990) has described a similar system run solely by traditional healers. This "involves the active participation of relatives of the mentally ill. In fact the relatives have to live with their ill member in the compound of the traditional healers to provide creature needs of the patient and also to participate in the healing rituals" (pp. 35–36). The treatment consists of administration of herbs (which typically include *Rauwolfia serpentina,* which has known antipsychotic properties, as an active component), performance of rituals, and recitation of incantations. Initially kept under restraints, patients are given greater freedom of movement and are involved in household chores and other village community activities as their mental state improves. Asuni notes that "even though it is not identified as such, rehabilitation is built into the system of care and treatment by traditional healers" (p. 36).

Among certain ethnic groups in the United States, indigenous healing not only provides an explanatory model for the patient and family but, according to Sandoval (1979), functionally permits mastery through manipulation of the powerful gods. Equally important are the human resources found in "cult houses" such as those of Haitian *Voodoo,* Afro-Cuban *Santería,* or Hispanic *Espiritismo.* Garrison (1978) has described an important social support system provided for schizophrenic Puerto Rican women by fellow believers in *Espiritismo* in New York. For many transplanted immigrants, the communal practice of ritual provides an extended kinship network augmenting or replacing missing family ties.

When community mental health centers started expanding in the United States in the early 1970s, there was widespread recognition of the need for culturally appropriate services. A number of centers around the country developed innovative services (Dana, 1982; Lefley, 1984; Lefley & Bestman, 1991; Ruiz & Langrod, 1976). In many of these centers there was a principled attempt to link patients with indigenous healers when necessary. Two examples from the University of Miami–Jackson Memorial (now New Horizons) Community Mental Health Center in Florida exemplify these efforts. The first demonstrates the integration of folk healing with clinical treatment, whereas the second deals with the differing conceptual models of etiology and treatment effects.

In the first case, a Haitian patient with a history of schizophrenia and previous crisis admissions was still floridly psychotic after ten days of inpatient treatment and maximum dosage antipsychotic medications. Haitian mental health professionals were not able to calm him, since according to the patient's belief system, he needed to be exorcised of the curse that prevented his recovery. Staff elicited the aid of a *houngan* (a *voodoo* priest) and curative rituals were performed. The patient immediately quieted down, was stabilized on medications, and was soon discharged (see Lefley, 1984).

In the second example, an African-American woman of Bahamian descent, Mrs. Z, was complaining of depression. She believed her lover had another girlfriend, who had placed a love curse or a hex on her. The hex was causing problems with her children and her job and cooling the interest of her lover. Mrs. Z perceived her "blues" as being caused by the curse itself rather than as a reaction to her situation. She knew that the girlfriend had gone to a Bahamian *obeah* man to provide the hex, so Mrs. Z herself went to an even more powerful Haitian spiritual healer to counteract the malevolence. The healer cleansed her with special perfumes, oils, and herbs, and he gave her special tasks to perform that would align her with the benign forces of the universe. To finalize the therapeutic intervention, the healer took Mrs. Z to a cemetery at midnight, lowered her into an unfilled grave, and sprinkled her with grave dirt. After the ritual "burial," Mrs. Z was euphoric and in a short period of time reported that she had received a raise at work and her children were acting better. She also issued an ultimatum to the boyfriend to get rid of the other woman, after which she got rid of him. Mrs. Z was then able to form a therapeutic alliance and proceed with her counseling at the community mental health center.

In commenting on the explanatory models of the two systems involved in this case, Haitian anthropologist Claude Charles (personal communication, 1991) has pointed out that the clinician would conceptualize this case in terms of *psychodynamics,* whereas the healer would view it in terms of *exchange.* In the therapist's perception, the symbolic burial enabled Mrs. Z to shed her ineffectual self, her weakness and vulnerability, and to take control of her life though symbolic rebirth. In the conceptual system of the spiritual healer, however, purification and burial are a reordering or rebalancing of universal forces. Mrs. Z is under the influence of a malevolent spirit evoked by the girlfriend's curse. All bad spirits come from the cemetery, so the healer goes directly to that forcefield and puts the person in the ground. By burying the carrier, one buries the evil spirit. When the person is taken out of the grave, the malevolent influence remains in the ground and the person is free (see Lefley, 1991).

It is important to recognize also that in the lives of many of our clients, personal effort and hard work do not always pay off, and much is attributed to one's good or bad luck. It is healers, not therapists, who are most adept at manipulating luck (Sandoval, 1979). When a client's culture offers a time-honored rationale for a lover's diminishing interest or similar misfortunes, appropriate remedies are found with spiritual healers rather than in the mental health system.

In Puerto Rico, anthropologist Koss-Chioino (1992) had a long-standing Therapist-Spiritist Training Project that brought together mental health professionals, medical doctors, and spirit mediums. In many mental health systems in the mainland United States, traditional healers have been incorporated as educators, consultants, and cotherapists (Lefley, 1984; Ruiz & Langrod, 1976).

Western therapists treating newly entrant groups such as Southeast Asians will try to use psychoeducational approaches and explanatory models that incorporate salient elements of the clients' belief systems. We have long known that in most traditional cultures Cartesian mind-body dualism is unknown, so many patients do not conceptualize mind and emotions as distinct from bodily experience. In dealing with Southeast Asian refugees who have gone through multiple traumatic transitions in their escape and subsequent entry to the United States, Kinzie and his associates (1986) have developed an extremely creative therapeutic technique. Utilizing the principle of mind-body unity, they have patients link a history of their experiences with a drawing of the human brain and body. The patients recall stressful transitional periods such as a fearful sojourn in a displaced persons camp, or a difficult boat journey. The therapists then point out visually on the drawing what was happening in the patients's brain and body as they responded to these stressors and what is happening as they relive the experience.

Other innovative approaches are used in clinics that treat immigrants from diverse cultures. The Department of Psychiatry of the University of California, San Francisco, maintains ethnic minority focus units in their teaching hospital, San Francisco General, training residents in transcultural psychiatry in an inpatient setting (Zatrick & Lu, 1991). In the same hospital, "a Cambodian woman complaining of insomnia was offered sleeping pills and also encouraged to seek a blessing from a krou khmer, a native healer. . . . Illiterate hill tribesmen from Laos are taught how to take their pills, which are taped to an index card under pictures of the sun and moon at different places in the sky" (Gross, 1992). In many clinics staff have learned the importance of humoral medicine concepts, such as taking pills with warm water rather than cold to balance yin and yang for Chinese patients, and hot-cold elements of disease in the belief systems of many Hispanic and Caribbean patients.

CULTURAL FACTORS IN PROGNOSIS AND REHABILITATION

In his chapter in this book, Juris Draguns has described the findings of the World Health Organization's International Pilot Study of Schizophrenia

(IPSS). This nine-culture study demonstrated transcultural agreement on the symptom clusters diagnosed as schizophrenia, reinforcing the growing evidence that this is a biologically based panhuman disorder. At follow-up, however, the IPSS also found better prognosis in the developing countries than in the industrialized West (Sartorius et al., 1986).

It should be noted at this point that even in the developing countries, there is a core group of individuals who do not have a good prognosis. Studies from various sources suggest that approximately one-third do not stabilize and do poorly over the long term (Lin & Kleinman, 1988; Mendis, 1990; Westermeyer, 1989). Nevertheless, the developing countries seem to provide a more favorable climate for many patients to avoid progressive social disability.

Explanations for the more benign course of illness have usually postulated lower stress and higher social support in the developing countries, together with a world view that both expects recovery and frees the patient and family of blame (Lin & Kleinman, 1988). Opportunities for productive labor, supportive families and extended kinship networks, and externalization of causality have all been considered factors in lowering stress levels and facilitating recovery (Lin & Kleinman, 1988; Lefley, 1990a). A brief summary of these views regarding the relationship of culture and prognosis follows.

Externalized Causality. In traditional cultures psychiatric symptoms are typically viewed in terms of a somatic or supernatural model of etiology. This generates less social rejection and less self-devaluation of patients and creates expectations that this is a temporary aberration. Because there are many culture-bound syndromes that are brief and self-limiting (see Chapter 14), this expectation leads to lack of stigmatization in first-episode or short-term cases of major disorders and facilitates remission of symptoms. (In cases of recurrent episodes, however, and particularly when there is a long history of bizarre antisocial behavior, the person becomes defined as chronically mentally ill and is then highly stigmatized in many traditional cultures.)

Different Concepts of Selfhood. Major psychotic disorders such as schizophrenia tend to fragment the self, but cultural concepts of personhood are a key to how self-disorganization is experienced and evaluated. In less individualistic cultures, people's concept of self is merged with that of the group. This tends to mitigate a sense of responsibility and guilt for personal deficiencies, unless they are connected with the group's common good. Fabrega (1989) has suggested that in Western culture, with its highly individualistic ethos, the loss of the sense of self in conditions such as schizophrenia involves a loss of control, autonomy, and meaning that makes it difficult for afflicted persons to distance themselves from their disorder. There is a fusion of identity with the illness. The person self-identifies as a mental patient, a "loser," which leads to alienation and despair and induces chronicity.

Estroff (1989) similarly has argued that culture affects prognosis by mediating the relationship between the self and the sickness. In Western cultures, persons are seen as unique beings with an enduring core of meaning and knowledge; thus the loss of the former personality and of positive social roles are seen as chronic conditions that fundamentally alter the person. Because self-disorganization is viewed as a temporary condition in traditional cultures (particularly those in which trance possession and other ritual dissociative states are common), self-evaluation and interpersonal relationships are not so readily affected.

Work. One of the big problems in rehabilitation in the United States is that mental patients, many with education and skills, often have to work in demeaning entry-level jobs and sometimes find even that work too demanding in terms of hours or pace of activity. In developing countries patients can work in agrarian economies in normalized roles and usually at their own pace. Thus there is no message from the culture that diminishes their value as productive human beings.

Different Concepts of Dependency and Interdependence. According to noted anthropologist Francis Hsu (1972), the overarching North American core value is fear of dependency. The emphases on self-reliance and personal autonomy that so characterize the Western value system have been generalized to the most basic treatment philosophies. Throughout the deinstitutionalization and rehabilitation literature, the phrase "return the patient to independent living" appears constantly, regardless of whether the goal is realistic or even advisable for all classes of patients. Emphasis on self-reliance carries over into psychotherapy. An African psychologist from an interdependent tribal background expressed his concern at reconciling his own cultural norms with the major psychotherapeutic goal of loosening dependency ties on significant others (Uzoka, 1979). The Japanese psychiatrist Takeo Doi (1973), describing the central Japanese concept of *amae*—a reciprocal honoring of adult dependency roles—reported his surprise at finding the concept entirely missing from the English lexicon.

In community-based treatment for persons with severe mental illnesses, aftercare planning in the United States has rarely made provisions for supportive networks. Day treatment and rehabilitation programs have had high-expectancy goals based on the implicit value of a client's attaining ultimate separation from the program. The linguistic terminology of mental health programs embodies expectations of linear progress: "transitional," "step-level," "half-way," and "three-quarter way."

Experiences with severely mentally ill people suggest that this orientation may be far too demanding and may exacerbate precisely those feelings of anxiety and apartness that are central to their illness. A "transitional" policy in mental health planning imposes a built-in impermanence in the lives of people who may need long-term stability in order to remain intact. In traditional societies, families provide this stability through a permanent caregiving role. The concept of interdependence, which characterizes most sociocentric societies, provides roles for mentally ill people. It also enables them to accept and benefit from familial caregiving without the personal and interpersonal conflicts that plague dependent adults in Western cultures.

Family Structure and Differential Family Burden. The extended family network in traditional cultures has also been postulated as a factor in prognosis (see Leff & Vaughn, 1985; Lin & Kleinman, 1988). In many cases this provides a large and benign support system for the mentally ill person. In most nuclear families there are typically only two adults and often only one person with the major responsibilities of care giving. In contrast to the charged atmosphere of most overburdened nuclear households, the extended family provides both financial and emotional buffering mechanisms to dilute the problems of living with a dysfunctional adult whose difficult behavior must be tolerated and forgiven. The network may also have a greater capacity for providing occasional work or other productive roles.

In the West, a growing literature indicates extensive family burden in caring for persons with severe and persistent mental illness (Fisher, Benson, & Tessler, 1990; Lefley, 1985). This may involve dealing with bizarre, abusive, and sometimes assaultive behavior in the household. The family's experience also includes time and energy spent in negotiating the mental health and welfare systems, stigmatization, curtailment of social activities, disruptions of household functioning, altered relations with friends, neighbors, and relatives, and the endurance of constant crises that often involve the police and psychiatric emergency rooms. Families are caught in an ongoing tension of balancing their own rights and those of other family members with those of the person with mental illness, and in balancing expectations that may be too high or too low. They also suffer empathic pain for a loved one, perhaps once bright with promise, who typically leads an impoverished life and must relinquish former aspirations.

In the United States a critical aspect of family burden, reported by many families in surveys of their experiences, has come from frustrating and often humiliating interactions with mental health service providers (see Fisher, Benson, & Tessler, 1990; Lefley & Johnson, 1990). Although family education is standard procedure when patients are hospitalized for medical conditions, for many years relatives of persons with mental disorders, seeking this type of education, experienced responses from professionals ranging from evasiveness to outright rejection. Professional-family relations are now changing in the West, but these types of interactions have been quite unknown in traditional cultures.

CULTURAL DIFFERENCES IN FAMILY-PROFESSIONAL RELATIONSHIPS

In all societies, long-term hospitalization in remote institutions has tended to isolate mentally ill persons from their families and to foster abandonment. In the West, however, for many years patients were deliberately distanced

from their relatives because of theories of family pathogenesis and requirements of psychodynamic treatment models. To avoid contamination of
transference and preservation of the therapeutic alliance, psychotherapists
rejected contact with families and excluded them from any involvement in
treatment. Under an all-inclusive definition of confidentiality, families were
often denied essential information needed for the care-giving role. Some
professionals agreed to meet and then expressed open hostility toward families because of their presumed role in causing their patients' illness (see
Lefley & Johnson, 1990).

Later, family systems models catapulted family members into family therapy on the unproven premise that psychotic symptoms would cease when
they were no longer needed to maintain homeostasis of a dysfunctional family system. With little empirical support and unsatisfactory outcomes, most
systematic family therapies moved away from the treatment of schizophrenia
toward nonpsychotic disorders. Family members who had experienced this
earlier therapeutic approach recalled bewilderment and anger that their expressed needs for information, support, and illness management techniques
were consistently ignored (Fisher, Benson, & Tessler, 1990). Subsequently
psychoeducational family interventions were developed that did meet these
needs and that were not based on any presumptions of family psychopathology. They also provided empirical research evidence of their effectiveness
(Anderson, Reiss, & Hogarty, 1986; Falloon, Boyd, & McGill, 1985).

The present era has seen some remarkable changes in the West as a result
of developments in several domains. The proliferation of biological and genetic research findings has led to widescale abandonment of theories of family causation of major disorders such as schizophrenia or major affective
illnesses. Corollary research on family burden has alerted professionals to the
devastating experience of living with mental illness in the household. The
pragmatic needs of deinstitutionalization have made it necessary for professionals to work more closely with family caregivers. Perhaps the most notable advances have come from the emergence of a powerful family
movement, the National Alliance for the Mentally Ill (NAMI), which has
over 1,000 affiliates throughout the United States. Similar family groups
have developed in Canada and the Caribbean and are developing in Europe
and Asia.

Focusing on advocacy for basic research, public education, destigmatization of mental illness, and improved funding for mental health services,
NAMI has become a powerful political force in little over a decade since its
inception. State and government funding sources have mandated family and
consumer participation on mental health planning and governance bodies,
and professionals have found it beneficial to ally with the large constituencies
of AMI groups for legislative advocacy. When they meet the families of their
patients in different roles, moreover, professionals have reported that their

former prejudices have changed to admiration for families' coping strengths under conditions of extreme stress (see Lefley & Johnson, 1990).

Relations in Traditional Cultures

In non-Western cultures relationships between families and practitioners have been quite different. In both traditional healing and psychiatric practice, family members have been welcomed as partners in the therapeutic process (see Asuni, 1990; Lefley, 1985, 1990a; World Health Organization, 1990). Family members typically accompany their ill relative to the hospital and often live in nearby compounds provided by the hospital, fulfilling an auxiliary nursing and feeding role until the patient is discharged (Bell, 1982). In traditional cultures, it would be inappropriate for a healer to withhold information from a patient's relatives, so the family is almost always informed of diagnosis, indicated therapeutic modalities, and prognosis. Above all, in cultures that have different explanatory models of mental illness, theories of family pathogenesis present cognitive dissonance and family blaming is largely unknown. Two prominent Indian psychiatrists describe relationships of families and professionals in India:

The family has always been regarded by professionals as a working partner. . . . [There is] an absence of conceptual dogma dictating professional-family interaction. In contrast to those in the West, mental health professionals in India generally have not dealt with families on the basis of any etiological presupposition regarding their role in the causation of illness. Because of this, professional-family interactions have been on a relatively even keel and the ideological see-saw from viewing families as schizophrenogenic in the 1950's to viewing families as equal treatment partners in the 1980's has not taken place. (Shankar & Menon, 1991, p. 86)

Culture and Expressed Emotion Research

Some important clues to both treatment and etiology have come from the international research on expressed emotion (EE). Early work of Brown, Birley, and Wing (1972) in Great Britain suggested that family members' responses to the Camberwell Family Interview (CFI) were associated with certain types of patient outcome in schizophrenia. Remarks indicating criticism, hostility, or emotional overinvolvement above a certain cutoff point on the CFI were scored as high EE, whereas those below the cutoff were scored as low EE. A consistent association was found between high EE of at least one family member and relapse in patients, a finding since replicated in numerous studies throughout the world.

A very large literature has emerged regarding EE as a construct, its validity and stability over time, and the direction of the relationship between patients' symptoms and behavior and their relatives' level of EE. Despite attempts to control for patients' level of psychopathology, researchers are still conflicted about whether familial EE levels actually predict relapse, or whether patients' characteristics mediate both familial EE and their potential for relapse. Moreover, although the correlation between high EE and relapse remains constant in the short term (typically one-year follow-up), a large number of recent studies indicate that the association seems to disappear or diminish over time (Lefley, 1992).

All EE researchers have explicitly denied any implication of family pathogenesis; rather, they have ascribed relapse to "ordinary family interactions" that may be too stressful for persons with the core deficits of schizophrenia. Some major investigators have described high-EE families as intrusive, excitable, critical, and overprotective, and low-EE families as empathic, calm, patient, and respectful (Leff & Vaughn, 1985), whereas others dispute any type of trait definitions. Clinicians and researchers have suggested that high EE is not specific to families, and that EE analogues should be sought in clinical and rehabilitative environments (see Lefley, 1992).

Despite the misconceptions of many clinicians, studies from Scotland, India, England, and Denmark, and from Mexican-descent families in the United States have demonstrated that the majority of persons with schizophrenia live in low-EE families (Jenkins & Karno, 1992; Lefley, 1992). It was primarily among urban Anglo-Americans and urban Australians that the number of high-EE relatives exceeded those of low-EE relatives. In terms of the trait definitions previously cited, the majority of families of persons with schizophrenia are empathic, calm, patient, and respectful, disputing a vast clinical literature on family characteristics.

Leff has linked the better prognosis in developing countries to lower EE in families (Leff & Vaughn, 1985). He suggests that criticism, hostile remarks, or emotional overinvolvement are more likely to be found in the overwhelmed nuclear family, whereas the extended families are better able to diffuse burden. This may be one piece in the tapestry of variables that affect the course of serious mental illness. It is important to note, however, that family structure is embedded within cultural systems that determine how people view illness roles and the obligations of human beings to each other.

INDIVIDUALISTIC AND SOCIOCENTRIC CULTURES

The concepts of selfhood, views of dependency and disability, and attitudes toward patients' families are closely interrelated with the degree of importance assigned to the individual versus the group, and the responsibility of the group towards its members. These types of cultural norms are very much related to how a society conceptualizes and cares for its disabled, dysfunctional, and dependent citizens—in that case, persons with long-term mental illnesses. They determine the rights and prerogatives of these individuals, society's obligations to care for them, and the type of mental health system developed to serve them.

In traditional cultures, adults typically live in the parental home until they marry, and there is no specific age ceiling for leaving. Disabled adults continue living with their families of origin, and families are expected to care for them. The question of individual autonomy is unrelated to these living arrangements. The notion that it is pathological for adult children to remain under parental supervision, a basic premise of some family therapies (Haley, 1980), is culturally dystonic in many traditional societies. Paternalistic concern with the affairs of an adult child would be considered appropriate behavior, rather than emotional overinvolvement. In such cultures there is little evidence of the independence-dependency conflicts that are so characteristic of family-patient relationships in Western society and that frequently consume the therapeutic hours of Western practitioners.

In certain political systems, however, individualist philosophy has been suppressed as a matter of course. A visiting Russian psychiatrist captured the perils of a sociocentric model that minimizes the rights of individuals in his comparison of psychiatric treatment in the United States and the former Soviet Union (Yegorov, 1992). He marveled that "contrary to Soviet practice, it would never occur to anyone in a U.S. psychiatric hospital to monitor patients' outgoing mail or to impede its delivery, no matter how deranged its content may be" (p. 8). But he also noted that Russian psychiatrists feel that "the strict guarantee of the rights of the mentally ill that is required by U.S. laws may result in certain negative medical and social consequences to some patients" (p. 12), particularly with respect to constraints on involuntary hospitalization and preventive detention of persons who may be dangerous to society. Yet because of these differences in world view, Yegerov (1992) admits, service models of the former Soviet Union may have been to the disadvantage of many patients. "In our country we have not particularly bothered with such issues as the rights of the mentally ill to express their wishes. Rather, we have committed them either to psychiatric nursing homes of the welfare system for the rest of their lives or to rural psychiatric hospitals for many years" (p. 12).

CONSUMERISM AND THE CONCEPT OF PATIENTS' RIGHTS

Societies that are sociocentric by tradition, religion, or political ideology expect the subordination of individual rights to those of the group or the body politic. Thus, there may be a commonality of views among the traditional cultures of developing countries and those of industrial countries such as the former Soviet Union and Japan. These tend to be sociocentric vis-à-vis the more individualistic views of Western Europe, the United States and Canada. Sociocentric cultures are far less likely to be concerned with the balance between rights and needs of mentally ill persons, a problem of increasing concern in Western culture.

The rights of mental patients has been a prominent issue in the United States and various Western European countries since deinstitutionalization began. Western culture has seen an increasingly vigorous advocacy for the civil liberties of persons with mental illnesses. This advocacy was long overdue. In the United States for example, for many years citizens had been automatically stripped of their civil rights when they entered a mental institution. Regardless of their willingness to seek treatment voluntarily, patients were deprived of their rights to vote, marry or divorce, keep bank accounts, sign contracts, and the like. Persons who had committed no crime were treated like felons and were forced to go to court and demonstrate their symptoms were in remission in order to reinstate their civil liberties. In institutional settings, they often had no redress against abuse.

With the forward surge of deinstitutionalization, our cultural emphasis on the rights of individuals spurred a large number of lawsuits and generated new legislation in many states. These have resulted in rigorous limitations on involuntary commitment and treatment. In 1986 federal protection and advocacy legislation was passed that set up programs in each state to ensure that patients were not being mistreated and were receiving appropriate services in public institutions.

The issue of civil liberties of patients is intertwined with the antipsychiatry movement that developed during the 1960s. Exemplified in the writings of "antiestablishment" psychiatrists, mental illness was viewed as a purely social construct without biological or psychological validity (Szasz, 1961) or as an alternative path to superior enlightenment. In this school of thought, the practice of psychiatry itself continues to be viewed as abusive and as an intrument of social coercion and control. Psychiatrists with this mode of thinking have increasingly been allied with the mental patients' liberation movement.

In the United States protest organizations with such names as the Insane Liberation Front (Portland, Oregon) or the Mental Patients Liberation Project (New York City) were formed in the early 1970s by former psychiatric patients. Later, two national organizations emerged. The National Association of Mental Patients, now renamed the National Association of Psychiatric Survivors, remains essentially a protest movement that adamantly opposes any form of involuntary treatment, promotes initiatives to make electroshock therapy illegal, and views both psychotropic medications and hospitalization as largely harmful. The National Mental Health Consumers' Association, which was organized primarily to improve rather than reject the mental health system, is generally opposed to involuntary treatment but acknowledges the validity of mental illness and the need for treatment. In open societies that tend to indulge and often applaud antiestablishment views, the movement of former mental patients, called the consumer movement, continues to grow and thrive.

The development of the consumer movement, however, has also provided a forum for destigmatization and growth of people who would have formerly languished in institutions or been isolated in homes. The consumer movement in the United States now boasts articulate speakers, researchers, and service providers. With great encouragement and funded support from the Community Support Program of the National Institute of Mental Health, formerly hospitalized mental patients are now functioning as paid research assistants, knowledge disseminators, case managers, operators of residences and drop-in centers for persons with mental illnesses, and support persons in crisis management teams. The current era has seen a remarkable social change in the way mentally ill persons are portrayed in the media, and research suggests that prognosis is far better than was once anticipated (Harding, Brooks, Ashikaga, Strauss, & Breier, 1987). By validating their potential for recovery, Western cultures may begin to provide a fertile basis for self-fulfilling prophecy.

FUTURE DIRECTIONS

Cross-cultural comparisons typically focus on differences among human groups. Often, however, it is commonalities that tell us even more about etiologies and treatments of disorders that increasingly are found to be pan-human. Most of our findings on genetic influences have come from the Scandinavian countries. Epidemiologic profiles, formerly based on scattered studies of uneven scientific rigor, are becoming more uniform and more sophisticated. Incidence and prevalence may be related to growing research evidence of possible ecological, dietary, and viral influences on intrauterine development of the fetus who later will develop a serious mental disorder, as well as to cultural influences on the course of illness (see Lefley, 1990a). There is cross-fertilization among nations such as Japan and the United States that ranges from Morita therapy to parallel biological research on cerebral functioning in schizophrenia (Utena & Niwa, 1992).

In terms of cultural influence on mental health systems, the philosophic and political distinctions between sociocentric and individualistic cultures may be the most important factors in predicting the form of service delivery in the future. In the United States the advent of the Reagan-Bush era with its antifederalist philosophy and block grants to the states saw the decentralization of community mental health services and the end of federal oversight. The old concept of catchment area–wide services largely disappeared. Today many community mental health centers are reducing their service delivery to persons with chronic mental illnesses while soliciting fee-paying patients with private insurance and less serious problems in living (see Lefley & Bestman, 1991).

The states are rapidly eroding their commitment to institutional care for even the most seriously disturbed patients. There is an increasing emphasis on "independent living" and assumption of personal autonomy for mentally ill individuals who continue to be severely disabled. During this decade Americans have begun to see numerous displaced homeless people, one-third of whom are untreated and severely disabled mentally ill. Many social commentators have claimed that homelessness of mentally ill people is directly due to a zealous civil libertarian philosophy that made individual rights to refuse treatment, regardless of cognitive capacity, more important than social need or even the individual's potential for survival.

The current era is seeing a rise of "communitarianism," a movement first espoused by sociologist Amitai Etzioni of George Washington University and exemplified in a new journal, *The Responsive Community*. Based on the notion that social responsibility is as important as individual rights, the centrist and bipartisan communitarian philosophy is now spreading among many academicians and prominent public figures. Communitarians suggest that an excessive zeal for protecting the prerogatives of individuals has ignored the pressing needs of society, making it difficult to hospitalize mentally ill people, imprison criminals, and otherwise protect the common good. The new movement favors gun control and mandatory drug and alcohol testing of persons who hold others' lives in their hands, such as airline pilots and railway engineers. If this philosophy takes hold, it may be predicted that a growing sociocentric emphasis may revitalize society's commitment to caring for the mentally ill but also make it easier to defend involuntary treatment and the subjugation of individual rights to the common good.

The move toward consumerism in the United States is finding some parallels in other countries. Many European countries now have active consumer groups, and family movements such as NAMI in the United States are spreading in Europe, Australia, and Asia. A WHO meeting on consumer involvement in mental health services was held in Mannheim, Federal Republic of Germany, in November 1988 (see World Health Organization, 1990).

It is of interest that in the United States the patient consumer groups generally focus on greater autonomy and patients' rights, whereas the family movement, NAMI, focuses on sponsoring basic research and improving services. The WHO meeting supported patients' empowerment, rights to representation in psychiatric facilities, and access to medical records; it also vigorously affirmed the rights of consumers to participate actively in the planning and implementation of mental health care. However, the WHO report specifically took note of cultural differences and warned against developing patient advocacy groups that might pit their agendas against those of their families.

In many developing countries the family is the most important unit for survival . . . [and] patients are completely dependent on the family for basic needs as well as for social and emotional support. Under these circumstances, it can be seen that family involvement in decisions which affect individuals with serious psychiatric disorders can be crucial. Furthermore, development of individual consumer advocacy groups comprised of patients would not only meet with disapproval and lack of success but would also leave patients without access to housing, food and shelter, and basic social contact and support, i.e., encouraging independence may be culturally and socially unacceptable. (World Health Organization, 1990, p. 16)

In the United States, approximately 65 percent of patients are discharged to their families, and at least 40 percent live with their families on an on-going basis (Lefley, 1985). Along with a reduction of housing initiatives connected with the official mental health system, there is now a growing movement toward independent residential arrangements for people who are sometimes too dysfunctional to survive on their own. Many families have to become reinvolved in care giving, and this is an increasing burden for aging parents who have difficulty living with disturbed adult children and worry about what will happen when the parents are gone (Lefley, 1985).

As indicated previously, the cross-cultural research suggests that living with mentally ill persons is particularly difficult in small nuclear family settings. However, the developing nations also are seeing attrition of joint and extended family structure. Internal and external migration patterns, including movements toward urban centers in search of economic opportunities, are rapidly eroding the extended family systems. We increasingly see nuclear families and single-parent households in the developing countries. In cultures where traditionally families have maintained physically and mentally disabled members at home, these developments bode ill for a continued care-giving capability. The fragmentation of families and their movement to urban centers may also mean fewer opportunities for any productive roles for a psychiatrically disabled person.

If this is the case, then prognoses for major mental illnesses in developing countries may no longer be as benign unless compensatory mechanisms are developed. It can only be hoped that any erosion of cultural supports is counterbalanced by greater sophistication and distribution of psychotropic medications and by more effective rehabilitative technologies. The Schizophrenia Research Foundation (SCARF) in Madras, India, is an example of a comprehensive rehabilitative and social support system developed by professionals to serve patients in a traditional culture (Nagaswami, 1990). Meanwhile, Western nations are beginning to understand the benefits of extended support systems and normalizing productive roles for persons with major mental illnesses. Data from multiple sources—from longitudinal studies in rural North America (Harding et al., 1987) to the multicultural World Health Organization Collaborative Study on Determinants of Outcome of Severe Mental Disorders (Sartorius et al., 1986) to the successful cooperative ventures of northern Italy—tell us much about what mentally ill persons are able to accomplish given the right cultural context. With decreased stigmatization, adequate support systems, and appropriate expectations—all culturally determined—together with increasingly perfected psychopharmacy and rehabilitative technologies, the future for mentally ill persons may be brighter in the years ahead.

Epilogue

Florence L. Denmark

Within the last three decades the need for awareness of cross-cultural comparisons has increased dramatically, as has the impact of current comparisons. Countless areas of human endeavor have been affected, among them business and industry, government, applied research, education, and especially the helping professions, where sensitivity to cross-cultural concerns is crucial if not essential. Yet all too often psychologists and other behavioral scientists are immersed in their own culture and are unaware of the perspectives of those whose customs and lifestyles may differ appreciably from their own. In response to this need for training and sensitivity, cross-cultural psychology has evolved and has become a rapidly growing enterprise involving interdisciplinary effort in which human behavior can best be understood from a global perspective (Segall in Adler, 1989).

Rapid technological advances have had a far-reaching impact globally as advanced methods of communication and the internationalization of trade continue to increase and develop. While expanding technologically, our world is in effect shrinking into what has been called a "global village" (Moghaddam, Taylor, & Wright, 1993). Despite our coming closer together in one's community, there remains a pride and commitment to maintaining one's own ethnic and cultural customs, which may serve to provide a sense of stability in what appears to be an almost explosively expanding worldwide community. However, without ignoring one's own culture and experience, one's monocultural perspectives must now give way to the multiculturalism of the present day, which is the way of the future. Thus a wider view of social science is evolving in which it is becoming increasingly imperative to achieve a greater breadth of human understanding when the individual steps outside of his or her own values, norms, and traditions. It is no longer sufficient simply to report on studies from other countries; rather, one must take these investigations a step farther by comparing and contrasting what is known about one culture with that of another in order to arrive at a greater appreciation of differences as well as similarities within, among, and between groups. Although some countries, more scientifically advanced than others, can provide excellent techniques, methodologies, and devices to study human behavior, they should not rush in to impose their own ethnocentric views on other cultures, regardless of whether the research conducted is in social science or business. A willingness to appreciate diverse cultural values and behaviors is needed by the professional who engages in multicultural work, particularly in light of the concept of global community and its direct relationship to greater multicultural exposure.

This book, edited by Leonore Loeb Adler and Uwe P. Gielen, both experts in cross-cultural psychology, represents a great step forward in psychology. Whereas other books have been written about doing psychotherapy with different cultures or counseling specific client groups based on ethnicity, the book is unique in its encompassing of many areas of psychology. It not only looks at service delivery but relates the importance of cultural sensitivity and competency as it affects research methodology, psychological testing, and multinational trade. It also presents developmental issues, and several authors address the impact of cross-cultural themes as they relate to childhood and old age. Personality formation, specific cultural gender issues, language and communication, beliefs about psychopathology, and provision of mental health service delivery are among the topics addressed by the contributors to this volume, all scholars from various ethnic backgrounds. In sum, this volume addresses many fields within psychology, providing a needed cross-cultural focus.

The general theme unifying this collection of papers is the recognition and emphasis of culture and how it influences all aspects of interpersonal relations and human behavior. This book is useful not only to prepare undergraduate and graduate students in psychology (and more specifically for its relevance to the major targeted in cross-cultural psychology) but in its capacity to be a very valuable adjunct to other courses. The recognition and need for well-trained and knowledgeable cross-cultural professionals in other fields such as teaching, consulting, and communications is becoming clearly more vital.

Although such a volume cannot in and of itself furnish the reader with cross-cultural competency, it can serve as a catalyst by heightening the reader's awareness and enhancing his or her motivation to learn more about human diversity. Thus this compilation of timely chapters can provide the impetus for cross-cultural research, particularly in its promotion of pioneering investigations. As such, this book illustrates where psychology, and perhaps the world, *should* be headed.

References

Adler, L. L. (Ed.). (1977). *Issues in cross-cultural research. Annals of the New York Academy of Sciences, 285.* New York: New York Academy of Sciences.

Adler, L. L. (Ed.). (1982). *Cross-cultural research at issue.* New York: Academic Press.

Adler, L. L. (1989, April). *A personal appreciation of Wilhelm Maximilian Wundt.* Paper presented at the Annual Meeting of the New York State Psychological Association, New York, NY.

Adler, L. L. (Ed.). (1989). *Cross-cultural research in human development: Life-span perspectives.* New York: Praeger.

Adler L. L. (1990–1991). *Androgynous self-perception by college students.* Unpublished study conducted at Molloy College.

Adler, L. L. (1991). In appreciation of Wilhelm Maximilian Wundt. *The New York State Psychologist, 42*(1), 18–19.

Adler, L. L. (Ed.). (1991). *Women in cross-cultural perspective.* New York: Praeger.

Adler, L. L. (1993, February 19–21). *Gender roles of the elderly in cross-cultural perspective.* Paper presented at the Annual Convention of the Society for Cross-Cultural Research, Washington, DC.

Adler, L. L., Denmark, F. L., & Ahmed, R. A. (1991). A critical evaluation of attitudes toward mother-in-law and stepmother: A cross-cultural study. In W. Oxman-Michelli & M. Weinstein (Eds.), *Proceedings of the 1989 Conference: Critical thinking: Focus on social and cultural inquiry.* Upper Montclair, NJ: Montclair State College.

Adler, L. L., & Graubert J. G. (1975). Projected social distances from mental patient-related items by male and female volunteers and nonvolunteers. *Psychological Reports, 37,* 515–521.

Adler, L. L. & Graubert, J. G. (1976). Projected social distances from mental patient-related stimuli in cross-national perspective: Four English speaking countries. *International Journal of Group Tensions, 6,* (3,4), 15–25.

Adler, L. L., & Iverson, M. A. (1975). Projected social distance as a function of praise conditions and status orientation: A comparison with physical interpersonal spacing in the laboratory. *Perceptual and Motor Skills, 41,* 659–664.

Adler, Leonore Loeb, Denmark, F. L., Miao, S.-C. Y., Ahmed, R. A., Takooshian, H., Adler, H. E., & Wesner, R. W. (1992). Cross-cultural comparisons of projected social distances toward family members: A programatic study. In U. P. Gielen, L. L. Adler, & N. A. Milgram (Eds.), *Psychology in international perspective*. Lisse, the Netherlands: Swets and Zeitlinger, 260–270.

Adorno, T. W., Frenkel-Brunswik, E., Levinson, D. J., & Sanford, R. N. (1950). *The authoritarian personality*. New York: Harper & Row. (Reprinted: W. W. Norton, 1969.)

Ahmed, R. A. (1984). *Sudanese University men's preferred educational level of future brides*. Unpublished study conducted at Cairo University, Khartoum Branch.

Ahmed, R. A. (1989). The development of number, space, quantity, and reasoning concepts in Sudanese schoolchildren. In L. L. Adler (Ed.), *Cross-cultural research in human development: Life-span perspectives*. New York: Praeger.

Ahmed, R. A. (1991). Women in Egypt and the Sudan. In L. L. Adler (Ed.), *Women in cross-cultural perspective* (pp. 107–133). New York: Praeger.

Ahmed, R. A., Gielen, U. P., & Avellani, J. (1987). Perceptions of parental behavior and the development of moral reasoning in Sudanese students. In C. Kağitçibaşi (Ed.), *Growth and progress in cross-cultural psychology* (pp. 196–206). Lisse, Netherlands: Swets & Zeitlinger.

Ainsworth, M. (1967). *Infancy in Uganda*. Baltimore, MD: Johns Hopkins University Press.

Akimoto, H., Sunazaki, T., Okada, K., & Hanashiro, S. (1942). Demographische und psychiatrische Untersuchung über abgegrenzte Kleinstadtbevölkerung. *Psychiatria et Neurologia Japonica, 47,* 351–374.

Alcock, James. (1981). Parapsychology: Science or Magic? Oxford: Pergamon Press.

Allen, L., & Santrock, J. W. (1993). *Psychology: The contexts of behavior*. Dubuque, IA: Brown & Benchmark.

Allport, G. W., & Odbert, H. S. (1936). Trait names: A psycho-lexical study. *Psychological Monographs, 47,*(1, Whole No. 211), 1–171.

Allport, G. W. (1937). *Personality: A psychological interpretation*. New York: Holt.

American Psychiatric Association. (1987). *Diagnostic and statistical manual of mental disorders* (3rd rev. ed.). Washington, DC: Author.

Amir, Y., & Sharon, I. (1987). Are social psychological laws cross-culturally valid? *Journal of Cross-Cultural Psychology, 18,* 383–470.

Amoss, P., & Harrell, S. (1981). *Other ways of growing old*. Stanford, CA: Stanford University Press.

Anastasi, A. (1988). *Psychological testing* (6th ed.). New York: Macmillan.

Anderson, C. M., Reiss, D. J., & Hogarty, G. E. (1986). *Schizophrenia and the family: A practitioner's guide to psychoeducation and assessment*. New York: Guilford.

Antonucci, T., Fuhrer, R., & Jackson, J. (1990). Social support and reciprocity: A cross-ethnic and cross-national perspective. *Journal of Social and Personal Relationships, 7,* 519–530.

Ardila, R. (1991). Women in Latin America. In L. L. Adler (Ed.), *Women in cross-cultural perspective* (pp. 27–37). New York: Praeger.

Argyle, M. (1986). Rules for social relationship in four cultures. *Australian Journal of Psychology, 38,* 309–318.

Aronson, E., Ellsworth, P. C., Carlsmith, J. M., & Gonzales, M. H. (1990). *Methods of research in social psychology*. (2nd ed.). New York: McGraw-Hill.

Aronson, L., Tobach, E., Rosenblatt, J. S., & Lehrman, D. S. (1972). *Selected writings of T. C. Schneirla* San Francisco: W. H. Freeman and Company.

Asuni, T. (1990). Nigeria: Report on the care, treatment, and rehabilitation of people with mental illness. *Psychosocial Rehabilitation Journal, 14,* 35–44.

Australian. (1986, April 8). Science index sparked off in laboratory flash. *Computers*.

Axtell, Roger E. (Ed.). (1990). *Do's and taboos around the world* (2nd ed.). New York: Wiley.

Bacon, W., & Ichikawa, V. (1988). Maternal expectations, classroom experiences, and achievement among kindergartners in the United States and Japan. *Human Development, 31,* 378–383.

Bagby, J. W. (1957). A cross-cultural study of perceptual predominance in binocular rivalry. *Journal of Abnormal and Social Psychology, 54,* 331–334.

Baldauf, R. B., Jr. (1977). Acculturation and educational achievement in American Samoan adolescents. *Journal of Cross-Cultural Psychology, 8,* 241–255.

Baldauf, R. B., Jr. (1986). Linguistic constraints on participation in psychology. *American Psychologist, 41,* 220–224. (Comment)

Baldauf, R. B., Jr., (1988). Developing alternatives to standardized achievement tests: Examples from American Samoa and Micronesia. In G. Davidson (Ed.), *Ethnicity and cognitive assessment: Australian perspectives* (pp. 44–53). Darwin: DIT Press.

Baldauf, R. B., Jr., & Jernudd, B. H. (1983). Language of publication as a variable in scientific communication. *Australian Review of Applied Linguistics, 6,* 97–108.

Baldauf, R. B., Jr., & Jernudd, B. H. (1986). Aspects of language use in cross-cultural psychology. *Australian Journal of Psychology, 38,* 381–392.

Baldauf, R. B., Jr., & Jernudd, B. H. (1987). Academic communication in a foreign language: The example of Scandinavian psychology. *Australian Review of Applied Linguistics, 10*(1), 98–117.

Barker, R. G. (1963). *The stream of behavior: Explorations of its structure and content*. New York: Meredith.

Barker, R. G. (1968). *Ecological psychology: Concept and methods for studying the environment of human behavior*. Stanford, CA: Stanford University Press.

Barker, R. G., & Gump, P. (1964). *Big school, small school*. Stanford, CA: Stanford University Press.

Barker, R. G., & Wright, H. F. (1951). *One boy's day*. New York: Harper.

Barker, R. G., & Wright, H. (1955). *Midwest and its children*. New York: Harper & Row.

Barnouw, V. (1985). *Culture and personality*. Chicago: Dorsey Press.

Barringer, F. (1993, April 7). Disability rates of elderly drop, study finds, challenging theory. *New York Times*.

Bart, P. (1969). Why women's status changes in middle age: The times of the social ferris wheel. *Sociological Symposium, 3,* 1–18.

Beatty, J. (1980). An analysis of some verbs of motion in English. *Studia Anglica Posnaniensia,* Vol. 11, Poznan.

Beatty, J., & Takahashi, J. (1994). *Bunka to Komyunikeeshon*. Tokyo: Tamagawa Daigaku Press.

Becker, J. H. (1984). German-language psychological journals: An overview. *German Journal of Psychology, 8,* 323–344.

Beddoe, I. B. (1980). *Assessing principled moral thinking among student teachers in Trinidad and Tobago.* Unpublished manuscript, University of the West Indies, St. Augustine, Trinidad.

Bell, J. (1982). The family in the hospital: Experiences in other countries. In H. Harbin (Ed.), *The psychiatric hospital and the family* (pp. 255–276). New York: Spectrum.

Bem, S. L. (1974). The measures of psychological androgyny. *Journal of Consulting and Clinical Psychology, 42,* 155–162.

Bendix, E. H. (1979). Linguistic models as political symbols: Gender and the generic "he" in English. In J. Orasanu, M. K. Slater, & L. L. Adler (Eds.), *Language, sex and gender: Does "la différence" make a difference?* Annals of the New York Academy of Science, Vol. 327.

Benedict, R. F. (1934). *Patterns of culture.* Boston: Houghton Mifflin.

Benedict, R. F. (1946). *The chrysanthemum and the sword.* Boston: Houghton Mifflin.

Berlin, B., & Kay, P. (1969). *Basic color terms: Their universality and evolution.* Berkeley: University of California Press.

Berry, J. W. (1969). On cross-cultural comparability. *International Journal of Psychology, 4,* 119–128.

Berry, J. W. (1980). Introduction to methodology. In H. C. Triandis & J. W. Berry (Eds.), *Handbook of cross-cultural psychology: Vol. 2. Methodology* (pp. 1–28). Boston: Allyn & Bacon.

Berry, J. W. (1983). The sociogenesis of social sciences: An analysis of the cultural relativity of social psychology. In B. Bain (Ed.), *The Sociogenesis of language and human conduct.* New York: Plenum Press.

Berry, J. W., & Annis, R. C. (1974). Ecology, culture, and psychological adaptation. *International Journey of Psychology, 9,* 173–193.

Bertenthal, B. I. (1987). Emerging discontinuities in the Piagetian legacy. *Contemporary Psychology, 32,* 9–11.

Bhagat, Ravi S., & Triandis, Harry C. (1984). *Management across cultures.* Glenview, IL: Scott Foresman.

Bickman, L., & Henchy, T. (1973). *Beyond the laboratory: Field research in social psychology.* New York: McGraw-Hill.

Bilmes, J., & Boggs, S. T. (1979). Language and communication: The foundations of culture. In A. J. Marsella, R. G. Tharp, & T. J. Ciborowski (Eds.), *Perspectives in cross-cultural psychology* (pp. 47–76). New York: Academic Press.

Binitie, E. (1975). A factor analytic study of depression across cultures. *British Journal of Psychiatry, 127,* 559–563.

Bird, L. (1993). Life in the South Pacific: New Zealand/Aotearoa. In L. L. Adler (Ed.), *International handbook of gender roles.* Westport, CT: Greenwood Press.

Birdwhistell, R. L. (1970). *Kinesics and context.* Philadelphia: University of Pennsylvania Press.

Birns, B., & Hay, D. F. (Eds.). (1988). *The different faces of motherhood.* New York: Plenum Press.

Blount, B. G. (1981). The development of language in children. In R. H. Monroe,

R. L. Monroe, & B. B. Whiting (Eds.), *Handbook of cross-cultural human development*. New York: Garland STPM.

Blumberg, S. H., Solomon, G. E., & Perloe, S. I. (1981). *Display rules and the facial communication of emotion*. Unpublished manuscript, Haverford College.

Bochner, S. (1980). Unobtrusive methods in cross-cultural experimentation. In H. C. Triandis & J. W. Berry (Eds.), *Handbook of cross-cultural psychology: Vol. 2. Methodology* (pp. 319–387). Boston: Allyn & Bacon.

Bock, P. K. (1980). *Continuities in psychological anthropology*. San Francisco: W. H. Freeman.

Bogardus, E. S. (1925). Measuring social distances. *Journal of Applied Sociology, 9,* 299–308.

Bond, M. (1989). (Ed.). *The cross-cultural challenge to social psychology*. Newbury Park, CA: Sage.

Bond, M. H., Nakasato, H., & Shiraishi, D. (1975). Universality and distinctiveness in dimensions of Japanese person perception. *Journal of Cross-Cultural Psychology, 6*(3), 346–357.

Bond, M. H., & Yang, K-S. (1982). Ethnic affirmation versus cross-cultural accommodation: The variable impact of questionnaire language on Chinese bilinguals from Hong Kong. *Journal of Cross-Cultural Psychology, 13,* 169–185.

Bornstein, M. H., Azuma, H., Tamis-LeMonda, C., & Ogino, M. (1990). Mother and infant activity and interaction in Japan and in the United States: I. A comparative microanalysis of naturalistic exchanges. *International Journal of Behavioral Development, 13,* 267–287.

Botwin, & Buss, D. M. (1989). Structure of act-report data: Is the five-factor model of personality recaptured? *Journal of Personality and Social Psychology, 56*(6), 988–1001.

Bowerman, M. (1981). Language development. In H. C. Triandis & A. Heron (Eds.), *Handbook of cross-cultural psychology: Vol. 4. Developmental psychology*. Boston: Allyn & Bacon.

Boyd, B. (1988, December 17). Women in the board room. *Detroit News*, p. C1.

Boyes, M. C., & Walker, L. J. (1988). Implications of cultural diversity for the universality claims of Kohlberg's theory of moral reasoning. *Human Development, 31,* 44–59.

Brandt, M. E., & Boucher, J. D. (1986). Concepts of depression in emotion lexicons of eight language communities. *International Journal of Intercultural Relations, 10,* 321–346.

Brewer, M. B., & Kramer, R. M. (1985). The psychology of intergroup attitudes and behavior. *Annual Review of Psychology, 36,* 219–243.

Brill, A. (1913). Pibloktoq or hysteria among Perry's Eskimos. *Journal of Nervous and Mental Diseases, 40,* 514–520.

Brislin, R. W. (1970). Back-translation for cross-cultural research. *Journal of Cross-Cultural Psychology, 1,* 185–216.

Brislin, R. W. (Ed.). (1976). *Translation: Applications and research*. New York: Wiley/Halsted.

Brislin, R. W. (1980). Translation and content analysis of oral and written materials. In H. C. Triandis & J. W. Berry (Eds.), *Handbook of cross-cultural psychology: Vol. 2. Methodology* (pp. 389–444). Boston: Allyn & Bacon.

Brislin, R. W. (1983). *Handbook of intercultural training.* New York: Pergamon Press.

Brislin, R. W. (1986). The wording and translation of research instruments. In W. J. Lonner & J. W. Berry (Eds.), *Field methods in cross-cultural research.* Beverly Hills, CA: Sage.

Brislin, R. W., & Keating, C. F. (1976). Cultural differences in perception of the three-dimensional Ponzo illusion. *Journal of Cross-Cultural Psychology, 7,* 397–411.

Brislin, R. W., Lonner, W. J., & Thorndike, R. M. (1973). *Cross-cultural research methods.* New York: Wiley.

Bronfenbrenner, U. (1970). *Two worlds of childhood.* New York: Russell Sage Foundation.

Brown, G. W., Birley, J. L. T., & Wing, J. K. (1972). Influence of family life on the course of schizophrenic disorder: A replication. *British Journal of Psychiatry, 121,* 241–258.

Brown, J. (1982). Cross-cultural perspectives on middle-aged women. *Current Anthropology, 23,* 143–156.

Brown, R. (1965). *Social psychology.* New York: Free Press.

Brugger, C. (1931). Versuch einer Geisteskrankenzählung in Thüringen. *Zeitschrift für die Gesamte Neurologie Psychiatrie, 133,* 352–390.

Bullinger, A. (1985). The sensorimotor nature of the infant visual system: Cognitive problems. In V. L. Shulman, L. C. R. Restaino-Bauman, & L. Butler (Eds.), *The future of Piagetian theory: The neo-Piagetians.* New York: Plenum Press.

Burling, R. (1964). Componential analysis: God's truth or Hocus pocus? *American Anthropologist, 66,* 20–28.

Butler, R. (1982). Toward a psychiatry of the late life cycle. In S. Zarith (Ed.), *Readings in aging and death.* New York: Harper & Row.

Butzin, C. A., & Anderson, N. H. (1973). Functional measurement of children's judgments. *Child Development, 44,* 529–537.

Candell, G. L., & Hulin, C. L. (1986). Cross-language and cross-cultural comparisons in scale translations: Independent sources of information about item nonequivalence. *Journal of Cross-Cultural Psychology, 17,* 417–440.

Campbell, D. T. (1964). Distinguishing differences in perception from failures of communication in cross-cultural studies. In F. Northop & H. Livingston (Eds.), *Cross-cultural understanding: Epistemology in anthropology.* New York: Harper & Row.

Campbell, D. T. (1975). On the conflicts between biological and social evolution and between psychology and moral tradition. *American Psychologist, 30,* 1103–1126.

Carothers, J. (1948). A study of mental derangement in Africans and an attempt to explain its peculiarities more especially in relation to the African attitude to life. *Psychiatry, 11,* 47–86.

Carroll, J. B. (1956). *Language, thought and reality: selected writings of Benjamin Lee Whorf.* Cambridge: MIT Press.

Carson, R. C. (1989). Personality. In M. R. Rosenzweig & L. W. Porter (Eds.), *Annual Review of Psychology, 40,* (227–248). Palo Alto, CA: Annual Reviews.

Casati, I., & Lezine, I. (1968). *Les étapes de l'intelligence sensorimotrice* (Manual). Paris: Centre de Psychologies Appliquée.

Cashmore, J. A., & Goodnow, J. J. (1986). Influences on Australian parents' values: Ethnicity versus socioeconomic status. *Journal of Cross-Cultural Psychology*, *17*, 441–454.

Cawte, J. E., & Kiloh, L. G. (1967). Language and pictorial representation in Aboriginal children: Implications for transcultural psychiatry. *Social Science and Medicine*, *1*, 67–76.

Chapman, D. W., & Carter, J. F. (1979). Translation procedures for the cross-cultural use of measurement instruments. *Educational Evaluation and Policy Analysis*, *1*, 71–76.

Chen, C., & Uttal, D. H. (1988). Cultural values, parents' beliefs, and children's achievement in the United States and China. *Human Development*, *31*, 351–358.

Chipman, H. (1985). Aspects of language acquisition: Developmental strategies. In V. L. Shulman, L. C. R. Restaino-Baumann, & L. Butler (Eds.), *The future of Piagetian theory: The neo-Piagetians*. New York: Plenum Press.

Chomsky, N. (1965). *Aspects of the theory of syntax*. Cambridge: MIT Press.

Chu, C., Sallach, H. S., Zakena, S. A. et al. (1985). Differences in psychopatholgy between black and white schizophrenics. *International Journal of Social Psychiatry*, *31*, 252–257.

Cleland, J. (1928). Mental diseases amongst Australian Aborigines. *Journal of Tropical Medicine*, *31*, 326–330.

Clyne, M. (1987). Cultural differences in the organization of academic texts: English and German. *Journal of Pragmatics*.

Cochran, M., Larner, M., Riley, D., Gunnarsson, L., & Henderson, C. R., Jr. (1990). *Extending families: The social networks of parents and their children*. Cambridge: Cambridge University Press.

Condon, J. C., & Yousef, F. (1975). *An introduction to intercultural communication*. New York: MacMillan.

Converse, J. M., & Schuman, H. (1974). *Conversation at random: Survey research as interviewers see it*. New York: Wiley.

Cook, T. D., & Campbell, D. T. (1979). *Quasi-experimentation: Design and analysis issues for field settings*. Chicago: Rand McNally.

Costa, P. T., & McCrae, R. R. (1985). *The NEO-PI personality manual*. Odessa, FL: Psychological Assessment Resources.

Costa, P. T., & McCrae, R. R. (1988). Personality in adulthood: A six-year longitudinal study of self reports and spouse ratings of the NEO Personality Inventory. *Journal of Personality and Social Psychology*, *54*, 853–863.

Costello, B. R., & Taylor, J. L. (1991). Women in Australia. In L. L. Adler (Ed.), *Women in cross-cultural perspective* (pp. 242–254). New York: Praeger.

Cowgill, D., & Holmes, L. (1972). *Aging and modernization*. New York: Appleton-Century-Crofts.

Cronbach, L. J. (1960). *Essentials of psychological testing* (2nd ed). New York: Harper & Row.

Dana, R. H. (Ed.). (1982). *Human services for cultural minorities*. Baltimore: University Park Press.

Darwin, C. (1872). *The expression of emotion in man and animals*. New York: Philosophical Library.

Dasen, P. R. (Ed.). (1977). *Piagetian psychology: Cross-cultural contributions.* New York: Gardner Press.

Dasen, P. R. (1982). Cross-cultural aspects of Piaget's theory: The competence-performance model. In L. L. Adler (Ed.), *Cross-cultural research at issue.* New York: Academic Press.

Dasen, P. R., & Heron, A. (1981). Cross-cultural tests of Piaget's theory. In H. C. Triandis & A. Heron (Eds.), *Handbook of cross-cultural psychology* (Vol. 4). Boston: Allyn & Bacon.

Dasen, P. R., Inhelder, B., Lavallee, M., & Retschitzki, J. (1978). *Naissance de l'intelligence chez l'enfant Baoule de Cote d'Ivoire.* Bern: Hans Huber.

Daton, N., Antonovsky, A., & Maoz, B. (1985). Tradition, modernity and transitions in five Israeli subcultures. In J. Brown & V. Kearns (Eds.), *In her prime: A new view of middle-aged women.* South Hadley, MA: Bergin and Garvey.

Davidson, A. R., Jaccard, J. J., Triandis, H. C., Morales, M. L., & Diaz-Guerrero, R. (1976). Cross-cultural model testing: Toward a solution of the etic-emic dilemma. *International Journal of Psychology, 11,* 1–13.

Dean, A., & Ensel, W. (1982). Modelling social support, life events, competence, and depression in the context of age and sex. *Journal of Community Psychology, 10,* 392–408.

De Hoyos, A., & De Hoyos, G. (1965). Symptomatology differentials between negro and white schizophrenics. *International Journal of Social Psychiatry, 11,* 245–255.

DeVos, G. (1986). The relation of guilt towards parents to achievement and arranged marriage among the Japanese. In T. S. Lebra and W. P. Lebra (Eds.), *Japanese culture and behavior.* Honolulu: University of Hawaii Press.

Deka, N. (1993). India. In L. L. Adler (Ed.), *International handbook on gender roles* (Chap. 10). Westport, CT: Greenwood Press.

DeLint, J. (1975). Current trends in the prevalence of excessive alcohol use and alcohol-related health damage. *British Journal of Addictions, 70,* 3–13.

Denmark, F. L. (1977). The psychology of women: An overview of an emerging field. *Personality and Social Psychology Bulletin, 3,* 356–367.

Denmark, F. L., Schwartz, L., & Smith, K. M. (1991). Women in the United States of America and Canada. In L. L. Adler (Ed.), *Women in cross-cultural perspective* (1–18). New York: Praeger.

Depner, C., & Ingersoll-Dayton, B. (1985). Conjugal social support: Patterns in later life. *Journal of Gerontology, 40,* 761–766.

Deregowski, J. B. (1980). Perception. In H. C. Triandis & W. Lambert (Eds.), *Handbook of cross-cultural psychology* (3rd ed.). Boston: Allyn & Bacon.

de Ribaupierre, A., Rieben, L., & Lautrey, J. (1985). Horizontal decalogues and individual differences in the development of concrete operations. In V. L. Shulman, L. C. R. Restaino-Baumann, & L. Butler (Eds.), *The future of Piagetian theory: The neo-Piagetians.* New York: Plenum Press.

DeRidder R., Zawi, B. & Hendricks, E. (In preparation). Sociocultural variations in the selective functioning of belief systems.

Deutscher, I. (1973). Asking questions cross-culturally: Some problems of linguistic comparability. In D. P. Warwick & S. Osherson (Eds.), *Comparative research methods (pp. 163–203).* Englewood Cliffs, NJ: Prentice Hall.

Diaz-Guerrero, R. (1967). Sociocultural premises, attitudes, and cross-cultural research. *International Journal of Psychology, 2,* 79–88.

Diaz-Guerrero, R. (1970). *Estudios de psicología del mexicano* (2nd ed.) Mexico: Trillas.

Diaz-Guerrero, R. (1971). La enseñanza de la investigación psicológica en Latinoamérica: Un paradigma. *Revista Latinoamericana de Psicología, 3,* (1), 5–36.

Diaz-Guerrero, R. (1972). Una escala factorial de premisas histórico-socioculturales de la familia mexicana. *Revista Interamericana de Psicología, 6,* 235–244.

Diaz-Guerrero, R. (1977a). Culture and personality revisited. In L. L. Adler (Ed.), *Issues in cross-cultural research. Annal of the New York Academy of Sciences, 285* (pp. 119–130). New York: New York Academy of Sciences.

Diaz-Guerrero, R. (1977b). A Mexican psychology. *American Psychologist, 32* (11), 934–944.

Diaz-Guerrero, R. (1982). The psychology of the historic-sociocultural premise, I. *Spanish Language Psychology, 2,* 383–410.

Diaz-Guerrero, R. (1984). Tristeza y psicopatología en México. *Salud Mental, 7*(2), 3–9.

Diaz-Guerrero, R. (1985). Holtzman Inkblot Technique (HIT) differences across Mexican, Mexican-American and Angloamerican cultures. In E. E. Roslam (Ed.), *Measurement and personality assessment* (pp. 247–259). Amsterdam: Elsevier Science.

Diaz-Guerrero, R. (1986a). Historio-sociocultura y personalidad. Definición y características de los factores de la familia mexicana. *Revista de Psicología Social y Personalidad, 2*(1), 13–42.

Diaz-Guerrero, R. (1986b, July). A Mexican ethnopsychology. In J. W. Berry & U. Kim (Organizers), *Indigenous psychology.* Symposium presented at the 8th Congress of the International Society of Cross-Cultural Psychology, Istanbul, Turkey.

Diaz-Guerrero, R. (1987). Historic-sociocultural premises and ethnic socialization. In J. S. Phinney & M. J. Rotheram (Eds.), *Children's ethnic socialization, pluralism and development* (pp. 239–250). Newbury Park, CA: Sage.

Diaz-Guerrero, R. (1989a). Towards an ecosystemic psychology. In J. A. Keats, R. Taft, R. A. Heath, & S. H. Lovibond (Eds.), *Mathematical and Theoretical Systems* (pp. 229–240). Amsterdam: North-Holland.

Diaz-Guerrero, R. (1989b). Una etnopsicologia Mexicana. *Ciencia y Desarrollo, 15*(86), 69–85.

Diaz-Guerrero, R., & Diaz-Loving, R. (1992). Interpretation in cross-cultural personality assessment. In C. R. Reynolds & R. Kamphaus (Eds.), *Handbook of psychological and educational assessment* (Vol. 2, Chap. 28). New York: Guilford.

Diaz-Guerrero, R., & Iscoe, I. (1984). El impacto de la cultura Iberoamericana tradicional y del estrés económico sobre la salud mental y física: Instrumentación y potencial para la investigación transcultural, I. *Revista Latinoamericana de Psicología, 16*(2), 167–211.

Diaz-Guerrero, R., & Rodriguez de Diaz, M. L. (1993). Mexico. In L. L. Adler (Ed.), *International handbook on gender roles* (Chap. 15). Westport, CT: Greenwood Press.

Diaz-Loving, R., Diaz-Guerrero, R., Helmreich, R. L., & Spence, J. T. (1981).

Comparación transcultural y análisis psicométrico de una medida de rasgos masculinos (instrumentales) y femeninos (expresivos). *Revista de la Asociación Latinoamericana de Psicología Social, 1*(1), 3–37.

Digman, G. M., & Inouye, J. (1986). Further specification of the five robust factors of personality. *Journal of Personality and Social Psychology, 50,* 116–123.

Digman, G. M., & Takemoto-Chock, N. K. (1981). Factors in the natural language of personality: Re-analysis and comparison of six major studies. *Multivariate Behavioral Research, 16,* 149–170.

DiNicola, V. F. (1990). Anorexia multiforme: Self-starvation in historical and cultural context: P. 2, Anorexia nervosa as a culture-reactive syndrome. *Transcultural Psychiatric Research Review, 27,* 245–286.

Diop, M. (1967). La dèpression chez le noir africain. *Psychopathologie africaine, 3,* 183–195.

Dohrenwend, B. P., & Dohrenwend, B. S. (1969). *Social status and psychological disorder.* New York: Wiley.

Doi, T. (1973). *The anatomy of dependence.* Tokyo: Kodansha.

Doi, T. (1985). *The anatomy of self.* Tokyo: Kodansha.

Doi, T. (1986). *Amae:* A key concept for understanding Japanese personality structure. In T. S. Lebra & W. P. Lebra (Eds.), *Japanese culture and behavior.* Honolulu: University of Hawaii Press.

Doise, W. (1985). On the social development of the intellect. In V. L. Shulman, L. C. R. Restaino-Bauman, & L. Butler (Eds.), *The future of Piagetian research: The neo-Piagetians.* New York: Plenum Press.

Doob, L. W. (1965). Exploring eidetic imagery among the Kamba of Central Kenya. *Journal of Social Psychology, 67,* 3–22.

Doob, L. W. (1980). The inconclusive struggles of cross-cultural psychology. *Journal of Cross-Cultural Psychology, 11,* 59–73.

Draguns, J. G. (1973). Comparison of psychopathology across cultures: Issues, findings, directions. *Journal of Cross-Cultural Psychology, 4,* 9–47.

Draguns, J. G. (1980). Disorders of clinical severity. In H. C. Triandis & J. G. Draguns (Eds.), *Handbook of cross-cultural psychology: Vol. 6. Psychopathology* (pp. 99–174). Boston: Allyn & Bacon.

Draguns, J. G. (1986). Culture and psychopathology: What is known about their relationship? *Australian Journal of Psychology, 38,* 329–338.

Draguns, J. G. (1990). Normal and abnormal behavior in cross-cultural perspective: Toward specifying the nature of their relationship. In J. J. Berman (Ed.), *Nebraska symposium on motivation 1989* (pp. 236–277). Lincoln: University of Nebraska Press.

Draguns, J. G. (1990a). Applications of cross-cultural psychology in the field of mental health. In R. W. Brislin (Ed.), *Applied cross-cultural psychology* (pp. 302–324). Newbury Park, CA: Sage.

Dunlap, D. A. (1990). Rural psychiatric rehabilitation and the interface of community development and rehabilitation services. *Psychosocial Rehabilitation Journal, 14,* 67–89.

Durkheim, E. (1912/1915). *The elementary forms of religious life.* London: Allen & Unwin.

Durkheim, E. (1951). *Suicide* (J. A. Spaulding & G. Simpson, trans.). Glencoe, IL: Free Press.

Ebigno, P. (1982). Development of a culture specific screening scale of somatic complaints indicating psychiatric disturbance. *Culture, Medicine and Psychiatry, 6,* 29–43.

Ebin, V. (1979). *The body decorated.* London: Blacker Calmann Cooper Ltd.

Eckensberger, L. H. (1993). Moralische Urteile als handlungsleitende Regelsysteme im Spiegel der kulturvergleichenden Forschung. In A. Thomas (Ed.), *Einführung in die kulturvergleichende Psychologie* (pp. 259–295). Göttingen: Hogrefe. (in German)

Eckland, B. K. (1968). Theories of mate selection. *Eugenics Quarterly, 15,* 17–23.

Edwards, C. P. (1981). The comparative study of the development of moral judgement and reasoning. In R. H. Munroe, R. L. Munroe, & B. B. Whiting (Eds.), *Handbook of cross-cultural human development* (pp. 501–528). New York: Garland.

Edwards, C. P. (1986). Cross-cultural research on Kohlberg's stages. The basis for consensus. In S. Modgil & C. Modgil (Eds.), *Lawrence Kohlberg: Consensus and controversy* (pp. 419–430). London: Falmer Press.

Efron, D. (1972). *Gesture, race and culture.* The Netherlands: Mouton.

Egeland, J. A., Hofstetter, A. M., & Eshleman, S. K. (1983). Amish Study III. The impact of cultural factors on diagnosis of bipolar illness. *American Journal of Psychiatry, 140,* 67–71.

Eibl-Eibesfeldt, I. (1972). Similarities and differences between cultures in expressive movements. In R. A. Hinde (Ed.), *Nonverbal communication.* Cambridge: Cambridge University Press.

Ekman, P. (1980). *The face of man: Expressions of universal emotion in a New Guinea village.* New York: Garland Press.

Ekman, P. (1972). Universals and cultural differences in facial expressions of emotion. In J. Cole (Ed.), *Nebraska symposium of motivation, 1971* (Vol. 19). Lincoln: University of Nebraska Press.

Ekman, P. (1973). *Darwin and facial expression: A century of research in review.* New York: Academic Press.

Ekman, P., & Friesen, W. V. (1971). Constants across cultures in face and emotion. *Journal of Personality and Social Psychology, 17,* 124–129.

Ekman, P., Friesen, W. V., O'Sullivan, M., Chan, A., Diacoyanni-Tarlatzia, I., Heider, K., Krause, R., LeCompte, W., Pitcairn, T., Ricci-Bitti, P., Scherer, K., Tomita, M., & Tzavaras, A. (1987). Universals and cultural differences in the judgments of facial expressions of emotion. *Journal of Personality and Social Psychology, 53,* 712–717.

Ekman, P., Friesen, W. V. & Ellsworth, P. (1972). *Emotion in the human face: Guidelines for research and integration of findings.* New York: Pergamon Press.

Ekman, P., Sorenson, E. R., & Friesen, W. V. (1969). Pancultural elements in facial displays of emotion. *Science, 164,* 86–88.

El-Shikh, S. A. (1985). A study of moral thinking in Egyptian adolescents and adults. In F. A. Abou-Hatab (Ed.), *The yearbook of psychology, 4* (123–169). Cairo: Anglo-Egyptian Bookshop. (in Arabic)

Erikson, E. (1963). *Childhood and society* (2nd ed). New York: W. W. Norton.

Estroff, S. (1989). Self, identity, and subjective experiences of schizophrenia: In search of the subject. *Schizophrenia Bulletin, 15,* 189–196.

Evans-Pritchard, E. (1937). *Witchcraft, oracles, and magic among the Azande.* Oxford: Clarendon Press.

Fabrega, H. (1989). The self and schizophrenia: A cultural perspective. *Schizophrenia Bulletin, 15,* 277–290.

Fabrega, H., Mezzich, J., & Ulrich, R. F. (1988). Black-white differences in psychopathology in an urban psychiatric population. *Comprehensive Psychiatry, 29,* 285–297.

Falloon, I. R. H., Boyd, J. L., & McGill, C. W. (1985). *Family management of schizophrenia.* Baltimore: Johns Hopkins University Press.

Farkas, M., & Anthony, W. (1989). *Psychiatric rehabilitation: Putting theory into practice.* Baltimore: Johns Hopkins University Press.

Feldman, C. F., Lee, B., McLean, J. D., Pillemer, D. B., & Murray, J. R. (1974). *The development of adaptive intelligence.* San Francisco: Jossey-Bass.

Fernando, S. (1988). *Race and culture in psychiatry.* London: Croom Helm.

Festinger, L., Schachter, S., & Riecken, H. (1958). *When prophecy fails.* Minneapolis: University of Minnesota Press.

Fioravanti, M., Gough, H. G., & Frere, L. J. (1981). English, French, and Italian adjective check lists. *Journal of Cross-Cultural Psychology, 12,* 461–472.

Fischer, M. (1991). Women in the Arctic (Alaska): A culture in transition. In L. L. Adler (Ed.), *Women in cross-cultural perspective* (pp. 20–25). New York: Praeger.

Fishbein, H. D. 1984. *The psychology of infancy and childhood: Evolutionary and cross-cultural perspectives.* Hillsdale, NJ: Erlbaum.

Fishbein, M., & Raven, B. (1962). The AB scale: An operational definition of belief and attitude. *Human Relations, 15,* 35–44.

Fisher, G. A., Benson, P. R., & Tessler, R. C. (1990). Family response to mental illness: Developments since deinstitutionalization. In J. R. Greenley (Ed.), *Research in community and mental health: Mental disorder in social context* (pp. 203–236). Greenwich, CT: JAI Press.

Forgas, J. P., & Michael O'Driscoll. (1984). Cross-cultural and demographic differences in the perception of nations. *Journal of Cross-Cultural Psychology,* June, 199–222.

Fowler. F. J. (1993). *Survey research methods* (2nd ed.). Newbury Park, CA: Sage.

Frackowiak, J., & Jasinska-Kania, A. (1992). *Moral development and the life course: The Polish case.* Unpublished paper, Warsaw University.

Francis, D. (1978). *Trial run.* London: Michael Joseph.

Frazier, C., & Douyon, C. (1989). Social support in the elderly: A cross-cultural comparison. In L. L. Adler (Ed.), *Cross-cultural research in human development: Life-span perspectives.* New York: Praeger.

Fries, J. (1980). The compression of morbidity. *Milbank Memorial Fund Quarterly/Health and Society, 61,* 397–419.

Friesen, W. V. (1972). *Cultural differences in facial expressions in a social situation: An experimental test of the concept of display rules.* Unpublished doctoral dissertation, University of California, San Francisco.

Fry, C. (1990). Cross-cultural comparisons of aging. In K. Ferraro (Ed.), *Perspectives and issues.* New York: Springer.

Fukada, N. (1991). Women in Japan. In L. L. Adler (Ed.), *Women in cross-cultural perspective* (205–219). New York: Praeger.

Gardiner, H. W. (1972). *Indicators of cognitive development among Thai children.* Paper presented at 1st meeting of the International Association of Cross-Cultural Psychology, University of Hong Kong.

Gardiner, H. W., Singh, U. P. & D'Orazio, D. E. (1974). The liberated woman in three cultures: Marital preferences in Thailand, India, and the United States. *Human Organization, 33,* 413–415.

Gardiner, H. W., & Sommoonpin Gardiner, O. (1991). Women in Thailand. In L. L. Adler (Ed.), *Women in cross-cultural perspective* (175–187). New York: Praeger.

Gardiner, O. S., & Gardiner, H. W. (1991). *A cross-cultural study of mathematics achievement in the United States and Thailand.* Unpublished paper.

Garfield, E. (1983). Review of *The foreign language barrier: Problems in scientific communication* by J. A. Large. 1983. *Nature, 303,* 554.

Garrison, V. (1978). Support systems of schizophrenic and nonschizophrenic Puerto Rican migrant women in New York City. *Schizophrenia Bulletin, 4,* 56–596.

German, J. (1972). Aspects of clinical psychiatry in sub-Saharan Africa. *British Journal of Psychiatry, 121,* 461–479.

Gielen, U. P. (1986). Moral reasoning in radical and non-radical German students. *Behavior Science Research, 20,* 71–109.

Gielen, U. P. (1990). Some recent work on moral values, reasoning, and education in Chinese societies. *Moral Education Forum, 15* (2), 3–22.

Gielen, U. P. (1991a, July). Moral reasoning in cross-cultural perspective. In U. P. Gielen (Chair), *Moral reasoning in cross-cultural perspective.* Symposium conducted at the meeting of the International Association for Cross-Cultural Psychology (IACCP), Debrecen, Hungary.

Gielen, U. P. (1991b). Research on moral reasoning. In L. Kuhmerker, with U. P. Gielen & R. L. Hayes, *The Kohlberg legacy for the helping professions* (pp. 39–60). Birmingham, AL: R. E. P. Books.

Gielen, U. P. (1993). Traditional Tibetan societies. In L. L. Adler (Ed.), *International handbook on gender roles* (Chap. 29). Westport, CT: Greenwood Press.

Gielen, U. P., Ahmed, R. A., & Avellani, J. (1992). The development of moral reasoning and perceptions of parental behavior in students from Kuwait. *Moral Education Forum, 17* (3), 20–37.

Gielen, U. P., Cruickshank, H., Johnston, A., Swanzey, B., & Avellani, J. (1986). The development of moral reasoning in Belize, Trinidad-Tobago and the USA. *Behavior Science Research, 20,* 178–207.

Gielen, U. P., Markoulis, D., & Avellani, J. (1992). *Development of moral reasoning and perceptions of parental behavior in Greek students.* Unpublished paper, St. Francis College, Brooklyn, NY.

Gielen, U. P., Miao, E., & Avellani, J. (1990). Perceived parental behavior and the development of moral reasoning in students from Taiwan. *Proceedings of CCU-ICP-International Conference: Moral values and moral reasoning in Chinese societies* (pp. 464–506). Taipei: Chinese Culture University.

Gilligan, C. (1982). *In a different voice: Psychology theory and women's development.* Cambridge: Harvard University Press.

Gladwin, T., & Sarason, S. B. (1953). *Truk: Man in paradise.* Chicago: University of Chicago Press.

Glascock, A., & Feinman, S. (1981). Social asset or social burden: Treatment of the aged in non-industrial societies. In C. Fry (Ed.), *Dimensions: Aging, culture, and health*. New York: Praeger.

Goldberg, L. R. (1981). Language and individual differences: The search for universals in personality lexicons. In L. Wheeler (Ed.), *Review of personality in social psychology* (Vol. 2, pp. 141–165). Beverly Hills, CA: Sage.

Goldberg, L. R. (1982). From Ace to Zombie: Some explorations in the language of personality. In C. D. Spielberger & J. N. Butcher (Eds.), *Advances in personality assessment* (Vol. 1, pp. 203–234). Hillsdale, NJ: Erlbaum.

Goldberg, S. (1972). Infant care and growth in urban Zambia. *Human Development, 15,* 77–89.

Goodnow, J. J., & Bethon, G. (1966). Piaget's tasks: The effects of schooling and intelligence. *Child Development, 37,* 573–582.

Gove, W., Hughes, M., & Style, C. (1983). Does marriage have positive effects on the psychological well-being of the individual? *Journal of Health and Social Behavior, 24,* 122–131.

Graubert, J. G., & Adler, L. L. (1982). Attitudes toward stigma-related and stigma-free stimuli: A cross-national perspective. In L. L. Adler (Ed.), *Cross-cultural research at issue*. New York: Academic Press.

Greenberg, J. (1978, July 29). Adulthood comes of age. *Science News, 74*–79.

Greenfield, P. M. (1979). Response to "Wolof 'magical' thinking: Culture and conservation revisited" by Judith T. Irvine. *Journal of Cross-Cultural Psychology, 10,* 251–256.

Greenfield, P. M., & Childs, C. P. (1977). Understanding sibling concepts: A developmental study of kin terms in Zinacatan. In P. Dasen (Ed.), *Piagetian psychology: Cross-cultural contributions*. New York: Garden City Press.

Griffin, J. (1984). Emotional support providers and psychological distress among Anglo- and Mexican-Americans. *Community Mental Health Journal, 20,* 182–201.

Gross, J. (1992, June 28). Clinics help Asian immigrants feel at home. *New York Times, 141* (49,011), p. 10.

Grzymała-Moszczyńska, H. (1991). Women in Poland. In L. L. Adler (Ed.), *Women in cross-cultural perspective* (54–66). New York: Praeger.

Gudykunst, W. B., Kim, Y. Y. *Communicating with strangers*. New York: Random House.

Gurland, B., & Zubin, J. (1982). The United States–United Kingdom Cross-National Project: Issues in cross-cultural psychogeriatric research. In L. L. Adler (Ed.), *Cross-cultural research at issue* (pp. 323–334). New York: Academic Press.

Guthrie, G. M., Jackson, D. N., Astilla, E., & Elwood, B. (1983). Personality measurement: Do the scales have similar meaning in another culture? In S. H. Irvin & J. W. Berry (Eds.), *Human assessment and cultural factors*. New York: Plenum Press.

Guthrie, G. M., & Lonner, W. J. (1986). Assessment of personality and psychopathology. In W. J. Lonner & J. W. Berry (Eds.), *Field methods in cross-cultural research*. Beverly Hills: Sage.

Gutmann, D. (1977). The cross-cultural perspective: Notes towards a comparative psychology of aging. In J. Birren & K. Schaie (Eds.), *Handbook of the psychology of aging*. New York: Van Nostrand Reinhold.

Haley, J. (1980). *Leaving home: The therapy of disturbed young people.* New York: McGraw-Hill.

Hall, E. T. (1959). *The silent language.* Garden City, NY: Doubleday.

Hall, E. T. (1966). *The hidden dimension.* Garden City, NY: Doubleday.

Halpern, R., & Myers, R. (1985). Effects of early childhood intervention on primary school progress and performance in the developing countries (mimeo). Ypsilanti, MI: High/Scope Educational Research Foundation.

Handel, G. (Ed.). (1988). *Childhood socialization.* New York: Aldine de Gruyter.

Harding, C. M., Brooks, G., Ashikaga, T., Strauss, J. S., & Breier, A. (1987). The Vermont Longitudinal Study of Persons with Severe Mental Illness, II. Long-term outcome of subjects who retrospectively met DSM–III criteria for schizophrenia. *American Journal of Psychiatry, 144.* 727–735.

Harris, Philip R., & Robert T. Moran. (1987). *Managing cultural differences* (2nd ed.). Houston, TX: Gulf Publishing.

Harvey, Michael G. (1985). The executive family: An overlooked variable in international assignments. *Columbia Journal of World Business,* Spring, 84–92.

Hatch, E. (1983). *Culture and morality: The relativity of values in anthropology.* New York: Columbia University Press.

Hau, K. T. (1983). *A cross-cultural study of a moral judgment test (The DIT).* Master's thesis, Chinese University, Hong Kong.

Havighurst, R. (1952). *Developmental tasks and education.* New York: McKay.

Haynes, J. P. (1983). An empirical method for determining core psychological journals. *American Psychologist, 38,* 959–961. (Comment)

Henley, N. (1977). *Body politics: Power, sex, and nonverbal communication.* Englewood Cliffs, NJ: Prentice Hall.

Henry, G. T. (1990). *Practical sampling.* Newbury Park, CA: Sage.

Herskovits, M. (1948). *Man and his works.* New York: Knopf.

Hess, R. D., Halloway, S., McDevitt, T., Azuma, H., Kashiwagi, K., Nagano, S., Miyake, K., Dickson, W. P., Price, G., & Hatano, G. (1986). Family influences on school readiness and achievement in Japan and the United States: An overview of a longitudinal study. In H. Stevenson, H. Azuma, & K. Hakuta (Eds.), *Child development and education in Japan.* New York: W. H. Freeman.

Heyduk, R. G., & Fenigstein, A. (1984). Influential works and authors in psychology: A survey of eminent psychologists. *American Psychologist, 39,* 556–559. (Comment)

Hinde, R. A. (Ed.). (1972). *Non-verbal communication.* Cambridge: Cambridge University Press.

Ho, D.Y.F. (1976). On the concept of face. *American Journal of Sociology, 81,* 867–884.

Ho, D.Y.F. (1977). Culture-specific belief stereotypy and some of its personality, attitudinal, and intellective correlates. In Y. H. Poortinga (Ed.), *Basic problems in cross-cultural psychology* (pp. 289–298). Amsterdam: Swets & Zeitlinger.

Ho, D.Y.F. (1988). Asian psychology: A dialogue on indigenization and beyond. In A. C. Paranjpe, D.Y.F. Ho, & R. W. Rieber (Eds.), *Asian contributions to psychology* (pp. 53–77). New York: Praeger.

Ho, D.Y.F., & Kang, T. K. (1984). Intergenerational comparisons of child-rearing attitudes and practices in Hong Kong. *Developmental Psychology, 20,* 1004–1016.

Ho, D. Y. F., & Lee, L. Y. (1974). Authoritarianism and attitudes toward filial piety in Chinese teachers. *Journal of Social Psychology, 92,* 305–306.

Hockett, C. F. (1960). The origin of speech. *Scientific American,* Sept.

Hofstede, G. (1979). Value systems in 40 countries: Interpretation, validation and consequences for theory. In L. H. Eckensberger, W. J. Lonner & Y. H. Poortinga (Eds.), *Cross-cultural contributions to psychology.* Lisse, Netherlands: Swets & Zeitlinger.

Hofstede, G. (1980). *Culture's consequences: International differences in work-related values.* Beverly Hills: Sage.

Hofstede, G. (1982). Dimensions of national cultures. In R. Rath, H. S. Asthana, D. Sinha, & J. B. H. Sinha (Eds.), *Diversity and unity in cross-cultural psychology.* Lisse, Netherlands: Swets & Zeitlinger.

Hofstede, G. (1983). Dimensions of national cultures in 50 countries and 3 regions. In J. B. Deregowksi, S. Dziurawiec, & R. C. Annis (Eds.), *Explications in cross-cultural psychology.* Lisse, Netherlands: Swets & Zeitlinger.

Hogan, R. T. (1983). A socioanalytic theory of personality. In M. Page (Ed.), *1982 Nebraska symposium on motivation* (pp. 55–89). Lincoln: University of Nebraska Press.

Holtzman, W. H., Diaz-Guerrero, R., & Swartz, J. D. (1975). *Personality development in two cultures.* Austin: University of Texas Press.

Horton, D. (1943). The functions of alcohol in primitive societies: A cross-cultural study. *Quarterly Journal Studies of Alcohol, 4,* 199–320.

House, J. (1987). Social support and social structure. *Sociological Forum, 2,* 135–146.

Hsu, F. L. K. (1972). American core values and national character. In F. L. K. Hsu (Ed.), *Psychological anthropology.* Cambridge, MA: Schenkman.

Hudson, R. A. (1980). *Sociolinguistics.* Cambridge: Cambridge University Press.

Hudson, W. (1960). Pictorial depth perception in sub-cultural groups in Africa. *Journal of Social Psychology, 52,* 183–208.

Hui, C. H., & Triandis, H. C. (1985). Measurement in cross-cultural psychology: A review and comparison of strategies. *Journal of Cross-Cultural Psychology, 16,* 131–152.

Hui, C. H., & Triandis, H. C. (1986). Individualism-Collectivism: A study of cross-cultural researchers. *Journal of Cross-Cultural Psychology, 17,* 225–248.

Hulin, C. L. (1987). A psychometric theory of evaluations of item and scale translations: Fidelity across languages. *Journal of Cross-Cultural Psychology, 18,* 115–142.

Hyde, J. S. (1985). *Half the human experience: The psychology of women.* Lexington, MA: Remson University.

Hymes, D. (1962). The ethnography of speaking. In *Anthropology and Human Behavior.* Anthropological Society of Washington, Washington.

Hymes, D. (1972). Models of the interaction of language and social life. In *Directions in sociolinguistics: The ethnography of communication.* Oxford: Basil Blackwell.

Imamoglu, O., & Imamoglu V. (1992). Life situations and attitudes of Turkish elderly toward institutional living within a cross-cultural perspective. *Journal of Gerontology, 47,* 102–108.

Irvine, J. T. (1978). Wolof "magical thinking": Culture and conservation revisited. *Journal of Cross-Cultural Psychology, 9,* 300–310.

Izard, C. E. (1971). *The face of emotion.* New York: Appleton-Century-Crofts.

Izraeli, D. N., & Safir, M. P. (1993). Israel. In L. L. Adler (Ed.). *International handbook on gender roles.* Westport, CT: Greenwood Press.

Jablensky, A., Sartorius, N., Gulbinat, W., & Ernberg, G. (1981). Characteristics of depressive patients contacting psychiatric services in four cultures. *Acta Psychiatrica Scandinavica, 63,* 367–383.

Jahoda, G. (1977). Cross-cultural study of factors influencing orientation errors in reproduction of Kohs-type figures. *British Journal of Psychology, 69,* 45–57.

Jahoda, G. (1977). Psychology and anthropology: Possible common ground in cross-cultural research. In L. L. Adler (Ed.), *Issues in cross-cultural research. Annals of the New York Academy of Sciences, 285* (pp. 13–18). New York: New York Academy of Sciences.

Jahoda, G. (1982). *Psychology and anthropology: A psychological perspective.* London: Academic Press.

Jahoda, G. 1986. A cross-cultural perspective on developmental psychology. *International Journal of Behavioral Development, 9,* 417–437.

Jahoda, G., & Lewis, I. M. 1988. *Acquiring Culture: Cross-Cultural Studies in Child Development.* London: Croom Helm.

Jakobson, R. O. (1968). *Child language, aphasia and phonological universals.* Mouton: The Hague.

James, W. (1968). The self. In C. Gordon & K. J. Gergen (Eds.), *The self in social interaction* (Vol. 1). New York: Wiley.

Jenkins, J. H., & Karno, M. (1992). The meaning of expressed emotion: Theoretical issues raised by cross-cultural research. *American Journal of Psychiatry, 149,* 9–21.

Jilek-Aal, L. (1988). Suicidal behavior among youth: A cross-cultural comparison. *Transcultural Psychiatric Research Review, 25,* 87–106.

Jones, E. E. (1976). How do people perceive the causes of behavior? *American Scientist, 64,* 300–305.

Jones, K., & Poletti, A. (1985). The Italian transformation of the asylum: A commentary and review. *International Journal of Mental Health,* Spring-Summer, 210.

Judd, C. M., Smith, E., & Kidder, L. H. (1991). *Research methods in social relations* (6th ed.). New York: Harcourt Brace Jovanovich.

Kagitcibasi, C., & Berry, J. (1989). Cross-cultural psychology: Current research and trends. *Annual Review of Psychology, 40,* 493–531.

Kahn, J. V. (1982). Moral reasoning in Irish children and adolescents as measured by the Defining Issues Test. *Irish Journal of Psychology, 2,* 96–108.

Kalu, W., & Kalu, O. (1993). Nigeria. In L. L. Adler (Ed.), *International handbook on gender roles,* (Chap. 17). Westport, CT: Greenwood Press.

Kamara, A. I. 1971. *Cognitive development among school-age Themne children of Sierra Leone.* Unpublished doctoral dissertation, University of Illinois.

Katz, A. M., Katz, V. T. (Eds.). (1983). *Foundations of nonverbal communication.* Southern Illinois University Press.

Katz, M. M., Marsella, A., Dube, K. C. et al. (1988). On the expression of psychosis in different cultures: Schizophrenia in an Indian and in a Nigerian community. *Culture, Medicine, & Psychiatry, 12,* 331–355.

Katz, S., Branch, L., Branson, M., Papsidero, J., Beck, J., & Greer, D. (1983). Active life expectancy. *New England Journal of Medicine, 309,* 1218–1224.

Keith, J., Fry, C., & Ikels, C. (1990). Community as context for successful aging. In J. Sokolovsky (Ed.), *The cultural context of aging: Worldwide perspectives.* New York: Bergin and Garvey.

Kelly, M. R. 1977. Papua, New Guinea and Piaget—An eight year study. In P. Dasen (Ed.), *Piagetian psychology: Cross-cultural contributions.* New York: Gardner Press.

Kemper, T. (1984). Power, status, and emotions: A sociological contribution to a psychophysiological domain. In K. Scherer & P. Ekman (Eds.), *Approaches to emotion.* New York: Erlbaum.

Kerlinger, F. N. (1986). *Foundations of behavioral research* (3rd ed.). New York: Holt, Rinehart & Winston.

Kertzer, D. (1978). Theoretical developments in the study of age-group systems. *American Ethnologist, 5,* 368–374.

Khubalkar, R., Gupta, O. P., & Jain, A. P., (1986). *Dhat* syndrome in rural India: Some observations. *Proceedings of the Annual Conference of the Indian Association of Clinical Psychology.* Saugar University.

Kiesling, R. (1981). Underdiagnosis of manic-depressive illness in a hospital unit. *American Journal of Psychiatry, 138,* 672–673.

Kilbride, P. L., & Leibowitz, H. W. (1975, October). *The Ponzo illusion among the Baganda of Uganda.* Paper presented at the 3-day Conference on Issues in Cross-Cultural Research. Sponsored by The New York Academy of Sciences; Organized by Leonore Loeb Adler.

Kilbride, P. L., & Leibowitz, H. W. (1977). The Ponzo illusion among the Baganda of Uganda. In L. L. Adler (Ed.), *Issues in cross-cultural research. Annals of the New York Academy of Sciences, 285* (pp. 408–417). New York: New York Academy of Sciences.

Kilbride, P. L., & Leibowitz, H. W. (1982). The Ponzo illusion among the Baganda of Uganda: Implications for ecological and perceptual theory. In L. L. Adler (Ed.), *Cross-cultural research at issue.* New York: Academic Press.

Kim, T. L. (1993). Korea. In L. L. Adler (Ed.), *International handbook on gender roles* (Chap. 14). Westport, CT: Greenwood Press.

Kim, U., & Berry, J. W. (1993). *Indigenous psychologies, research and experience in cultural context.* Newbury Park, CA: Sage Publications.

Kimmel, D. (1980). *Adulthood and aging: An interdisciplinary developmental view* (2nd ed.). New York: Wiley.

Kimura, B. (1965). Vergleichende Untersuchungen über depressive Erkrankungen in Japan und Deutschland. *Fortschritte der Psychiatrie und Neurologie, 33,* 202–215.

King, L. M. (1978). Social and cultural influences upon psychopathology. *Annual Review of Psychology, 29,* 405–434.

Kinzie, J. D. (1986). The establishment of outpatient mental health services for Southeast Asian refugees. In C. L. Williams & J. Westermeyer (Eds.), *Refugee mental health in resettlement countries* (pp. 217–231). Washington, DC: Hemisphere.

Kirmayer, L. (1984). Culture, affect, and somatization. Parts 1 and 2. *Transcultural Psychiatric Research Review, 21,* 159–188, 237–262.

Kirmayer, L. J. (1991). The place of culture in psychiatric nosology: *Taijin Kyofushu* and DSM-IIIR. *Journal of Nervous and Mental Disease, 179,* 19–28.

Kleck, R., Buck, P. L., Goller, W. L., London, R. S., Pfeiffer, J. R., & Vukcevic, D. P. (1968). Effect of stigmatizing conditions on the use of personal space. *Psychological Reports, 23,* 111–118.

Kleinman, A. (1977). Depression, somatization, and the "new transcultural psychiatry." *Social Science and Medicine, 11,* 3–9.

Kleinman, A. (1982). Neurasthenia and depression: A study of somatization and culture in China. *Culture, Medicine, and Psychiatry, 6,* 117–190.

Kleinman, A. (1986). *Social origins of distress and disease.* New Haven, CT: Yale University Press.

Klineberg, O. (1940). *Social psychology.* New York: Henry Holt.

Klineberg, O. (1980). Historical perspectives: Cross-cultural psychology before 1960. In H. C. Triandis & W. W. Lambert (Eds.), *Handbook of cross-cultural psychology: Perspectives* (Vol. 1, pp. 31–67). Boston: Allyn & Bacon.

Kluckhohn, C., & Murray, H. A. (Eds.). (1953). *Personality in nature, society, and culture.* New York: Knopf.

Kluckhohn, F., & Strodtbeck, F. (1961). *Variations in value orientations.* Evanston, IL: Row, Peterson.

Kohlberg, L. (1984). *The psychology of moral development.* San Francisco: Harper & Row.

Kohlberg, L., & Gilligan, C. (1971). The adolescent as a philosopher: The discovery of self in a post-conventional world. *Daedalus, 100,* 1051–1086.

Koss-Chioino, J. (1992). *Women as healers, women as patients: Mental health care and traditional healing in Puerto Rico.* Boulder, CO: Westview Press.

Krause, N., Jay, G., & Liang, J. (1991). Financial strain and psychological well-being among the American and Japanese elderly. *Psychology and Aging, 6,* 170–181.

Kuhmerker, L. (1991). *The Kohlberg legacy for the helping professions.* Birmingham, AL: R.E.P. Books.

Kumar, U. (1991). Life stages in the development of the Hindu woman in India. In L. L. Adler (Ed.), *Women in cross-cultural perspective* (pp. 143–158). New York: Praeger.

Kupfer, Andrew. (1988, March 14). How to be a global manager. *Fortune,* pp. 52–58.

Kurian, G. (Ed.). (1986). *Parent-child interaction in transition.* New York: Greenwood Press.

LaBarre, W. (1947). The cultural basis of emotion and gestures. *Journal of Personality, 16,* 49–68.

Laboratory of Comparative Human Cognition. (1979). Cross-cultural psychology's challenges to our ideas of children and development. *American Psychologist, 34,* 827–833.

Laboratory of Comparative Human Cognition. (1983). Culture and cognitive development. In W. Kessen (Ed.), *Handbook of child psychology* (Vol. 1). New York: Wiley.

Laboratory of Comparative Human Cognition. (1986). Contributions of cross-cultural research to educational practice. *American Psychologist, 41,* 1049–1058.

Lamb, M. E. (Ed.). (1987). *The father's role: Cross-cultural perspectives.* Hillsdale, NJ: Erlbaum.

Lambert, W. (1987). The fate of old country values in a new land: A cross-national study of child rearing. *Canadian Journal of Psychology, 28,* 9–20.

Lambo, T. A. (1978). Psychotherapy in Africa. *Human Nature, 1,* 32–39.

Lancy, D. F. (1983). *Cross-cultural studies in cognition and mathematics.* New York: Academic Press.

Lange, L. (1985). Effects of disciplines and countries on citation habits: An analysis of empirical papers in behavioural sciences. *Scientometrics, 8,* 205–215.

Langer, Ellen. (1975). *The psychology of control.* Beverly Hills, CA.: Sage.

Large, J. A. (1983). *The foreign language barrier: Problems in scientific communication.* London: A. Deutsch.

La Rosa, J. (1986). *Escalas del locus de control y autoconcepto. Construcción y validación.* Unpublished doctoral dissertation, National University of Mexico, Mexico City.

La Rosa, J., & Diaz-Loving, R. (1988). Diferencial semántico del autoconcepto en estudiantes. *Revista de Psicología Social y Personalidad, 4*(1), 39–57.

Laurendeau-Bendavid, M. (1977). Culture, schooling and cognitive development: A comparative study of children in French Canada and Rwanda. In P. Dasen (Ed.), *Piagetian psychology: Cross-cultural contributions.* New York: Gardner Press.

Laws, R. (1886). *Women's work in heathen lands.* Paisley: Parlane.

LeBon, G. (1895). *The crowd.* London: Benn.

Leach, E. (1972). The influence of cultural context on nonverbal communication in man. In R. A. Hinde (Ed.), *Nonverbal communication.* Cambridge: Cambridge University Press.

Lebra, T. S. (1976). *Japanese patterns of behavior.* Honolulu: University of Hawaii Press.

Lee, G. (1985). Kinship and social support among the elderly: The case of the United States. *Ageing and Society, 5,* 19–38.

Lee, James A. (1966). Cultural analysis in overseas operations. *Harvard Business Review, 44,* March–April, 106–114.

Leff, J., Sartorius, N., Jablensky, A., Korten, A., & Ernberg, G. (1992). The International Pilot Study of Schizophrenia: Five-year follow-up findings. *Psychological Medicine, 22,* 131–145.

Leff, J., & Vaughn, C. (1985). *Expressed emotion in families.* New York: Guilford.

Lefley, H. P. (1984). Delivering mental health services across cultures. In P. B. Pedersen, N. Sartorius, & A. Marsella (Eds.), *Mental health services: The cross-cultural context.* Beverly Hills, CA: Sage.

Lefley, H. P. (1985). Families of the mentally ill in cross-cultural perspective. *Psychosocial Rehabilitation Journal, 8*(4), 57–75.

Lefley, H. P. (1990a). Culture and chronic mental illness. *Hospital & Community Psychiatry, 41,* 277–286.

Lefley, H. P. (1990b). Rehabilitation in mental illness: Insights from other cultures. *Psychosocial Rehabilitation Journal, 14,* 5–11.

Lefley, H. P. (1991). Dealing with cross-cultural issues in clinical practice. In P. A.

Keller & S. R. Heyman (Eds.), *Innovations in clinical practice: A sourcebook* (Vol. 10, pp. 99–115). Sarasota, FL: Professor Resource Exchange.

Lefley, H. P. (1992). Expressed emotion: Conceptual, clinical, and social policy issues. *Hospital & Community Psychiatry, 43,* 591–598.

Lefley, H. P., & Bestman, E. W. (1991). Public-academic linkages for culturally sensitive community mental health. *Community Mental Health Journal, 27,* 473–488.

Lefley, H. P., & Johnson, D. L. (Eds.). (1990). *Families as allies in treatment of the mentally ill: New directions for mental health professionals.* Washington, DC: American Psychiatric Press.

Leighton, A., Lambo, T., Hughes, C., Leighton, D., Murphy, J., & Macklin, D. (1963). *Psychiatric disorder among the Yoruba.* Ithaca, NY: Cornell University Press.

Leslie, G. R., & Korman, S. K. (1985). *The family in social context.* New York: Oxford University Press.

Leung, & Bond, M. (1989). On the empirical identification of dimensions for cross-cultural comparison. *Journal of Cross-Cultural Psychology, 20,* (2), 136–151.

Lewis, M. (1972a). Parents and children: Sex role development. *School Review, 80,* 229–240.

Lewis, M. (1972b). Culture and gender roles: There's no unisex in the nursery. *Psychology Today, 5,* 54–57.

Lewittes, H. (1982). Women's development in adulthood and old age: A review and critique. *International Journal of Mental Health: Women and Mental Illness, 11,* 115–134.

Lewittes, H., & Mukherji, R. (1989). Friends of older black and white women. In L. L. Adler (Ed.), *Cross-cultural research in human development: Life-span perspectives.* New York: Praeger.

Likert, R. (1932). A technique for the measurement of attitudes. *Archives of Psychology,* No. 140.

Lin, K-M, & Kleinman, A. M. (1988). Psychopathology and clinical course of schizophrenia: A cross-cultural perspective. *Schizophrenia Bulletin, 14,* 555–567.

Lind, G. (1986). Cultural differences in moral judgement competence? A study of West and East European university students. *Behavior Science Research, 20,* 208–225.

Lindsey, R. (1975, October 26). Economy mars belief in the American dream. *New York Times,* Sec. 1, pp. 1, 48.

Linton, R. (1956). *Culture and mental disorders.* Springfield, IL: Charles C. Thomas.

Little, K. B. (1965). Personal space. *Journal of Experimental Social Psychology, 1,* 237–247.

Longabaugh, R. (1980). The systematic observation of behavior in naturalistic settings. In H. C. Triandis and J. W. Berry (Eds.), *Handbook of cross-cultural psychology: Vol. 2. Methodology* (pp. 57–126). Boston: Allyn & Bacon.

Lonner, W. J. (1979). Issues in cross-cultural psychology. In A. J. Marsella, R. G. Tharp, & T. J. Ciborowski (Eds.), *Perspectives in cross-cultural psychology* (pp. 17–46). New York: Academic Press.

Lonner, W. J. (1980a). A decade of cross-cultural psychology: JCCP 1970–1979. *Journal of Cross-Cultural Psychology, 11,* 7–34.

Lonner, W. J. (1980b). The search for psychological universals. In H. C. Triandis & W. W. Lambert (Eds.), *Handbook of cross-cultural psychology: Vol. 1. Perspectives.* Boston: Allyn & Bacon.

Lonner, W. J., & Berry, J. W., (Eds.). (1986). *Field methods in cross-cultural research.* Beverly Hills, CA: Sage Publications.

Lorenz, K. (1965). *Evolution and modification of behavior.* Chicago: University of Chicago Press.

Lounsbury, F. (1964). A formal account of the Crow and Omaha-type kinship terminologies. In W. H. Goodenough (Ed.), *Explorations in cultural anthropology.* New York: McGraw Hill.

Lowenstein, L. F. & Lowenstein, K. (1991). Women in Great Britain. In L. L. Adler (Ed.), *Women in cross-cultural perspective.* (pp. 39–52) New York: Praeger.

Lynn, R. (1971). *Personality and national character.* Oxford: Pergamon Press.

Lynn, R. (1973). National differences in anxiety and the consumption of caffeine. *British Journal of Social and Clinical Psychology, 14,* 223–240.

Lynn, R. (1975). National differences in anxiety, 1935–1965. In I. G. Sarason & C. D. Spielberger (Eds.), *Stress and anxiety* (Vol. 2). Washington, DC: Hemisphere.

Lynn, R., & Hampson, S. L. (1975). National differences in extraversion and neuroticism. *British Journal of Social and Clinical Psychology, 14,* 223–240.

Lynn, R., & Hampson, S. L. (1977). Fluctuations in national level of neuroticism and extraversion, 1935–1970. *British Journal of Social and Clinical Psychology, 16,* 131–137.

MacAndrew, C., & Edgerton, R. B. (1969). *Drunken comportment: A social explanation.* Chicago: Aldine.

Mackey, W. C. (1985). *Fathering behaviors: The dynamics of the man-child bond.* New York: Plenum Press.

Mail, P. D., & McDonald, D. P. (1980). *Tulapai to Tokay: A bibliography of alcohol use and abuse among Native Americans of North America.* New Haven, CT: HRAF Press.

Maloney, Clarence (Ed.). (1976). *The evil eye.* New York: Columbia University Press.

Malpass, R. S. (1985). Editor's notes. *Journal of Cross-Cultural Psychology, 16,* 3–7.

Malpass, R. S., & Poortinga, Y. H. (1988). Strategies for design and analysis. In W. J. Lonner & J. W. Berry (Eds.), *Field methods in cross-cultural research.* Beverly Hills: Sage.

Mandler, G. (1967). Organization and memory. In K. W. Spence & J. T. Spence (Eds.), *Psychology of learning and motivation* (pp. 327–372). New York: Academic Press.

Manten, A. A. (1980). Publication of scientific information is not identical with communication. *Scientometrics, 2,* 303–308.

Marano, L. (1982). Windigo psychosis: The anatomy of an emic-etic confusion. In R. C. Simons & C. C. Hughes (Eds.), *The culture-bound syndromes: Folk illnesses of psychiatric and anthropological interest* (pp. 411–448). Boston: Reidel.

Marin, G., & Triandis, H. C. (1985). Allocentrism as an important characteristic of the behavior of Latin Americans and Hispanics. In R. Diaz-Guerrero (Ed.), *Cross-cultural and national studies in social psychology* (pp. 85–104). Amsterdam: Elsevier Science.

Markoulis, D. (submitted). *Antecedent variables for sociomoral reasoning development: Evidence from two cultural settings.* University of Thessaloniki.

Marsella, A. J. (1979). Cross-cultural studies of mental disorders. In A. J. Marsella, R. G. Tharp, & T. J. Ciborowski (Eds.), *Perspectives on cross-cultural psychology.* New York: Academic Press.

Marsella, A., Sartorious, N., Jablensky, A., & Fenton, F. (1985). Cross-cultural studies of depressive disorders: An overview. In A. Kleinman & B. Good (Eds.), *Culture and depression.* Berkley: University of California Press.

Matsumoto, D. (1986). *Cross-cultural communication of emotion.* Unpublished doctoral dissertation, University of California, Berkeley.

Matsumoto, D. (1990). *Cultural similarities and differences in display rules.* Manuscript submitted for publication.

Matsumoto, D. (in press). American-Japanese cultural differences in the recognition of universal facial expressions of emotion. *Journal of Cross-Cultural Psychology.*

Matsumoto, D., & Ekman, P. (1989). American-Japanese cultural differences in judgments of facial expressions of emotion. *Motivation and Emotion, 13,* 143–157.

Matsumoto, D., Wallbott, H., & Scherer, K. (1989). Emotions in intercultural communication. In M. Asante & W. Gudykunst (Eds.), *Handbook of intercultural and international communication.* Beverly Hills: Sage.

Maxwell, E., & Maxwell, R. (1980). Contempt for the elderly: A cross-cultural analysis. *Current Anthropology, 21,* 569–70.

McArdle, J. L., & Yeracaris, C. (1981). Respect for the elderly in preindustrial societies as related to their activity. *Behavior Science Research, 16*(3 & 4), 307–339.

McCrae, R. R., & Costa, P. T. (1985). Updating Norman's "Adequate Taxonomy": Intelligence and personality dimensions in natural language and in questionnaires. *Journal of Personality and Social Psychology, 49*(3), 710–721.

McCrae, R. R., & Costa, P. T. (1986). Clinical assessment can benefit from recent advances in personality psychology. *American Psychologist, 41*(9), 1001–1003.

McCrae, R. R., & Costa, P. T. (1987). Validation of the five factor model of personality across instruments and raters. *Journal of Personality and Social Psychology, 52*(1), 81–90.

McDougall, W. (1903). Cutaneous sensations. *Reports of the Cambridge Anthropological Expedition to Torres Strait, 2,* 189–195.

Mead, M. (1967). *Cooperation and competition among primitive people.* Boston: Beacon Press.

Mead, M. (1975). Review of Darwin and facial expression. *Journal of Communication, 25,* 209–213.

Mendis, N. (1990). A model for the care of people with psychosocial disabilities in Sri Lanka. *Psychosocial Rehabilitation Journal, 14,* 45–52.

Merenda, R., & Mattioni, M. (1993). Italy. In L. L. Adler (Ed.)., *International Handbook on Gender Roles.* Westport, CT: Greenwood Press.

Messick, D. M., & Mackie, D. M. (1989). Intergroup relations. *Annual Review of Psychology, 40,* 45–81.

Michael, D. N. (1953). A cross-cultural investigation of closure. *Journal of Abnormal and Social Psychology, 48,* 225–230.

Miller, G. E. (1956). The magical number 7, plus-or-minus 2: Some limits on our capacity for processing information. *Psychological Review, 63,* 81–97.

Miller, P., Ingham, J., & Davidson, S. (1976). Life events, symptoms, and social support. *Journal of Psychosomatic Research, 20,* 515–522.

Minai, N. (1981). *Women in Islam: Tradition and transition in the Middle East.* London: John Murray.

Minturn, L., & Lambert, W. (1964). *Mothers of six cultures.* New York: Wiley.

Mischel, W. (1968). *Personality and assessment.* New York: Wiley.

Mischel, W. (1973). Toward a cognitive social learning reconceptualization of personality. *Psychological Review, 80,* 252–283.

Mishler, E. (1986). *Research interviewing: Context and narrative.* Cambridge, MA: Harvard University Press.

Modgil, S., & Modgil, C. (1976). The Growth of logic: Concrete and formal operations. In *Piagetian research* (Vol. 3). Atlantic Highlands, NJ: Humanities Press.

Moghaddam, F. M., Taylor, D. M., & Wright, S. C. (1993). *Social psychology in cross-cultural perspective.* New York: W. H. Freeman.

Montada, L. (1985). Retrieving German psychological literature: Services available to U.S. psychologists. *American Psychologist, 40,* 1413. (Comment)

Montagu, A. M. F. (1971). *Touching.* New York: Columbia University Press.

Moon, Y. L. (1986). A review of cross-cultural studies on moral judgment development using the Defining Issues Test. *Behavior Science Research, 20,* 147–177.

Moravscik, N. J. (1985). *Strengthening the coverage of Third World science: The bibliographic indicators of the Third World's contribution to science.* Eugene: University of Oregon. (Final Report)

Morris, C. (1938). *Foundation of the theory of sign.* Chicago: University of Chicago Press.

Morris, Desmond. (1979). *Gestures.* New York: Stein and Day.

Mounoud, P., & Vinter, A. (1985). A theoretical developmental model: Self-images in children. In L. C. Shulman, L. C. R. Restaino-Baumann, & L. Butler (Eds.), *The future of Piagetian theory: The neo-Piagetians.* New York: Plenum Press.

Mukherjee, S., Shukla, S., Woodle, J., et al. (1983). Misdiagnosis of schizophrenia in bipolar patients: A multiethnic comparison. *American Journal of Psychiatry, 140,* 1571–1574.

Mundy-Castle, A. C., & Okonji, M. O. (1976). *Mother-infant interaction in Nigeria.* Unpublished manuscript, University of Lagos.

Munroe, R. H., & Munroe, R. L. (1971). Household density and infant care in East African Society. *Journal of Social Psychology, 83,* 3–13.

Munroe, R. H., Munroe, R. L., & Whiting, B. B. (Eds.). (1981). *Handbook of cross-cultural human development.* New York: Garland Press.

Murdock, G. P. (1945). The common denominator of culture. In R. Linton (Ed.), *The science of man in world crisis* New York: Columbia University Press.

Murdock, G. P. (1971). *Outline of cultural material* (4th rev. ed). New Haven, CT: HRAF Press.

Murdock, G. P. (1975). *Outline of world cultures* (5th ed.). New Haven, CT: HRAF Press.

Murphy, H. B. M. (1982). *Comparative psychiatry*. Berlin: Springer-Verlag.

Murphy, H. B. M., & Raman, A. C. (1971). The chronicity of schizophrenia in indigenous tropical peoples. *British Journal of Psychiatry, 118,* 489–497.

Murphy, H. B. M., Wittkower, E. W., & Chance, N. A. (1967). Cross-cultural inquiry into the symptomatology of depression: A preliminary report. *International Journal of Psychiatry, 3,* 6–15.

Muse, C. J. (1991). Women in Western Samoa. In L. L. Adler (Ed.), *Women in cross-cultural perspective* (pp. 221–240). New York: Praeger.

Musgrave, W., & Sison, A. (1910). Mali-mali: A mimic psychosis in the Philippine Islands. *Philippine Journal of Sciences, 5,* 335.

Myerhoff, B. (1978). Aging and the aged in other cultures: An anthropological perspective. In E. Bauwers (Ed.), *The anthropology of health*. St. Louis: C. V. Mosby.

Myers, C. S. (1903). Smell. *Reports of the Cambridge Anthropological Expedition to Torres Strait, 2,* 169–185.

Myers, D. G. (1990). *Social psychology* (3rd ed.). New York: McGraw-Hill.

Myers, D. G. (1993). *Social psychology* (4th ed.). New York: McGraw-Hill.

Nagaswami, V. (1990). Integration of psychosocial rehabilitation in national health care programmes. *Psychosocial Rehabilitation Journal, 14,* 53–65.

Nakane, C. (1970). *Japanese society*. Berkeley: University of California Press.

Naroll, R. (1970). The culture-bearing unit in cross-cultural surveys. In R. Naroll & R. Cohen (Eds.), *A handbook of method in cultural anthropology* (pp. 721–765). New York: Natural History Press. (Reprinted: New York: Columbia University Press, 1973.)

Naroll, R. (1971a). *Conceptualizing the problem, as seen by an anthropologist*. Paper presented at the American Political Science Association Annual Meeting, Chicago.

Naroll, R. (1971b). The double language boundary in cross-cultural surveys. *Behavioral Science Notes, 6,* 95–102.

Naroll, R. (1983). *The moral order: An introduction to the human situation*. Beverly Hills, CA: Sage.

Nason, J. D. (1981). Respected elder or old person: Aging in a Micronesian community. In P. T. Amoss & S. Harrell (Eds.), *Other ways of growing old* (pp. 155–174). Stanford, CA: Stanford University Press.

National Institute of Mental Health. (1990). *Clinical training in serious mental illness* (DHHS Pub. No. ADM 90–1679). Washington, DC: Superintendent of Documents, U.S. Government Printing Office.

Neugarten, B., and Bengtson, V. (1968). Cross-national studies of adulthood and aging. In E. Shanas & J. Madge (Eds.), *Methodological problems in cross-national studies in aging* (pp. 18–36). Basel: Karger.

Neugarten, B., Moore, J., & Lowe, J. (1965). Age norms, age constraints, and adult socialization. *American Journal of Sociology, 70,* 710–717.

Neugarten, B., & Neugarten, D. (1986). Age in the aging society. *Journal of the American Academy of Arts and Sciences, 115,* 31–49.

Nicholson, J. R., & Seddon, G. M. (1977). The influence of secondary depth cues on the understanding by Nigerian schoolboys of spatial relationships in pictures. *British Journal of Psychology 68,* 327–333.

Norman, W. T. (1963). Toward an adequate taxonomy of personality attributes. *Journal of Abnormal and Social Psychology, 66,* 574–583.

Nyiti, R. M. (1982). The validity of "cultural differences explanations" for cross-cultural variation in the rate of Piagetian cognitive development. In D. A. Wagner & H. W. Stevenson (Eds.), *Cultural perspectives on child development.* San Francisco: W. H. Freeman.

Odejide, A. O. (1979). Cross-cultural psychiatry: A myth or reality? *Comprehensive Psychiatry, 20,* 103–108.

Okafor, N. A. O. (1991). Some traditional aspects of Nigerian women. In L. L. Adler (Ed.), *Women in cross-cultural perspective* (pp. 135–141). New York: Praeger.

Olmsted, P. R., & Weikart, D. P. (1989). *How nations serve young children: Profiles of child care and education in 14 countries.* Ypsilanti, MI: High/Scope Press.

Orasanu, J., Slater, M. K., & Adler, L. L. (Eds.). (1979). *Language, sex and gender: Does la différence make a difference?* New York: New York Academy of Sciences. *Annals of the New York Academy of Sciences, 237.*

Osgood, C. E. (1967). Cross-cultural comparability in attitude measurement via multilingual semantic differentials. In M. Fishbein (Ed.), *Readings in attitude theory and measurement.* New York: Wiley.

Osgood, C. E., May, M. H., & Miron, M. S. (1975). *Cross-cultural universals of affective meaning.* Urbana: University of Illinois Press.

Osgood, C. E., Suci, G. J., & Tannenbaum, P. H. (1967). *The measurement of meaning.* Urbana: University of Illinois Press.

Palmore, E., & Manton, K. (1974). Modernization and the status of the aged: International correlations. *Journal of Gerontology, 25,* 205–210.

Pareek, U., & Rao, T. V. (1980). Cross-cultural surveys and interviewing. In H. C. Triandis & J. W. Berry (Eds.), *Handbook of cross-cultural psychology: Vol. 2. Methodology.* Boston: Allyn & Bacon.

Paris, J. (1991). Personality disorders, parasuicide, and culture. *Transcultural Psychiatric Research Review, 28,* 25–39.

Park, J. Y., & Johnson, R. C. (1984). Moral development in rural and urban Korea. *Journal of Cross-Cultural Psychology, 15,* 35–46.

Pepitone, A. (1976). Toward a normative and comparative biocultural social psychology. *Journal of Personality and Social Psychology, 4,* 641–653.

Pepitone, A. (1981). Lessons from the history of social psychology. *American Psychologist, 9,* 972–985.

Pepitone, A. (1986). Culture and the cognitive paradigm in social psychology. *Australian Journal of Psychology, 3,* 245–256.

Pepitone, A., & Triandis, H. (1987). On the universality of social psychological theories. *Journal of Cross-Cultural Psychology, 4,* 471–498.

Petzold, M. (1983). *Developmental psychology and the Third World: Some preliminary considerations.* Paper presented at the Biennial meeting of the International Society for the Study of Behavioural Development, Munich, West Germany.

Philip, H., & Kelly, M. (1974). Product and process in cognitive development: Some comparative data on the performance of school age children in different cultures. *British Journal of Educational Psychology, 44,* 248–265.

Piaget, J. (1972). Intellectual evolution from adolescence to adulthood. *Human Development, 15,* 1–12.

Price-Williams, D. (1979). Modes of thought in cross-cultural psychology: An historical overview. In A. J. Marsella, R. G. Tharp, & T. J. Ciborowski (Eds.), *Perspectives on cross-cultural psychology*. New York: Academic Press.

Prince, R. N. (1980). Variations in psychotherapeutic procedures. In H. C. Triandis & J. G. Draguns (Eds.), *Handbook of cross-cultural psychology: Vol. 6. Psychopathology* (pp. 291–349). Boston: Allyn & Bacon.

Prince, R. (1985). The concept of culture-bound syndromes: Anorexia nervosa and brain fag. *Social Science and Medicine, 21,* 197–203.

Raphael, D., & Davis, F. (1985). *Only mothers know: Patterns of infant feeding in traditional cultures*. Westport, CT: Greenwood Press.

Resnick, L. B. (1989). Developing mathematical knowledge. *American Psychologist, 44,* 162–169.

Rest, J. (1979). *Development in judging moral issues*. Minneapolis: University of Minnesota Press.

Rest, J. (1983). Morality. In P. Mussen (Ed.), *Handbook of child psychology: Vol. 4. Cognitive development* (pp. 556–629). New York: Wiley.

Rest, J. (1986a). *Manual for the Defining Issues Test: An objective test of moral development* (3rd ed.). Minneapolis: Center for the Study of Ethical Development. University of Minnesota.

Rest, J. (1986b). *Moral development: Advances in research and theory*. New York: Praeger.

Reynolds, C. R., Kamphaus, R. W., & Rosenthal, B. L. (1988). Factor analysis of the Stanford-Binet Fourth Edition for ages 2 years through 23 years. *Measurement and Evaluation in Counseling and Development, 21,* 52–63.

Rivers, W. H. R. (1901). Vision. In *Physiology and psychology: Part 1. Reports of the Cambridge Anthropological Expedition to Torres Strait*. Cambridge: Cambridge University Press.

Rivers, W. H. R. (1905). Observations on the senses of the Todas. *British Journal of Psychology, 1,* 321–396.

Robinson, J. P., Shaver, P. R., & Wrightsman, L. S. (Eds.). (1991). *Measures of personality and social psychological attitudes*. San Diego: Academic.

Rodrigues, A. (1982). Replication: A neglected type of research in social psychology. *Interamerican Journal of Psychology, 16,* 91–109.

Roetz, H. (forthcoming). Kohlberg and Chinese morality: A philosophical perspective. In U. P. Gielen, T. Lei, & E. Miao (Eds.), *Chinese morality: Values, reasoning, and education*.

Rogers, R., Rogers, A., & Belanger, A. (1992). Disability-free life among the elderly in the United States. *Journal of Aging and Health, 4,* 19–42.

Rogoff, B., & Morelli, G. (1989). Perspectives on children's development from cultural psychology. *American Psychologist, 44,* 343–348.

Rohner, R. P., Naroll, R., Barry, H., Divale, W., Erickson, E., Schaefer, J., & Sipes, R. (1978). Guidelines for holocultural research. *Current Anthropology, 19*(1), 128–129.

Rosch, E. (1975). Universals and cultural specifics in human categorization. In R. Brislin, S. Bochner, & W. Lonner (Eds.), *Cross-cultural perspectives on learning*. New York: Halstad-Sage.

Rotter, J. B. (1966). Generalized expectancies for internal versus external control of reinforcement. *Psychological Monographs, 80* (Whole No. 609).

Rulon, P. J. (1953). A semantic test of intelligence. *Proceedings, 1952 Invitational Conference on Testing Problems*. Princeton, NJ: Educational Testing Service.

Ruiz, P., & Langrod, J. (1976). The role of folk healers in community mental health services. *Community Mental Health Journal, 12*, 392–398.

Russell, J. G. (1989). Anxiety disorders in Japan: A review of the Japanese literature on *shinkeishitsu* and *taijin kyofusho*. *Culture, Medicine, and Psychiatry, 13*, 391–403.

Sadoun, R., Lolli, G., & Silverman, M. (1965). *Drinking in French culture*. New Brunswick, NJ: Rutgers Center of Alcohol Studies.

Saffiotti, Luisa (1990). *The selective use of beliefs to interpret major life events*. (Unpublished doctoral dissertation, University of Pennsylvania, Philadelphia.)

Safir, M. P., & Izraeli, D. N. (1991). Growing up female. A life-span perspective on women in Israel. In L. L. Adler (Ed.), *Women in cross-cultural perspective* (pp. 90–105). New York: Praeger.

Salisbury, R. (1966). Possession in the New Guinea Highlands: Review of literature. *Transcultural Research*.

Samovar, L. A., & Porter, R. E. (Eds.). (1982). *Intercultural communication: A reader*. 3rd ed. Belmore, CA: Wadsworth Publishing.

Sandoval, M. (1979). *Santeria* as a mental health care system: An historical overview. *Social Science & Medicine, 13B*(2), 137–151.

Sapir, E. (1933). The psychological reality of phonemes. In D. Mandelbaum (Ed.), *The Selected Writings of Edward Sapir*. Berkeley: University of California Press.

Sapir, E. (1949). *Culture, language and personality*. Berkeley: University of California Press.

Sartorius, N., & Harding, T. W. (1983). The WHO Collaborative Study on Strategies for Extending Mental Health Care: I. The genesis of the study. *American Journal of Psychiatry, 140*, 1470–1473.

Sartorius, N., Jablensky, A., Korten, A., Ernberg, G., Anker, M., Cooper, J. E., & Day, R. (1986). Early manifestations and first contact incidence of schizophrenia in different cultures: A preliminary report on the initial evaluation phase of the WHO Collaborative Study on Determinants of Outcome of Severe Mental Disorders. *Psychological Medicine, 16*, 909–928.

Sartorius, N., Shapiro, R., & Jablensky, A. (1974). The international pilot study of schizophrenia. *Schizophrenia Bulletin, 11*, 21–34.

Saussure, F. de (1959). *Course in general linguistics*. New York: The Philosophical Library.

Saville-Troike, M. (1982). *The ethnography of communication*. Oxford: Basil Blackwell.

Saxe, G. B. (1991). *Culture and cognitive development: Studies in mathematical understanding*. Hillsdale, NJ: Erlbaum.

Schmid-Kitsikis, E. (1985). Clinical investigations and Piagetian experimentation. In V. L. Shulman, L. C. R. Restaino-Baumann, & L. Butler (Eds.), *The future of Piagetian theory: The neo-Piagetians*. New York: Plenum Press.

Schwartz, T. (1981). The acquisition of culture. *Ethos, 9*, 4–17.

Schwendler, W. (1984). UNESCO's project on the exchange of knowledge for endogenous development. In D. Sinha & W. H. Holtzman (Eds.), *The Impact of psychology on Third World development*. Special Issue of the *International Journal of Psychology, 19*(1–2), 3–15.

Sechrest, L. (1970). Experiments in the field. In R. Naroll & R. Cohen (Eds.), *A handbook of method in cultural anthropology* (pp. 196–209). Garden City, NY: Natural History Press.

Sechrest, L. (1975). Another look at unobtrusive measures: An alternative to what? In W. Sinaiko & L. Broedling (Eds.), *Perspectives on attitude assessment: Surveys and their alternatives.* Washington, DC: Smithsonian Institution.

Sechrest, L. (Ed.). (1979). *Unobtrusive measurement today: New directions for methodology of behavioral science.* San Francisco: Jossey-Bass.

Sechrest, L., Fay, T., & Zaidi, H. (1972). Problems of translation in cross-cultural research, *Journal of Cross-Cultural Psychology, 3,* 41–56.

Sechrest, L., Fay, T., Zaidi, H., & Florez, L. (1973). Attitudes toward mental disorder among college students in the United States, Pakistan, and the Philippines. *Journal of Cross-Cultural Psychology, 4,* 342–360.

Segall, M. H. (1979). *Cross-cultural psychology: Human behavior in global perspective.* Monterey, CA: Brooks/Cole.

Segall, M. H. (1986). Culture and behavior: Psychology in global perspective. *Annual Review of Psychology, 37,* 523–564.

Segall, M. H. (1989). Foreword. In L. L. Adler, Ed., *Cross-cultural research in human development: Life span perspectives.* New York: Praeger.

Segall, M. H., Dasen, P. R., Berry, J. W., & Poortinga, Y. P. (1990). *Human behavior in global perspective: An introduction to cross-cultural psychology.* New York: Pergamon Press.

Segalowitz, N. S. (1981). Issues in the cross-cultural study of bilingual development. In H. C. Triandis & A. Heron (Eds.), *Handbook of cross-cultural psychology: Vol 4. Developmental psychology.* Boston: Allyn & Bacon.

Selvini Palazzoli, M. (1985). Anorexia nervosa: A syndrome of the affluent society. *Transcultural Psychiatric Research Review, 22*(3), 199–205.

Sexton, V. S., & Hogan, J. D. (Eds.) (1992). *International psychology: Views from around the world.* Lincoln: University of Nebraska Press.

Shankar, R., & Menon, M. S. (1991). Interventions with families of people with schizophrenia: The issues facing a community-based rehabilitation center in India. *Psychosocial Rehabilitation Journal 15,* 85–90.

Sherif, M., & Sherif, C. W. (1969). *Social psychology.* New York: Harper & Row.

Shouksmith, G. (1992). Psychology in New Zealand. In V. S. Sexton & J. D. Hogan (Eds.), *International psychology: Views from around the world.* Lincoln: University of Nebraska Press.

Shrimali, S., & Broota, K. (1987). Effect of surgical stress on belief in God and superstition. *Journal of Personality and Clinical Studies, 2,* 135–138.

Shulman, V. L., Restaino-Bauman, L. C. R., & Butler, L. (Eds.), (1985). *The future of Piagetian theory: The neo-Piagetians.* New York: Plenum Press.

Sigel, I. E. (1988). Cross-cultural studies of parental influence on children's achievement. *Human Development, 31,* 384–390.

Sigel, I. E., & Parke, R. D. (1987). Structural analysis of parent-child research models. *Journal of Applied Developmental Psychology, 8,* 123–127.

Silver, S. O., & Pollack, R. H. (1967). Racial differences in pigmentation of the fundus oculi. *Psychonomic Science, 7,* 159–160.

Silverman, P. (1987). *The elderly as modern pioneers.* Bloomington: Indiana University Press.

Silverman, P., & Maxwell, R. (1978). How do I respect thee? Let me count the ways: Deference towards elderly men and women. *Behavior Science Research, 13,* 91–108.

Simmons, L. (1945). *The role of the aged in primitive society.* New Haven, CT: Yale University Press.

Simmons, L. (1960). Aging in preindustrial societies. In C. Tibbitts (Ed.), *Handbook of social gerontology.* Chicago: University of Chicago Press.

Simpson, E. L. (1974). Moral development research: A case study of scientific cultural bias. *Human Development, 17,* 81–106.

Singhal, U., & Mrinal, N. R. (1991). Tribal women of India: The Tharu women. In L. L. Adler (Ed.), *Women in cross-cultural perspective* (pp. 160–173). New York: Praeger.

Sinha, D., & Holtzman, W. H. (1984). Foreword, In D. Sinha & W. H. Holtzman (Eds.), *The impact of psychology on Third World development* (p. 1). Special Issue of the *International Journal of Psychology, 19* (1–2).

Skolnick, A. S., & Skolnick, J. H. (1989). *Family in transition* (6th ed.). Boston: Little, Brown.

Skultans, V. (1991). Anthropology and psychiatry: The uneasy alliance. *Transcultural Psychiatric Research Review, 28,* 5–25.

Small, S. A., Zeldin, R. S., & Savin-Williams, R. C. (1981). *Professional behavior: A case for consistency.* Paper presented at the Annual Meeting of the Western Psychological Association, Los Angeles, CA.

Snarey, J. (1985). Cross-cultural universality of social-moral development: A critical review of Kohlbergian research. *Psychological Bulletin, 97,* 202–232.

Snarey, J., & Keljo, K. (1991). In a *Gemeinschaft* voice: The cross-cultural expansion of moral development theory. In W. Kurtines & J. Gewirtz (Eds.), *Handbook of moral behavior and development: Vol. 1. Theory* (pp. 395–424). Hillsdale, NJ: Erlbaum.

Snyder, C. R. (1958). *Alcohol and the Jews.* Glencoe, IL: Free Press.

Spence, J. T., & Helmreich, R. L. (1978). *Masculinity and femininity: Their psychological dimensions, correlates and antecedents.* Austin: University of Texas Press.

Spradley, J. P. (1968). A cognitive analysis of tramp behavior. In Proceedings of the Eighth International Congress of Anthropological and Ethnological Sciences. Tokyo: Japan Science Council.

Spradley, J. P. (1970). *You owe yourself a drunk: An ethnography of Urban nomads.* Boston: Little, Brown.

Spradley, J. P. (1971). Beating the drunk charge. In J. P. Spradley & D. W. McCurdy (Eds.), *Conformity and conflict: Readings in cultural anthropology,* pp. 351–358. Boston: Little, Brown.

Spradley, J. P. (1979). *The ethnographic interview.* New York: Holt, Rinehart and Winston.

Spradley, J. P. (1980). *Participant observation.* New York: Holt, Rinehart and Winston.

Spradley, J. P., & Mann, B. (1975). *The cocktail waitress: Women's work in a male world.* New York: Wiley.

Stevenson, H. W., Lee, S. Y., Chen, C., Stigler, J. W., Hsu, C. C., & Kitamura, S. (1990). Contexts of achievement: A study of American, Chinese, and Japanese children. *Monographs of the Society for Research in Child Development, 55*(1–2), Serial No. 221.

Stevenson, H. W., Lee, S., & Stigler, J. W. (1986). Mathematics achievement of Chinese, Japanese, and American children. *Science, 231*, 693–698.

Stivers, R. (1976). *A hair of the dog: Irish drinking and American stereotype.* University Park: Pennsylvania University Press.

Sudanow (1985, March). Sudanese monthly magazine, March, p. 7.

Super, C. M., & Harkness, S. (1986). The developmental niche: A conceptualization of the interface of child and culture. *International Journal of Behavioral Development, 9*, 545–570.

Swales, J. (1985). English language papers and author's first language: Preliminary explorations. *Scientometrics, 8*, 91–101.

Sweetland, R. C., & Keyser, D. J. (1983). *Tests.* Kansas City, MO: Test Corporation of America.

Symonds, P. M. (1939). *The psychology of parent-child relationships.* New York: Appleton-Century.

Szasz, T. (1961). *The myth of mental illness.* New York: Hoeber-Harper.

Tajfel, H. (1982). Social psychology of intergroup relations. *Annual Review of Psychology, 33*, 1–39.

Takooshian, H. (1985). Non-verbal reasoning. In D. J. Keyser & R. C. Sweetland (Eds.), *Test critiques* (vol. 4, pp. 463–468). Kansas City, MO: Test Corporation of America.

Takooshian, H. (1991). Soviet women. In L. L. Adler (Ed.), *Women in cross-cultural perspective.* (pp. 79–88) New York: Praeger.

Tanaka-Matsumi, J. (1979). *Taijin-kyofusho:* Diagnostic and cultural issues in Japanese psychiatry. *Culture, Medicine, and Psychiatry, 3*, 231–245.

Tapp, J. L. (1981). Studying personality development. In H. C. Triandis & A. Heron (Eds.), *Handbook of cross-cultural psychology: Vol. 4. Developmental psychology, 4.* (pp. 343–423). Boston: Allyn & Bacon.

Tarde, G. (1903). *The laws of imitation.* New York: Holt.

Terpstra, V., & Kenneth, D. (1985). *The cultural environment of international business* (2nd ed.). Cincinnati: South-Western Publishing.

Thoma, S. (1986). Estimating gender differences in the comprehension and preference of moral issues. *Developmental Review, 6*, 165–180.

Thomas, E., & Chamber, K. (1989). Phenomenology of life satisfaction among elderly men: Quantitative and qualitative views. *Psychology and Aging, 4*, 284–289.

Thorndike, R. L., Hagen, E. P., & Sattler, J. M. (1986). *Technical manual for the Stanford-Binet Intelligence Scale: Fourth Edition.* Chicago: Riverside.

Thouless, R. H. (1933). A racial difference in perception. *Journal of Social Psychology, 4*, 330–339.

Tomkins, S. S. (1962). *Affect, imagery, consciousness: Vol. 1. The positive affects.* New York: Springer.

Tomkins, S. S. (1963). *Affect, imagery, consciousness: Vol. 2. The negative affects.* New York: Springer.

Trevor-Roper, H. (1967). The European witchcraze of the sixteenth and seventeenth centuries. In *The crisis of the seventeenth century.* New York: Harper & Row.

Triandis, H. C. (1972). *The analysis of subjective culture.* New York: Wiley.

234   References

Triandis, H. C. (1988, September 2). *A strategy for cross-cultural research in social psychology.* Invited address, International Congress of Scientific Psychology, Sydney, Australia.

Triandis, H. C., Bontempo, R., Villareal, M. J., Asai, M., & Lucca, N. (1988). Individualism and collectivism: Cross-cultural perspectives on self-ingroup relationships. *Journal of Personality and Social Psychology, 54,* 323–338.

Triandis, H. C., & Heron, A. (Eds.). (1981). *Handbook of cross-cultural psychology: Developmental psychology, 4.* Boston: Allyn & Bacon.

Triandis, H. C., Lambert, W. W., Berry, J. W., Brislin, R. W., Draguns, J., Lonner, W., & Heron, A. (Eds.). (1980). *Handbook of cross-cultural psychology* (6 vols.). Boston: Allyn & Bacon.

Triandis, H. C., Malpass, R. S., & Davidson, A. (1972). Cross-cultural psychology. *Biennial Review of Anthropology,* 1–84.

Tseng, W. S., & McDermott, J. F. (1981). *Culture, mind, and therapy.* New York: Brunner/Mazel.

Tylor, E. B. (1889). On a method of investigating the development of institutions: Applied to laws of marriage and descent. *Journal of the Anthropological Institute of Great Britain and Ireland, 18,* 245–269.

Tyson, G. A., Doctor, E. A., & Mentis, M. (1988). A psycholinguistic perspective on bilinguals' discrepant questionnaire responses. *Journal of Cross-Cultural Psychology, 19,* 413–426.

Utena, H., & Niwa, S-I. (1992). The history of schizophrenia research in Japan, *Schizophrenia Bulletin, 18,* 67–84.

Uzgiris, I. C., & Hunt, J. McV. (1975). *Assessment in infancy: Ordinal scales of psychological development.* Urbana: University of Illinois Press.

Uzoka, A. F. (1979). The myth of the nuclear family: Historical background and clinical implications. *American Psychologist, 34,* 1095–1106.

Valsiner, J. (1989). *Human development and culture.* Lexington, MA: Lexington Books.

Van Brero, P. (1895). Latah. *Journal of Mental Science, 41,* 537–538.

Vasudev, J., & Hummel, R. (1987). Moral stage sequence and principled reasoning in an Indian sample. *Human Development, 30,* 105–118.

Veness, H., & Hoskin, J. O. (1968). Psychiatry in New Britain: A note on the "fruit tree experiment" as a measure of effect of language on association processes. *Social Science and Medicine, 1,* 419–424.

Vine, I. (1986). Moral maturity in socio-cultural perspective: Are Kohlberg's stages universal? In S. Modgil & C. Modgil (Eds.), *Lawrence Kohlberg: Consensus and controversy* (pp. 431–450). London: Falmer Press.

Wallace, A. F. C. (1965). The problem of the psychological validity of componential analysis. *American Anthropologist, 67*(5), Part 2, 229–248.

Watson, W. (1983). *A study of factors affecting the development of moral judgement.* Unpublished manuscript, Monash Chirering, Victoria, Australia.

Werner, E. E. (1979). *Cross-cultural child development: A view from the planet earth.* Monterey, CA: Brooks/Cole.

Werner, E. E. (1988). A cross-cultural perspective on infancy. *Journal of Cross-cultural Psychology, 19,* 96–113.

Werner, O., & Campbell, B. T. (1970). Translating, working through interpreters, and the problem of decentering. In R. Narroll & R. Cohens (Eds.), *A hand-*

book of method in cross-cultural anthropology (pp. 398–420). New York: Natural History Press.

Westermeyer, J. (1989). Psychiatric epidemiology across cultures: Current issues and trends. *Transcultural Psychiatric Research Review, 26,* 5–25.

White, M. (1987). *The Japanese educational challenge: A commitment to children.* New York: Free Press.

Whiting, B. B. (1963). *Six cultures: Studies of child rearing.* New York: Wiley.

Whiting, B. B., & Edwards, C. P. (1988). *Children of different worlds.* Cambridge, MA: Harvard University Press.

Whiting, B. B., & Whiting, J. W. M. (1975). *Children of six cultures: A psychocultural analysis.* Cambridge, MA: Harvard University Press.

Whiting, J. W. M., & Child, I. L. (1953). *Child training and personality.* New Haven, CT: Yale University Press.

Whiting, J. W. M., & Whiting, B. B. (1978). A strategy for psychocultural research. In G. D. Spindler (Ed.), *The making of psychological anthropology.* Berkeley: University of California Press.

Wiener, M. (1989). Psychopathology reconsidered: Depressions interpreted as psychosocial transactions. *Clinical Psychology Review, 9,* 295–322.

Wilder, D., & Gurland, B. (1989). Cross-cultural comparison of disability and depression among older persons in four community-based probability samples. In L. L. Adler (Ed.). *Cross-cultural research in human development: Life-span perspectives.* New York: Praeger.

Wilson, E. O. (1978). *On human nature.* Cambridge, MA: Harvard University Press.

Witkin, H. A. (1975). Psychological differentiation in cross-cultural perspective. *Journal of Cross-Cultural Psychology, 6,* 4–87.

World Health Organization. (1973). *Report of the International Pilot Study of Schizophrenia.* Geneva: Author.

World Health Organization. (1979). *Schizophrenia: An international follow-up study.* New York: Wiley.

World Health Organization. (1983). *Depressive disorders in different cultures: Report of the WHO collaborative study of standardized assessment of depressive disorders.* Geneva: Author.

World Health Organization. (1990). Report of a World Health Organization (WHO) Meeting on Consumer Involvement in Mental Health Services, Mannheim, Federal Republic of Germany, November 9–12, 1988. *Psychosocial Rehabilitation Journal, 14,* 13–20.

Wundt, W. (1910–1920). *Völkerpsychologie: Eine Untersuchung der Entwicklungsgesetze von Sprache, Mythos, und Sitte* (Vols. 1–10). Leipzig: Engelmann.

Yap, P. M. (1951). Mental disease peculiar to certain cultures: A survey of comparative psychiatry. *Journal of Mental Science, 97,* 313–327.

Yap, P. M. (1965). Phenomenology of affective disorder in Chinese and other cultures. In A. deReuck & R. Porter (Eds.), *Transcultural psychiatry.* Boston: Little, Brown.

Yegorov, V. F. (1992). And how is it over there, across the ocean? *Schizophrenia Bulletin, 18,* 7–14.

Yu, L. (1989). Cross-cultural perspective of the changing role of the care provider for the aged in a Chinese context. In L. L. Adler (Ed.), *Cross-cultural research in human development: Life-span perspectives.* New York: Praeger.

Yu, L. C., & Carpenter, L. (1991). Women in China. In L. L. Adler (Ed.), *Women in cross-cultural perspective.* (pp. 189–203). New York: Praeger.

Yucun, S., Changhui, C., Weixi, Z., Tingming, X., & Yunhua, T. (1990). An example of a community based mental health/home-care programme: Haidian District in the suburbs of Beijing, China. *Psychosocial Rehabilitation Journal, 14,* 29–34.

Zatrick, D. F., & Lu, F. G. (1991). The ethnic/minority focus unit as a training site in transcultural psychiatry. *Academic Psychiatry, 15,* 218–225.

Zeira, Yoram, & Moshe Banai. (1985). Selection of expatriate managers in MNCs: The host-environment point of view. *International Studies of Management & Organization,* Spring, 33–51.

Zeldine, G., Ahvi, R., Leuckx, R., Boussat, M., Saibou, A., Hanck, C., Collignon, R., Tourame, G., & Collomb, H. (1975). A propos de l'utilisation d'une échelle d'évaluation en psychiatrie transculturelle. *L'Encéphale, 1,* 133–145.

Zhernova, L. (1991). Women in the USSR. In L. L. Adler (Ed.), *Women in cross-cultural perspective* (pp. 68–77). New York: Praeger.

Index

Page numbers appearing in **bold** print denote pages containing notes or tables.

Unity of the human race. *See* Panhuman validity

Visual acuity research, 21
Visual Attitude Scale, 39
Völkerpsycholgie (folk psychology), 17
Voodoo, 185, 186

Wechsler scale, 54
Western Samoa: culture variations in, 20, 97; elderly in, 100; female education in, 94; women in power in, 92
Whiting, J.M.V., 19
WHO. *See* World Health Organization (WHO)
Whorf, Benjamin: language and, 47–48; Sapir influence on, 19
Whorfian hypothesis, 3
Windingo (cannibalistic frenzy), 172
Witchcraft, 144
Women: antecedent activities, feminist movement and, 91; cross-cultural

consideration of, 91–92; education and, 92–94; elderly, 98–100; families and, 97; in government, 91–92; in international management, 160–161; mate selection, marriage arrangements and, 94–97; overview of, 89–91, 100–101; in the workplace, 97
World Health Organization (WHO): community health care in developing countries and, 181; current attitudes, projects of, 197–199; indigenous healing with Western medicine, 185; schizophrenia research by, 166–168, 172, 180, 187–188
Wundt, Wilhelm, 17

Zambian sensorimotor intelligence research, 66
Zeitschrift für Völkerpsycholgie und Sprachwissenschaft (Journal of Folk Psychology and Language Science), 17

About the Editors and Contributors

LEONORE LOEB ADLER is the Director of the Institute for Cross-Cultural and Cross-Ethnic Studies and Professor Emerita in the Department of Psychology at Molloy College, Rockville Centre, New York. Dr. Adler is active in many professional organizations and recently was elected to the American Psychological Association's (APA) Committee on International Relations in Psychology. She is a Fellow of The New York Academy of Sciences, the APA's Divisions 1 and 35, and the American Psychological Society. Dr. Leonore Loeb Adler was for the past 30 years and is currently involved in several cross-cultural and cross-national research projects; she has published over 70 professional papers and chapters and is the author, editor, or coeditor of 14 books.

JOHN BEATTY is a Professor of Anthropology at Brooklyn College of the City University of New York. Dr. Beatty has held two Invited Professorships: in 1986 at the Universität des Saarlandes in Saarbrücken, Germany, and in 1991 at Ohu University in Koriyama, Japan. Dr. Beatty has written many articles on a variety of scientific topics and has contributed chapters to numerous edited works; in addition, he has published six books.

JUSTIN P. CAREY is Distinguished Professor of Management and Chair of the Department at St. John's University. He is a past president of the New York State Psychological Association (NYSPA) and of the Division of State Association Affairs of the American Psychological Association. Since 1981 he has been Executive Editor of *Psychology & Marketing* and has lectured, consulted, and presented his research on six continents. He was the guest of the Polish Academy of Sciences in Warsaw in 1991 and is currently completing a three-year project on the dynamics of entrepreneurship in Poland, the Czech and Slovak Federated Republic, and Lithuania.

FLORENCE L. DENMARK is the Robert Scott Pace Professor of Psychology at Pace University, where she is Chair of the Department of Psychology. She was president of the American Psychological Association, 1980–1981; the Eastern Psychological Association, 1985–1986; the New York State Psychological Association, 1972–1973; the International Council of Psychologists, 1989–1990; and Psi Chi, the National Honor Society in Psychology, 1978–1980. In addition, she has served as vice-president of the New York Academy of Sciences and the International Organization for the Study of Group Tensions and is currently a member of the Advisory Board of the Institute for Cross-Cultural and Cross-Ethnic Studies, Molloy College. Dr. Denmark has been the Thomas Hunter Professor of Psychology at Hunter College of the City University of New York. She has authored or edited 16 books and monographs and has written numerous chapters and articles.

ROGELIO DIAZ-GUERRERO is Research Professor, Faculty of Psychology at the National University of Mexico. He is also a member of the Advisory Board of the Institute for Cross-Cultural and Cross-Ethnic Studies at Molloy College. He has initiated research on Mexican culture and personality, as well as cross-cultural research. Besides having written many papers and books in psychology applied to Mexican problems, Dr. Diaz-Guerrero has made extensive contributions to research in the areas of culture and personality and cross-cultural psychology. Some highlights include Holtzman, Diaz-Guerrero, and Swartz, *Personality Development in Two Cultures* (1975); Diaz-Guerrero and Diaz-Loving, "Interpretation in Cross-Cultural Personality Assessment" (1990); Diaz-Guerrero and Szalay, *Understanding Mexicans and Americans* (1991).

ROLANDO DIAZ-LOVING is Professor in the Faculty of Psychology of the National University of Mexico, where he is also acting as Head of the Social Psychology Program and the Graduate School. His research interests span from applied work in the area contraceptive behavior and AIDS to basic research of couple relationships, personality, and cross-cultural psychology. In these areas he has published over 100 journal articles and chapters in specialized books. He is cofounder and past president of the Mexican Association of Social Psychology and cofounder and vice-president of the Mexican Institute of Family and Population Research.

LEONARD W. DOOB is Sterling Professor Emeritus in Psychology at Yale University. He is also Associate Director of the South African Research Program and Senior Research Associate at the Institute of Social and Policy

Studies. In addition, he is Editor of the *Journal of Social Psychology* and coeditor of the *Journal of Psychology*. Dr. Doob is a member of many professional organizations. He has authored, co-authored, and edited many journal articles, books, and other publications.

JURIS G. DRAGUNS is Professor of Psychology at The Pennsylvania State University. He has held research and clinical posts at Rochester State Hospital and Worcester State Hospital. He taught at Clark University and spent sabbaticals at the Johannes Gutenberg University in Mainz, Germany; East-West Center in Honolulu, Hawaii; Flinders University in Bedford Park, South Australia; and the Taiwan National University in Taipei. Dr. Draguns' research interests include cultural influences upon complex social behavior, especially in relation to psychological disturbance.

CYNTHIA L. FRAZIER is a clinical psychologist in private practice in Manhattan and Carmel, New York. In her work locally and abroad Dr. Frazier studies the influence of culture upon behavior and the determination of psychopathology. In 1984 she presented a minicourse on behavior therapy in Port-au-Prince sponsored by the Haitian Association of Mental Health. Later she and Dr. Chavannes Douyon conducted a cross-cultural study on social support in the elderly published in *Cross-Cultural Research in Human Development: Life-Span Perspectives,* edited by Dr. Leonore Loeb Adler (1989). Dr. Frazier currently teaches at the university level, consults with organizations and hospitals on therapeutic programming and management strategies, and conducts cross-cultural research. She has presented her findings internationally and has published several articles in the area of aging, Alzheimer's disease, and culture. Presently she is conducting a study on couple therapy in Indonesia.

HARRY W. GARDINER is Professor of Psychology at the University of Wisconsin-LaCrosse. He has been engaged in training, teaching, and research in Europe, Asia, and the United States of America. Dr. Gardiner has published more than 60 articles in professional journals and has presented research papers at numerous international meetings. He is coauthor of *Child and Adolescent Development* and is currently working on *Understanding Cross-Cultural Psychology.*

UWE P. GIELEN is Professor of Psychology and International Cultural Studies at St. Francis College and served as Chairman of its Psychology Department from 1980 to 1990. At present, he is coordinating a study of moral reasoning among students from twelve countries. He is coauthor of *The Kohlberg Legacy for the Helping Professions* (1991) and coeditor of *Psychology in International Perspective* (1992) and *Advancing Psychology and its Applications: International Perspectives* (1994). Professor Gielen is president

(1994–1995) of the International Council of Psychologists (ICP), an organization of more than 1,500 members in 83 countries. He has served on the Governing Board of the Society of Cross-Cultural Research (SCCR) and is Founding Editor of the new journal *World Psychology*.

ANTHONY P. GLASCOCK is Professor of Anthropology and Head, Psychology, Sociology, and Anthropology Department, Drexel University. For thirteen years, he taught at the University of Wyoming, where he was founder and co-chair of the Program in Aging and Human Development and was Visiting Faculty Fellow at the Andrus Gerontology Center, University of Southern California, in 1984. His most recent field research, supported by the National Institute on Aging, was conducted in a small community in the west of Ireland and focused on aging and life-stage transitions. Dr. Glascock has also conducted USAID-sponsored research in Somalia on the relationship between health and aging. He has published on the status and treatment of the elderly in nonindustrial societies and edited a special issue of *Experimental Aging Research* on "Engineering Design for an Aging Society." He was a founding member of the Society for Cross-Cultural Research, is a Fellow of the Gerontological Society of America, and is on the editorial board of the *Journal of Cross-Cultural Gerontology*.

DAVID YAU-FAI HO returned from North America to his birthplace, Hong Kong, in 1968, where he devoted his time to the introduction and development of clinical psychology in that society. He is committed to the development of an Asian psychology with indigenous roots in Asian cultures. His research interests have focused on personality development, psychopathology, and social behavior in Chinese culture. He has published extensively, with contributions in psychology, psychiatry, sociology, linguistics, and education. Dr. Ho has had multicultural experiences in North America, Hawaii, and the Far East. He was elected president of the International Council of Psychologists (1988–1989); he is also a member of the Advisory Board of the Institute for Cross-Cultural and Cross-Ethnic Studies, Molloy College.

JOHN D. HOGAN is Associate Professor at St. John's University, New York. He has published articles and chapters on a range of developmental topics including creativity, humor, Piaget, and death anxiety, and he is coeditor of the volume *International Psychology: Views from Around the World* (1992). His most recent publications focus on the history of psychology.

HARRIET P. LEFLEY, is Professor of Psychiatry, Office of Transcultural Education and Research, University of Miami School of Medicine in Miami, Florida. She has been Resident Consultant in Social Research to the Government of the Bahamas, Program Evaluation of the New Horizons Community Mental Health Center, Director of the University of Miami's

Cross-Cultural Training Institute for Mental Health Professionals, and Director of the Collaborative Family Training Project. Dr. Lefley has been involved in cross-cultural research, service, and training for more than 20 years. She has published six books and is the author of over 100 scientific papers, journal articles, and book chapters on cultural issues in mental health service delivery, community mental health models, and family support systems for the mentally ill.

DIOMEDES C. MARKOULIS is Associate Professor in the Department of Psychology and Education at the University of Thessaloniki in Greece. Dr. Markoulis is a member of many national and international professional organizations. His fields of interest focus on cognitive and sociocognitive development and sociomoral reasoning processes. He is the coauthor of *Prosocial and Antisocial Dimensions of Behavior* and has published many articles in professional journals.

DAVID MATSUMOTO is Associate Professor of Psychology at San Francisco State University. He has conducted cross-cultural research on human emotions for over a decade. His works include the development of a measure of individualism-collectivism on the individual level. In addition to a number of original research reports, he is author of *Japan Unmasked: The Feelings and Emotions of the Japanese* and *People: A Re-introduction to Psychology from a Multi-Cultural Perspective.*

PETER F. MERENDA is Professor Emeritus of Psychology and Statistics, University of Rhode Island. He has held joint appointment in the Departments of Psychology and of Computer Science and Statistics. Former Associate Dean of the Graduate School and University Coordinator of Research, he was also Fulbright-Hays Senior Research Scholar to Italy in psychology. Dr. Merenda is past president of the International Council of Psychologists; the Division of Psychological Assessment, International Association of Applied Psychology; the New England Psychological Association; and the Rhode Island Psychological Association. He is also former chair of the APA Committee on International Relations in Psychology and of the APA Committee on Academic Freedom and Conditions of Employment. He is currently a member of the Advisory Board of the Institute for Cross-Cultural and Cross-Ethnic Studies, Molloy College. Dr. Merenda has coauthored a book on multivariate statistics and on educational measurement and is a coauthor of teacher rating scales for young school children, personality assessment instruments, and multiple aptitude test batteries.

NIHAR R. MRINAL is a faculty member of the Department of Psychology of Nagpur University, India. His major areas of interest are research methods and clinical and cross-cultural psychology. Dr. Mrinal is a Fellow and executive member of the Indian Association of Clinical Psychology and a life member of the Indian Psychological Association, where he is an elected executive. He is also a life member of the Indian Science Congress and a member of the Advisory Board of the Institute for Cross-Cultural and Cross-Ethnic Studies, Molloy College. Dr. Mrinal has published and presented more than 50 articles in various journals and conferences. He is a consultant to the National Institute of Social Defence, Delhi; the Indian Institute of Youth Welfare, Nagpur; and the Bharatiya Adim-Jati Sevak Sangh (tribal welfare organization), Nagpur, India.

UMA SINGHAL MRINAL is Chair of the Department of Psychology, Bhagwandin Arya Kanya College, Lakhimpur Kheri, Uttar Pradesh, India. Her areas of interest are cross-cultural, community, and women's psychology. The author of various psychological tests and papers, Dr. Mrinal also writes articles on various topics in psychology to foster public awareness. She is associated with numerous social and cultural organizations and as a community activist pays much attention to the Tharu tribe, who live on the Indo-Nepal border. Dr. Mrinal is a member of several organizations. She is a life member of the Indian Science Congress Association and of the International Council of Psychologists (United States). She is also on the Advisory Board of the Institute for Cross-Cultural and Cross-Ethnic Studies, Molloy College.

ALBERT PEPITONE has been affiliated with the University of Pennsylvania since 1951. Pepitone has taught undergraduate courses and graduate seminars, supervised Ph.D students, and carried out programs of research on the dynamics of groups and social cognition—including cohesion, deindividuation, aggression, impression formation, decision making, and social judgment. He has received two Fulbright Awards for research at Groningen, the Netherlands, and Rome. Since the 1970s his research has focused on the influence of culture, particularly including human belief systems. Dr. Pepitone has been president of several scholarly societies—Cross-Cultural Research, Personality and Social Psychology (Division 8, APA), the Psychological Study of Social Issues (Division 9, APA), and the Advancement of Field Theory. He has also been vice president of the Interamerican Society of Psychology.

RONALD TAFT taught social psychology in Western Australia, Melbourne, and Monash universities and is now Professor Emeritus. Since 1952 he has pursued a systematic program of research into the adaptation of immigrants to their new society and into psychological aspects of ethnicity. He is a former president of the International Association for Cross-Cultural Psychology and executive member of the International Union of Psychological Sciences; he is a Fellow of the Academy of Social Science in Australia and an Honorary Fellow of the Australian Psychological Society.

HAROLD TAKOOSHIAN is Associate Professor in the Social Science Division of Fordham University. He served as Visiting Professor of Psychology in Latin America and as a U.S. Fulbright Scholar to the Soviet Union in 1987–1988, teaching and studying in Yerevan, Tbilisi, Moscow, and Leningrad (St. Petersburg). Dr. Takooshian is active with cross-cultural research and has published widely. He is affiliated with numerous professional associations and is most prominent in several Divisions of the American Psychological Association, the International Council of Psychologists, and the Society for Armenian Studies.

ALDO TARTAGLINI is a doctoral candidate in clinical psychology at St. John's University in New York. A native of Boston, he is currently completing a dissertation exploring some biological bases for psychopathology.